An

ENCYCLOPEDIA

of

HUMOR

A n

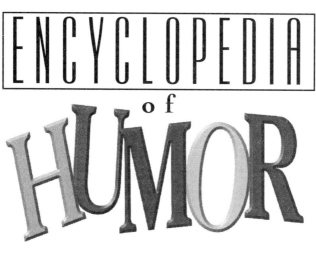

ENCYCLOPEDIA

of

HUMOR

Lowell D. Streiker

HENDRICKSON
PUBLISHERS

An Encyclopedia of Humor
Copyright © 1998 by Lowell D. Streiker, Ph.D.
Published by Hendrickson Publishers, Inc.
P.O. Box 3473
Peabody, Massachusetts 01961-3473

Disclaimer: The names of persons, businesses, and churches used in this collection are mostly fictitious. Any resemblance to persons, businesses, or churches living or dead is, for the most part, purely coincidental.

Printed in the United States of America

ISBN 1-56563-305-9

Second Printing—May 1998

Cover design by Paetzold Design, Batavia, Ill.
Interior design by Pinpoint Marketing, Kirkland, Wash.
Edited by Scott Pinzon, Margaret D. Smith, and Heather Stroobosscher

Library of Congress Cataloging-in-Publication Data

CONTENTS

AN
INTRODUCTION

Noted evangelist John Franklin was speaking at two different churches in a large city in the same week. A reporter was present at the first service. After the sermon the evangelist pleaded with the reporter not to publish in the local paper any of the jokes he had used that night since he was going to use the same stories the following night at the other church. The next morning the reporter published an excellent review of the evangelist's message and concluded with these words: "The Reverend Mr. Franklin also told many stories that cannot be published."

What follows is a collection of stories that definitely can be published! Here are nearly three thousand of my all-time favorite anecdotes, jokes, and witty comments about virtually every topic under the sun. I trust that they will be of value to you as you meet and communicate with others—whatever your vocation may be. Laughter is a powerful force, and it is yours to use whether you are a minister, a public speaker, a teacher, a salesman, an office worker, a psychologist, or a plumber!

The laughter encouraged by this collection is supportive of human dignity. It is life-affirming and life-giving. And it is, to borrow a word from religion, prophetic. It comforts the afflicted and afflicts the comfortable. It ennobles our spirits and extends our love to others.

And, above all, it's fun!

So remember four simple words:

Live. Love. Laugh. Bloom!

—Reverend Lowell

INTRODUCING LOWELL STREIKER

Lowell D. Streiker is an ordained minister in the United Church of Christ and holds a Ph.D. in religion from Princeton University. He has written, co-authored, edited, and contributed to more than twenty books. He has co-produced and moderated the television series *Counterpoint* for CBS. He has appeared on numerous radio and television programs including *The Oprah Winfrey Show, The Merv Griffin Show,* and CBS *Morning News.*

Visit his website, Reverend Lowell's Electronic Congregation, at http://www.revlowell.com. Your humor contributions and comments are always welcome.

MEET LOWELL IN PERSON!

Share Lowell's "good clean fun" words of inspiration with your business, church, or other audience. Lowell is available for speaking engagements, workshops, conferences, and preaching. During the past two years, he has spoken, sung, preached, and entertained in the United States, Norway, Germany, Holland, Finland, Russia, Poland, and Hungary. For more information, contact Lowell today at:

795 Reina del Mar Avenue
Pacifica, California 94044-3153
Phone: (650) 359-7123
Fax: (650) 359-0850
E-mail: revlowell@earthlink.net

1.
CHURCH LIFE

Sacred cows make the best hamburger. —Mark Twain

The new priest was trying to institute some liturgical reform in his very old-fashioned parish by teaching his parishioners the new responses. He said to them, "When I say, 'The Lord be with you,' you will reply all together, 'And with you also.' Then I will say, 'Let us pray.'"

The day came for the introduction of the new liturgy. Something happened to the microphone, and the priest, trying to adjust it, said in a loud voice, "There is something wrong with this microphone."

The congregation responded with one loud voice, "And with you also!" —King Duncan

I was preaching in a small Methodist church in Georgia and asked the congregation, "How many of you folks here this morning are Methodists?"

Everybody raised a hand, except one little old lady.

After the service, when she and I were shaking hands, I said, "Ma'am, I noticed you didn't raise your hand. That means you're not a Methodist. Would you mind telling me what you are?"

She said, "Well, I'm a Baptist."

Some of the people standing around didn't seem to appreciate her answer. So I asked her, "Ma'am, would you mind telling me why you're a Baptist?"

She said, "I really don't know, except my mother was a Baptist, my father was a Baptist, my grandmother and my grandfather were Baptists."

I said, "Ma'am, that's really not a good reason to be a Baptist. Suppose your mother and your father, and your grandmother and your grandfather had been morons, what would you have been?"

Without batting an eye, she said, "I guess I'd have been a Methodist."

Is it a sin to have sexual relations before receiving Communion?" the young woman asked her pastor.

"Only if you block the aisle," he replied.

We were traveling one summer in the Pocono Mountains and, like a good Presbyterian family, attended church while we were on vacation.

One lazy Sunday we found our way to a little Methodist church. It was a hot day, and the folks were nearly drowsing in the pews. The preacher was preaching on and on, until all of a sudden he said, "The best years of my life have been spent in the arms of another man's wife."

The congregation let out a gasp and came to immediate attention. The dozing deacon in the back row dropped his hymnbook.

Then the preacher added, "It was my mother."

The congregation tittered a little and managed to follow along as the sermon concluded.

I filed away this trick in my memory, since it was such a great way to regain the congregation's attention. The next summer, on a lazy Sunday, I was preaching and the flies were buzzing around and the ushers were sinking lower and lower in their seats in the back row until I could hardly see them.

Then I remembered our experience in the Pocono Mountains, and I said in a booming voice, "The best years of my life have been spent in the arms of another man's wife."

Sure enough, I had their attention. One of the ushers in the back row sat up so fast he hit his head on the back of the pew in front of him. I had them.

But you know something, I forgot what came next. All I could think to say was, "And for the life of me, I can't remember her name!"

—Pastor Roger Matthews

Mrs. Hansen had been a member of First Baptist church for twenty-five years. After the service, as she walked toward the pastor who stood waiting at the sanctuary door, it was obvious that she had something on her mind. She complained, "Reverend, if God were alive today, He would be shocked at the changes in this church!"

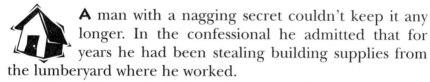 **A** man with a nagging secret couldn't keep it any longer. In the confessional he admitted that for years he had been stealing building supplies from the lumberyard where he worked.

"What did you take?" his parish priest asked.

"Enough to build my own home and enough for my son's house. And houses for our two daughters. And our cottage at the lake."

"This is very serious," the priest said. "I shall have to think of a far-reaching penance. Have you ever done a retreat?"

"No, Father, I haven't," the man replied. "But if you can get the plans, I can get the lumber."

Rev. Harold Watson, a Congregationalist minister, received a call from a woman who was quite distressed over the death of her pet cat, Samantha. She asked the minister to conduct a funeral service for her cat. The minister explained that it was contrary to Congregationalist policy to conduct funerals for animals and referred her to a friend, a Methodist pastor. Later, Watson learned that the Methodist minister had referred her to a Presbyterian minister, who had referred her to someone else.

A day later, the grieving pet owner called Watson back, still upset. She said she was at her wit's end, couldn't find a minister to conduct Samantha's funeral, and didn't know what to do. She said she planned to donate ten thousand dollars to the church of the minister who performed this service for Samantha.

Watson said to her, "Well, why didn't you tell me Samantha was a Congregationalist in the first place?"

The main course at the big civic dinner was baked ham with glazed sweet potatoes. Rabbi Cohen regretfully shook his head when the platter was passed to him.

Father Kelly scolded playfully, "When are you going to forget that silly rule of yours and eat ham like the rest of us?"

Without skipping a beat, Rabbi Cohen replied, "At your wedding reception, Father Kelly."

A man and his ten-year-old son were on a fishing trip miles from home. At the boy's insistence, they decided to attend the Sunday worship service at a small rural church.

As they walked back to their car after the service, the father complained. "The service was too long," he lamented. "The sermon was boring, and the singing was off key."

Finally the boy said, "Daddy, I thought it was pretty good for a dime."

A very dignified pastor was visiting a lady in a nursing home who was confined to a wheelchair. As he stood to leave, the lady asked him to have a word of prayer. He gently took her hand and prayed that God would be with her to bring her comfort, strength and healing.

When he finished praying, her face began to glow. She said softly, "Pastor, would you help me to my feet?"

Not knowing what else to do, he helped her up.

At first, she took a few uncertain steps. Then she began to jump up and down, then to dance and shout and cry with happiness until the whole nursing home was aroused.

After she was quieted, the solemn pastor hurried out to his car, closed the door, grabbed hold of the steering wheel and prayed this little prayer: "Lord, don't you ever do that to me again!"

A rabbi and a soap maker went for a walk together. The soap maker said, "What good is religion? Look at all the trouble and misery of the world! Still there, even after years—thousands of years—of teaching about goodness and truth and peace. Still there, after all the prayers and sermons and teachings. If religion is good and true, why should this be?"

The rabbi said nothing. They continued walking until he noticed a child playing in the gutter.

Then the rabbi said, "Look at that child. You say that soap makes people clean, but see the dirt on that youngster. Of what good is soap? With all the soap in the world, over all these years, the child is still filthy. I wonder how effective soap is, after all!"

The soap maker protested. "But, Rabbi, soap cannot do any good unless it is used!"

"Exactly!" replied the rabbi.

Just before I was to preach at a Baptist church in Maryland, the pastor, Carl Banks, said, "When you get through I want you to stand at the door with me, so that the people can greet you."

Afterwards I stood there, and folks came by. One woman grabbed my hand, looked me in the eye, and said, "Dr. Streiker, that was a sorry sermon."

Of course, I was shaken by that, but I was more shaken when I noticed her in line the second time. She grabbed my hand again, looked me in the eye, and said, ". . . a sorry sermon and you didn't even preach it well!" And she walked on.

Then she came back a third time, grabbed my hand, looked me in the eye, and said, ". . . a sorry sermon and you didn't preach it well, and I hope you never come back."

Well, I was devastated. I turned to the pastor and said, "Carl, what is with this woman?"

He said, "Don't pay any attention to her. She's not very bright. She just goes around repeating what she hears everybody else saying."

CHURCH SIGNBOARDS

Work for the Lord. The pay isn't much, but the retirement plan is out of this world.

Interested in going to heaven? Apply here for flight training!

Since you can't take it with you, why not leave it here?

You can't take it with you, but you can send it on ahead.

No parking. Violators will be turned into a pillar of salt.

We have a prophet-sharing plan for you.

The Lord loveth a cheerful giver. He also accepteth from a grouch.

Rev. Alan Hansen finished a powerful sermon on the Ten Commandments. One congregant was momentarily depressed but soon perked up. "Anyway," he told himself, "I've never made a graven image."

Pastor Sampson was visiting London. The guide showed him through Westminster Abbey where so many of the nation's renowned are entombed. The guide proudly announced, "England's Great sleep within these walls."

The minister muttered, "I feel right at home."

Visiting a newly-rich friend in the country, Wolcott Gibbs refused to be impressed by tennis courts, swimming pools, stables, and other forms of luxury.

Finally, returning to the house, the owner pointed to a magnificent elm growing just outside the library window and boasted, "That tree stood for fifty years on top of the hill. I had it moved down here so on pleasant mornings I can do my work in its shade."

Said Gibbs: "That just goes to show what God could do if he had money."

The pastor was growing concerned about sparse attendance, so he published this item in the church bulletin:

"This . . . is . . . the . . . way . . . the . . .church . . . sometimes . . . looks . . . to . . . the . . . pastor . . . when . . . he . . . goes . . . into . . . the . . . pulpit.

"Itwouldlooklikethisifeverybodybroughtsomebodyelsetochurch."

The minister selected a fifty-cent item at a convenience store but discovered he didn't have any money with him. "I could invite you to hear me preach in return," he said jokingly to the owner, "but I'm afraid I don't have any fifty-cent sermons."

"Perhaps," suggested the owner, "I could come twice."

Did you hear about the ostentatious bishop who had his car fitted with stained glass windows?

A visitor found in her Episcopal church a prayer book that obviously had been used by a novice server for Holy Communion prompting. At the appropriate places, he had written "sit," "stand," and "go to the altar." For one stage of the ritual he had added, and underlined, "Incense the people."

Billy Graham tells the amusing story of a fire that broke out in a small town church. When the fire brigade, sirens wailing, arrived on the spot, the minister recognized one of the men. "Hello there, Jim. I haven't seen you in church for a long time," he chided.

"Well," answered the sweating man struggling with the hose, "it's been a long time since there's been any kind of fire in this church."

The problem with mainline Christianity is that too many church members are singing "Standing on the Promises," when they are merely sitting on the premises.

Willard Scott, the irrepressible weather reporter on *The Today Show*, grew up in a Baptist church. On one occasion when he was twelve years old, he took Communion and had a most embarrassing thing happen to him. He describes it like this:

"In the Baptist church, they serve grape juice rather than wine, in tiny little individual-sized plastic cups. On this particular occasion, I was trying to get the last bit of juice out of the bottom of the cup with my tongue, when all of a sudden the suction grabbed hold and my tongue got stuck in the cup! I tried desperately to pull that doggone cup off, but it wouldn't budge. Then before I could make another attempt, the pastor asked everyone in the church to hold hands with the person next to him and sing 'Blest Be the Tie That Binds.' Well, I was the one in a bind. Here I was with this cup on my tongue, and the people next to me had grabbed my hands.

"Just when it seemed like I was about to be discovered, I had what I can only regard as a divine inspiration. I sucked the whole cup into my mouth and held it there until the hymn was over. Then, while no one was looking, I reached in and pulled it off my tongue."

—The Joy of Living

Shortly after the holy days of Lent and Passover, a priest, a minister, and a rabbi went off together on a fishing trip. They tried every kind of bait they could think of, but the fish weren't biting. So the priest got out of the boat and walked across the water to another spot. Then the rabbi got out of the boat and walked across the water. The minister got out of the boat, too— and started to sink. He floundered around, climbed back into the boat, and tried again. Once again he sank into the water. He clambered back into the boat, and tried once more, this time almost drowning. Finally the priest said to the rabbi, "Do you think we should tell him where the rocks are?"

The congregation of a small stone church in England decided that the stone which formed the step up to the front door had become too worn by its years of use, and would have to be replaced. Unfortunately, there were hardly any funds available for the replacement. Then someone came up with the bright idea that the replacement could be postponed for many years by simply turning over the block of stone.

They discovered that their great-grandparents had beaten them to it.

It seems the previous pastor was a paragon of virtue. He lived up to all the people's expectations and was willing to live on a very low salary, to boot. And he loved to work around the manse and keep both house and grounds in repair.

But the new pastor wasn't that type. He hired someone to do a lot of these chores, including the mowing of the manse and church lawns. Naturally, this cost more money.

This change of pattern was of concern to some of the elders of the church. One day one of them approached the new pastor and tried to bring up the matter tactfully. He said to the new pastor, "You know, our previous pastor mowed the lawn himself. Have you considered this approach?"

The new pastor responded, "Yes, I'm aware of this. And I asked him. But he doesn't want to do it anymore."

Every day, people are straying away from the church and going back to God.
—Lenny Bruce

 Pastor Phillips was delivering his sermon when a man in the back pew turned his head to one side, put his hand to his ear, and hollered, "Louder." The preacher raised his voice somewhat and continued with his sermon, which wasn't too interesting.

After a few minutes the man said again, "Louder!" The preacher strained even more and continued on, but by now the sermon had become quite boring.

The man shouted, "Louder!"

At this point a man in the front row couldn't stand it any longer and yelled back to the man in the rear, "What's the matter, can't you hear?"

"No," said the man in the back.

"Well," said the man down front, "move over, I'm coming back to join you."

During a flight between New York and Chicago the captain announced over the plane's intercom, "Our number four engine has just been shut off because of mechanical trouble. There is nothing to worry about, however. We can still finish the flight with just three engines. Besides, you will be reassured to know that we have four pastors on board."

One passenger called the flight attendant and said, "Would you please tell the captain that I would rather have four engines and three pastors?"
—Dick Underdahl-Peirce

The minister was sick, and a pastor noted for his never-ending sermons agreed to fill in. When he stood up in the pulpit, he was annoyed to find only ten worshipers present, including the choir. Afterward he complained to the sexton. "That was a very small turnout," he said. "Weren't they informed that I was coming?"

"No," replied the sexton, "but word must have leaked out."

A fella's talking to his priest. He said, "I gave up sex for Lent. Well, I tried to, but the last day of Lent my wife dropped a can of peaches and when she bent over to pick 'em up, I couldn't help it."

The priest said, "That's all right, son. A lot of people give in to temptation."

The fella asked, "You're not gonna throw us out of church?"

The priest said no.

The fella exclaimed, "Thank goodness. They threw us out of the supermarket!"   —George "Goober" Lindsey

One sunny Sunday morning, Henry Jones awoke to find his wife standing over him, shaking him by the shoulder.

"You have to get up," she urged. "We have to get ready for church."

"I don't want to go to church," he replied. "I want to stay in bed."

Crossing her arms over her chest, his wife demanded, "Give me three good reasons why you should stay in bed and not go to church."

"OK," he answered. "First, I don't get anything out of the service. Second, I don't like the people there. And third, no one there likes me. Now can you give me three good reasons why I should go to church?"

His wife responded, "First, it will do you some good. Second, there are people who really do like you, and they'll miss you if you aren't there. And third, you're the minister!"

Our former pastor, Jack Watson, invariably divided up his sermon into several major points on the basis of a number found in his selected Biblical text for the day. For instance, he would preach on the two angels who visited Lot in Sodom and divide his sermon into two parts. He would preach on the three men who approached the wounded man in the Parable of the Good Samaritan and divide his sermon into three parts. He would preach about a passage in the Book of Acts in which four anchors are dropped from a storm-tossed ship and divide his sermon into four parts. He would preach on the David and Goliath story, in which five smooth stones are mentioned, and divide the sermon into five parts. One Sunday morning, the congregation shook with terror when the preacher announced that he would now preach on the text from the twenty-first chapter of the Gospel of John—in which Peter throws out a net and catches 153 fish!

Twelve-year-old Norton was bitterly disappointed at not being cast as Joseph in the church school Nativity pageant. He was given the minor role of the innkeeper instead. Throughout the weeks of rehearsal he brooded on how he could avenge himself on his little brother, Wayne, who had been awarded the part of Joseph. On the day of the performance, Wayne (as Joseph) and his sister Kelly (as Mary) made their entrance and knocked on the door of the inn. Norton (the innkeeper) opened it a fraction and eyed them with suspicion.

Joseph implored, "Can you give us board and lodging for the night?" He then stood back awaiting the expected rejection. But Norton had not plotted all those weeks for nothing. He flung the door wide, smiled, and shouted, "Come in, come in! You shall have the best room in the hotel."

There was a long pause. Then with great presence of mind, Wayne turned and said to Kelly, "Hold on. I'll take a look inside first." He peered past the innkeeper, shook his head firmly and said, "I'm not taking my wife into a filthy place like this. Come on, Mary, I'd rather sleep in a stable."

The pageant was back on course.

During the hours before D-day, three chaplains—Reverend Paul Peterson, Father Mike O'Connor, and Rabbi Henry Birnbaum—sat together and solemnly discussed the possibility that one or more of them might be killed in the next few hours.

"It makes one feel the necessity of unburdening one's soul and making confession," said Father Mike. "I must own up to a terrible impulse to drink. Oh, I fight it, I do; but the temptation haunts me constantly, and sometimes I give in to it."

"Well," said Reverend Paul, "I don't have too much trouble with liquor, but I must own up to the terrible sexual urges I feel toward attractive women. I fight this temptation desperately, but every once in a while, I fail to resist."

After that, there was a pause. Finally both turned to the Jewish chaplain and one said, "And you, Henry, are you troubled with a besetting sin, too? What is your persistent temptation?"

Rabbi Birnbaum sighed and said, "I'm afraid I have a terrible, irresistible impulse to gossip."

At a mental hospital in California one Sunday morning a group of patients was being shepherded to the Catholic and Protestant chapels. One patient did not enter either chapel but continued walking toward the main gate. When an attendant caught up with him and asked where he was going, the patient replied, "I was told I could go to the church of my choice. It's in New York."

Which reminds me of the revivalist in Alaska who attracted a considerable crowd of visiting sailors because he condemned the town's prostitutes by name and address!

Henry Ward Beecher, the famous New England minister, entered his pulpit one Sunday morning. Awaiting him was an unmarked envelope. Opening it, he found a single sheet of paper on which was written the single word, "FOOL." After chuckling to himself, he held the paper up to the congregation and said, "I have known many an instance of a man writing letters and forgetting to sign his name. But this is the only instance I've ever known of a man signing his name and forgetting to write his letter."

Laughter reminds us how readily we misunderstand those who communicate with us.

There was a nice lady, a minister's widow, who was a little old-fashioned. She was planning a week's vacation in California at a church campground near Yosemite National Park, but she wanted to make sure of the accommodations first. Uppermost in her mind were bathroom facilities, but she couldn't bring herself to write "toilet" in a letter. After considerable deliberation, she settled on "bathroom commode," but when she wrote that down, it still sounded too forward. So, after the first page of her letter, she referred to the bathroom commode as "BC."

"Does the cabin where I will be staying have its own BC? If not, where is the BC located?" is what she actually wrote.

The campground owner took the first page of the letter and the lady's check and gave it to his secretary. He put the remainder of the letter on the desk of the senior member of his staff, without noticing that the staffer would have no way of knowing what "BC" meant. Then the owner went off to town to run some errands.

The staff member came in after lunch, found the letter, and was baffled by the euphemism. He showed the letter around to several counselors, but they couldn't decipher it either. The staff member's wife, who knew that the lady was the widow of a famous Baptist preacher, was sure that it must be a question about the local Baptist church. "Of course!" the first staffer exclaimed. "'BC' stands for 'Baptist Church.'"

The staffer was quite busy, so it took him a few days to answer the woman's letter. Finally, he sat down and wrote:

Dear Madam,

I regret very much the delay in answering your letter, but I now take the pleasure in informing you that the BC is located nine miles north of the campground and is capable of seating 250 people at one time. I admit it is quite a distance away if you are in the habit of going regularly, but no doubt you will be pleased to know that a great number of people take their lunches along and make a day of it. They usually arrive early and stay late.

The last time my wife and I went was six years ago, and it was so crowded we had to stand up the whole time we were there.

It may interest you to know that right now there is a supper planned to raise money to buy more seats. They are going to hold it in the basement of the 'BC.'

I would like to say that it pains me very much not to be able to go more regularly, but it is surely no lack of desire on my part. As we grow older, it seems to be more of an effort, particularly in cold weather.

If you decide to come down to our campground, perhaps I could go with you the first time, sit with you, and introduce you to all the folks. Remember, this is a friendly community.

Sincerely, . . .

Reverend Obediah Franklin wrote a sermon on "humility" then filed it away. He wanted to save it for a really big occasion when he could impress a lot of people.

Ministers are notorious for taking themselves too seriously. Leonard I. Sweet, President of United Theological Seminary in Dayton, Ohio, gave a vivid illustration from his own career:

It was my first stewardship campaign. I had been appointed by the bishop to the missionary church in a small-college community in New York's Genessee Valley. The first year had been a nervous one both for me (a young, not-dry-behind-the-ears pastor and wetback Ph.D.) and for the congregation, which was comprised of an odd and unconsummated coupling of rural folk and "academic types." But there was significant enough progress to warrant the belief that we could double the budget after my first year there. If only we had a slogan; some catchy motto or jingle around which to design our development campaign. . . . Or so I thought.

The weekend before the "Stewardship Sunday" kickoff, I sought solitary confinement in Toronto, Canada. There I hit first on a slogan and then an idea: why not have T-shirts made up for those "every-member canvassers" who could then call on parishioners emblazoned with my newly-brainstormed stewardship theme? It seemed the perfect plan.

During the "Community Concerns" time of the morning worship the next Sunday, the chair of the campaign, Doug Klapper, did an outstanding job of making the committee's case for our controversial financial leap forward. As soon as he finished, I bolted to the front, prevented him from returning to his seat, and presented him with a surprise gift that I announced confidently would give our campaign focus and force.

The color of Doug's face when he unwrapped his surprise should have alerted me to what was to come. His embarrassed refusal to hold up the T-shirt for the congregation to see ("You do it," he giggled) was another missed warning signal. But it was not until the moment that I held up that T-shirt and announced that there were enough of these "surprise gifts" for every one of our canvassers to wear that I realized exactly what I had done. Our stewardship slogan would be, I proudly read:

I Upped MY Pledge
Up YOURS

At first, there was a trickle of giggles, then a torrent of laughter. I tried to preach, but I had lost it. Convulsions of laughter drowned out my sermon at unpredictable moments, ebbing and flowing like a moonshine tide.

That moment of my greatest embarrassment and mistake, a moment from which that worship service never fully recovered, was the moment of my ministry's recovery in that community. For suddenly this upstart preacher and hotshot Ph.D. became human, and did something so outrageously stupid and foolish that it redeemed all his jarring strangeness. From that Sunday on, I became their pastor and was bonded to them for life. And for the next seven years, as I walked the streets of the village, I would find myself greeted with the query, "Are you the 'up-yours' preacher?"

Two fellows are talking religion. One says to the other, "Sometimes I'd like to ask God why he allows poverty, famine and injustice when he could do something about it."

"What's stopping you from asking?" asks the second.

The first replies, "I'm afraid God might ask me the same question."

If a minister preaches over ten minutes, he's long-winded. If his sermon is short, he didn't prepare it.

If his congregation's finances are in the black, he's too materialistic. If they're in the red, he's too other-worldly.

If he mentions money, he's money-mad. If he doesn't mention money, he's a lousy businessman.

If he visits his parishioners, he's nosy. If he doesn't, he's being snobbish.

If he has fairs, bazaars, and pancake breakfasts, he's bleeding the people. If he doesn't, there isn't any life in the parish.

If he takes time with his parishioners to help and advise, he's meddling. If he doesn't, he doesn't care.

If he celebrates liturgy in a quiet voice, he's boring. If he puts feelings into it, he's being histrionic.

If he starts the service on time, he's rushing the congregation. If he starts late, he's holding up the people.

If he tries to lead the people in music, he's showing off. If he doesn't, he doesn't care what the service is like.

If he decorates the church, he's wasting money. If he doesn't, he's letting it run down.

If he's young, he's not experienced. If he's old, he ought to retire.

But . . . if he dies . . . *no one can ever replace him.*

Willie Jensen, the sexton, was cleaning up the minister's office late one Thursday afternoon. The minister had gone to visit a parishioner at the hospital and had left the working manuscript of his sermon on his desk. Willie took a peek. Along the left margin were instructions such as:

"Pause here," "Wipe brow here," "Use angry fist gesture," and "Look upward."

Near the end was a long paragraph of text, opposite which the sexton wrote in large capital letters: "ARGUMENT WEAK HERE. YELL WITH ALL YOUR MIGHT!"

I was sitting in my office on the first Saturday of December. Outside in the courtyard of our church the men of the church were in the process of building the stage for a live nativity scene. Since my door was open, I heard two children discussing the process. One asked of the other, "What is this going to be?"

Answered the other, "Oh, they're building a live fertility scene."

—Walter Lauster

The church choir director was frustrated with the sporadic attendance of all the choir members for rehearsals for the Christmas Concert. At the final rehearsal he announced: "I want to personally thank the pianist for being the only person in this entire church choir to attend each and every rehearsal during the past two months."

At this, the pianist rose, bowed, and said, "It was the least I could do, considering I won't be able to be at the Christmas Concert tonight."

A party of clergymen was attending a conference in Scotland. Several of them set off to explore the district. Presently they came to a river spanned by a temporary bridge. Not seeing the notice that read, "Unsafe," they began to cross. The bridge-keeper ran after them to protest.

"It's all right," declared one pastor, not understanding the reason for the old man's haste. "We're Presbyterians from the conference."

"If ye dinna get off that bridge," he replied, "you'll all be Baptists!"

—On Top of the World News

Going to church doesn't make anybody a Christian any more than taking a wheelbarrow into a garage makes it an automobile.

—Billy Sunday

PASTOR QUITS SPORTS

TWELVE REASONS WHY A LOCAL CLERGYMAN
STOPPED ATTENDING ATHLETIC CONTESTS

1. Every time I went, they asked me for money.
2. The people with whom I had to sit didn't seem very friendly.
3. The seats were too hard and not comfortable.
4. The coach never came to call on me.
5. The referee made a decision with which I could not agree.
6. I was sitting with some hypocrites—they came only to see what others were wearing.
7. Some games went into overtime, so I was late getting home.
8. The band played some numbers that I had never heard before.
9. The games are scheduled when I want to do other things.
10. My parents took me to too many games when I was growing up.
11. Since I read a book on sports, I feel that I know more than the coaches, anyhow.
12. I don't want to take my children, because I want them to choose for themselves what sport they like best.

With apologies to those who use these same excuses for not coming to church.

—*Moody Monthly*

Pastor Susanne Phelps had preached a vigorous and thoughtful sermon, and several members of the congregation rushed up to congratulate her. One longtime member gushed, "Pastor, every sermon you preach is better than the next one!"

The church is the only outfit I know that shoots its wounded.

—Chuck Swindoll

A Methodist church tried to get a certain man to attend, but he never did. "Why don't you come?" the minister asked, and the man finally admitted it was because he didn't have proper clothes. So a member of the congregation took him to a clothing store and got him a nice suit, shirt, tie and shoes.

But on the following Sunday, he still did not show up. So the minister visited him again and asked why he didn't come.

"When I got dressed up in my new suit," the man explained, "I looked so good I decided to go to the Episcopal church."

The Lord created the world in six days. He rested on the seventh.

On the eighth day, he started to answer complaints.

A woman criticized D. L. Moody for his methods of evangelism in attempting to win people to the Lord. Moody replied, "I agree with you. I don't like the way I do it, either. Tell me, how do you do it?"

The woman replied, "I don't do it."

Moody retorted, "Then I like my way of doing it better than your way of not doing it."   —Christian Communications Laboratory

Lutherans believe you cannot get into heaven unless you bring a covered dish.   —Garrison Keillor

I feel sorry for Moses. He spent forty years wandering the desert, eating nothing but bread off the ground and the occasional bird, and every day a million people would come up to him and ask, "Are we there yet?"   —Robert G. Lee

The Bible tells us to love our neighbors, and also to love our enemies; probably because they are generally the same people.

—G. K. Chesterton

Sister Serafina was on a much desired mission assignment to the Apache Indians. She was so excited that she drove past the last gas station without noticing that her gas gauge was on "Empty." She ran out of gas about a mile down the road, and had to walk back to the station. The attendant told her that he would like to help her, but he had no container to hold the gas.

"Can't you find anything at all?" she asked him.

Sympathetic to her plight, he agreed to search through an old shed in the back for something that might suffice. He was doubtful, but the grateful nun told him that the bedpan he'd found would work just fine. She carried the gasoline back to her car, taking care not to drop an ounce.

A truck driver pulled alongside the car as the nun was emptying the bedpan's contents into the tank. He rolled down his window and yelled, "I wish I had your faith, Sister!"

Do you know what you get when you cross a Jehovah's Witness with an atheist? Someone who knocks on your door for no apparent reason. —Guy Owen

You know it's going to be a boring service when the ushers ask for your espresso order as they hand you a bulletin. —Bill Jones

Every week our preacher tells us to go out and "witness" to others. But nothing strikes more fear in my heart than having to share my faith with a complete stranger. It's gotten so bad I've enrolled in a Witness Relocation Program. —Robert G. Lee

Presbyterians are a rather conservative bunch. We're like Methodists without the excitement. We never raise our hands in church. We can't. We're afraid if we raise them too high, God might call on us. In fact, we're so conservative, Christ could come back tomorrow and we'd form a committee to look into it. —Robert G. Lee

In the town where I live, the Baptists and the Presbyterians share a single church building. The Presbyterians have their Sunday worship service at 9:30 A.M. and the Baptists at 11:00 A.M. The two congregations put up a banner over our main street directing the faithful to their services. Each church included an appropriate motto. The Baptists urge: "Repent and be saved!" The Presbyterians inquire: "Is your pledge up to date?"

A grandmother was told by her grandson that in Sunday school the teacher said Jesus was Jewish. The Presbyterian grandmother said, "Well, that may be, but I assure you, God is still a Presbyterian."

Marlin Hopkins, the pastor of Holy Apostles Covenant Church, was proud of his new "loose-leaf" Bible. He decided to use it as he began preaching a series from Genesis. The second week of his series he was on the story of the fall of man. As he was reading his text he read, "And Adam said to Eve . . ." Then he turned the page to complete the verse, but the rest of the text was missing.

He was puzzled for a few seconds. Then, finally realizing what had happened, he looked up rather embarrassed and said, "It looks like a leaf is missing!"

Jim Hansen, the pastor of St. Mark's Methodist Church, had just announced to the congregation that he would be leaving their church. There was a good deal of crying and lots of kind words. As the pastor was talking to one woman who had expressed her sadness at his leaving, he consoled her with these generous words: "Oh, don't feel bad. I'm sure our superintendent will come up with a much better replacement."

She turned and said, "Oh, that's what they said last time. In fact, that's what they say all the time. But it never happens!"

The Perfect Pastor has been found.

He preaches exactly twenty minutes and then sits down. He condemns sin, but never steps on anybody's toes. He works from eight in the morning until ten at night, doing everything from preaching sermons to sweeping. He makes $400 per week, gives $200 a week to the church, buys lots of books, wears fine clothes, and has a nice family. He's always ready to contribute to every other good cause, too, and to help panhandlers who drop by the church on their way to somewhere. He is thirty-six years old, and has been preaching forty years. He is tall on the short side, heavyset in a thin sort of way, and handsome. He wears his hair parted in the middle, left side dark and straight, right side brown and wavy. He has a burning desire to work with the youth and spends all his time with the senior citizens. He smiles all the time while keeping a straight face, because he has a keen sense of humor that finds him seriously dedicated. He makes fifteen calls a day on church members, spends all his time evangelizing non-members, and is always found in his study if he is needed.

Unfortunately he burnt himself out and died at the age of thirty-seven.

Jesus was walking along one day when he came upon a man crying, and he said, "My friend, what's wrong?"

The man replied, "I'm blind; can you help me?"

Jesus healed the man, and went on his way. Soon he came upon another man sitting and crying. "Good friend, what's wrong?"

The man answered, "I'm lame and can't walk; can you please help me?"

Jesus healed the man, and they both went down the road. As they continued, they came upon a third man crying. Jesus said, "Good friend, what's wrong?"

He said, "I'm a minister."

And Jesus sat down and wept with him.   —Phil Hines

Ad from a recent church music publication:

Position Wanted: Organist/Choirmaster. Lifelong, militantly loyal, dyed-in-the-wool traditional RC, seeks full time position in pre-Vatican II urban parish (will consider Tridentine) blessed with large church building designed by P.C. Keely, 19th-century American pipe organ of three or four manuals, and, most importantly, using or willing to implement the BACS hymnal (Hymns, Psalms, & Spiritual Canticles). All-male or professional mixed choir a must (no volunteers!) as is freedom from outside interference by liturgy committees, religious educators, or other so-called vested interests. Prefer Massachusetts (except Fall River diocese). Will consider other areas in Northeast. Write to . . .

When Jesus started his church, the pastor (Jesus) was executed. The chairman of the board (Peter) was cursing, swearing, and denying his position. The treasurer (Judas) committed suicide after embezzling funds. The other board members (the disciples) ran away. The only ones left were a few from the Women's Fellowship. You see, your church is not all that bad!

—Robert Sarpalius

Son: "Dad, what's a religious traitor?"
Father: "A person who leaves our church and joins another."
Son: "And what is a person who leaves another church and joins ours?"
Father: "A convert, son, a blessed convert."

Paul Harvey reports:

A young couple invited their parson for Sunday dinner. While they were in the kitchen preparing the meal, the minister asked their son what they were having. "Goat," the little boy replied.

"Goat?" replied the startled man of the cloth. "Are you sure about that?"

"Yep," said the youngster. "I heard Pa say to Ma, 'Might as well have the old goat for dinner today as any other day.'"

 And the Lord said unto Noah: "Where is the ark which I have commanded thee to build?"

And Noah said unto the Lord: "Verily, I have had three carpenters off ill. The gopher-wood supplier hath let me down, yea, even though the gopher-wood hath been on order for nigh upon twelve months. What can I do, O Lord?"

And God said unto Noah: "I want that ark finished even after seven days and seven nights."

And Noah said: "It will be so."

And it was not so. And the Lord said unto Noah: "What seemeth to be the trouble this time?"

And Noah said unto the Lord: "Mine subcontractor hath gone bankrupt. The pitch which Thou commandest me to put on the outside and on the inside of the ark hath not arrived. The plumber hath gone on strike. Shem, my son who helpeth me on the ark side of the business, hath formed a pop group with his brothers Ham and Japheth. Lord, I am undone."

And the Lord grew angry and said, "And what about the animals, the male and female of every sort that I ordered to come unto thee to keep their seed alive upon the face of the earth?"

And Noah said: "They have been delivered unto the wrong address but should arriveth on Friday."

And the Lord said: "How about the unicorns, and the fowls of the air by sevens?"

And Noah wrung his hands and wept, saying: "Lord, unicorns are a discontinued line; thou canst not get them for love nor money. And fowls of the air are sold only in half-dozens. Lord, Lord, Thou knowest how it is."

And the Lord in His wisdom said, "Noah, my son, I knowest. Why else dost thou think I have caused a flood to descend upon the earth?"

—*Journal of Eastern Region of the Royal Institute of British Architects*

In Minnesota three pastors got together for coffee one day and found all their churches had bat-infestation problems. "I got so mad," said Pastor Johnson, "I took a shotgun and fired at them. It made holes in the ceiling, but did nothing to the bats."

"I tried trapping them alive," said Pastor Linquist. "Then I drove fifty miles before releasing them, but they returned."

"I haven't had any more problems," said Pastor Stephens.

"What did you do?" asked the others amazed.

"I simply baptized and confirmed them," he replied. "I haven't seen them since."

Ruth Troutman, the Sunday school teacher, was very keen on religious ceremonies and had spent an entire session talking to the class about the correct way to pray.

"Now," she said finally, "suppose we want to pray to God for forgiveness. What must we do first of all?"

"Sin?" suggested one little boy.

A Methodist minister, a Catholic priest, and a Jewish rabbi were talking.

The Methodist bragged, "One of my ancestors wrote over a hundred hymns."

Not to be outdone, the priest responded, "One of my ancestors translated the Bible into English."

"That's nothing," said the rabbi. "One of my ancestors wrote the Ten Commandments."

Mike and Lefty grew up together in Chicago. They both became lawyers. Then, much to the amazement of Mike, Lefty became a Sunday school teacher.

"I bet you don't even know the Lord's Prayer," said Mike.

"Everybody knows that," replied Lefty. "It goes, 'Now I lay me down to sleep. . . .'"

"You win," said Mike. "I didn't know you knew so much about the Bible."

When my friend Ralph was rector of a small Episcopal chapel in West Virginia, he presided at so many shotgun weddings he renamed his church Winchester Cathedral.

I had been invited to speak as a visiting minister at Christ Episcopal Church in Mount Pocono. "Do you wish to wear a surplice?" asked the rector.

"Surplice!" I cried. "I'm a Congregationalist. What do I know about surplices? All I know about is deficits!"

The Bible is a very ancient book, yet it is always relevant to our lives. People in it have the same problems we do. Think of Noah . . . it took him forty days to find a place to park.

A favorite story of Lyndon Johnson's:

A preacher was becoming terribly distracted by a man who came to church every Sunday and slept through the entire sermon. One Sunday the preacher decided to do something about it. As he began to preach, the man, true to form, fell fast asleep. Whereupon the preacher said quietly, "Everyone who wants to go to heaven, stand up." The entire congregation immediately stood up, except the sleeping man. When they sat down, the preacher shouted at the top of his voice, "Everyone who wants to go to hell, stand up!"

This startled the dozing man. Still half asleep, he jumped up, looked around to see what was going on, then said to the preacher, "I don't know what we're voting on but it looks like you and I are the only ones in favor of it."

The following story is attributed to Mark Twain:

"I once heard a preacher who was powerful good. I decided to give him every cent I had with me. But he kept at it too long. Ten minutes later I decided to keep the bills and give him my loose change. Another ten minutes and I was darned if I'd give him anything at all. When he finally stopped and the plate came around, I was so exhausted, I stole two dollars from the plate in sheer spite."

At the church I attend there is a young woman whose husband is an usher. During last Sunday's morning service, she became terribly worried that she might have left a roast cooking in the oven. She wrote a note to her husband and passed it to him by way of another usher. The latter, thinking it was a note for the pastor, handed it to the minister with the morning's offering.

The minister was just about to begin his sermon. He shuffled the note in with his sermon manuscript and paid no attention to it until he was well into his oration. Imagine his surprise when halfway through the sermon his eyes fell on the following words: "Please go home and turn off the gas."

A stranger came to church, and the minister was pleased to see him come sit in one of the empty seats at the front. Afterwards he greeted the newcomer and said, "I'm glad you felt free to sit well forward, even though you are a visitor."

"Well," said the person, "I'm a bus driver—and I wanted to see if I could learn how you get everyone to move to the rear all the time."

—King Duncan

An enthusiastic minister was exhorting his congregation to become more active in church affairs, to get the church on its feet. "Brothers and sisters," he proclaimed. "What this church needs is the energy to get up and walk."

One of his deacons said, "Let her walk, brother, let her walk!"

The preacher raised his voice a little and added, "But we cannot be satisfied with walking, we've got to pick up speed and run."

The same deacon chimed in, "Let her run, my brother, let her run!"

The preacher was really getting into his message now. "But running's not enough, either. One of these days this church has got to fly!"

That same deacon echoed, "Let her fly, brother, let her fly!"

The preacher paused for a moment and said solemnly, "But if this church is going to fly, we are all going to have to work harder and give more money!"

The deacon said softly, "Let her walk, brother, let her walk."

—King Duncan

We were all surprised one Sunday morning to find the president of our congregation at the pulpit. He explained that the pastor had the flu and had called him on Saturday to ask him to conduct the worship service.

"After agreeing to do it," the man said, "I began to panic at the thought of preparing a talk on such short notice. The panic subsided when I thought of those comforting words, 'Ask and ye shall receive.' I remembered that all I had to do is ask for anything I wanted, so I did."

He paused a moment before adding, "But, as you can see, I didn't catch the flu, and I still had to come here this morning."

—Carolyn A. Edwards (Metairie, LA) in *Reader's Digest*

We expect so little out of church nowadays. I once asked Angel Fernando, pastor of a church in northern California, "Do your people come to church expecting something?"

He replied, "Yes, they expect to be out by twelve."

Flanagan knelt in the confessional. "Yes, my son?" said the priest.

"Bless me, Father, for I have sinned," Flanagan whispered. "Yesterday I killed two lawyers and a politician. . . . "

"I'm not interested in your civic activities," interrupted the priest. "Just tell me your sins!"

Father Victor Owens, the parish priest, was being honored at a dinner on the twenty-fifth anniversary of his pastorate. A leading local politician, who was a lawyer and a member of the priest's congregation, was to give the keynote speech at the dinner, but found himself delayed in court. The toastmaster decided to proceed without him.

After all the laudations had been heaped upon the venerable priest, he rose to acknowledge the tributes given him.

"The seal of the confessional," he said, "can never be broken, and so I can only hint gently of my impressions when I first came here twenty-five years ago. Oh, I thought I had been assigned a terrible place. The very first chap who entered my confessional told me how he had stolen a television set, and when stopped by a policeman, had almost murdered the officer. Further, he told me he had embezzled money from his place of business and had an adulterous affair with his partner's wife. I was appalled. If that was only the first one, I thought, what were the others like? But as the days went on I knew that my people were not all like that and I had, indeed, a fine parish full of understanding and loving people."

Just as Father Owens finished his thanks, the politician arrived full of apologies and rushed to the dais to make the gift presentation speech.

"I'll never forget the first day our pastor arrived in this parish," said the politician. "In fact, I had the honor of being the first one to go to him in confession."

Twenty-three-year-old Kevin Pearson asked his minister, "Can I live a good Christian life on one hundred dollars a week?"

"Sure," the minister replied. "In fact, that's all you can do!"

My friend, Pastor Crawford Flanders, tells me that during the first five years of his ministry, he had a sign on his desk reading, "Win the world for Christ."

The next five years the sign read, "Win five for Christ."

After ten years, he changed the sign to read, "Don't lose too many."

The details of insurance benefits and premiums are almost never completely understandable. Not long ago, the clergy of the Spokane, Washington, Roman Catholic diocese got into a hassle with Blue Cross. The diocese held a group medical policy on its sixty-six priests. Blue Cross had added thirty cents a month to the premium for each policy—for maternity benefits.

—Joseph L. Felix, *It's Easier for a Rich Man to Enter Heaven*

The pastor of the church had bemoaned the fact that no one seemed to feel involved in worship service. The people could not be motivated to go into the world properly, because they held back so much in worship. He found an architect who promised to build a badly needed worship center if the church would agree to keep the plans secret until its unveiling on the day it was first to be used.

The big day finally arrived. The building looked quite normal from the outside. The big difference was on the inside. A great crowd gathered early that first Sunday. Each person was seated in a pew near the door, one pew at a time. When the pew was filled, it was rolled automatically to the front! This process continued until the entire sanctuary was filled. The minister was so carried away by having his audience at the front, he preached on and on. In fact, he didn't even really get warmed up until twelve o'clock!

Suddenly another innovative architectural feature made itself known. In the middle of one of his most fervent appeals, at two minutes past twelve, a trap door opened, and the preacher dropped into the basement.

—Don Emmitte

A woman joined a convent before she learned that as a nun, she could talk only once a year. The first year she said to the Mother Superior, "My room is cold."

"We'll get you a blanket," was the response.

The second year she said, "My bed is hard."

"We'll get you a mattress," was the response.

The third year she said, "My room is too dark."

"We'll get you a brighter lamp." was the response.

The fourth year she had done some thinking and said, "I quit."

"Well," came the response, "we were thinking about letting you go, anyway. You're always complaining." —*A Clear Sign*

A church in California's San Fernando Valley stopped buying from its regular office supplier. Why? When they ordered small pencils to be used in the pews for visitors to register with, the dealer sent golf pencils—each stamped with the words PLAY GOLF NEXT SUNDAY.

Father Truman Johns, the Episcopal priest, asked for a discount at the hardware store, saying: "I'm a poor preacher."

"I know," said the storekeeper. "I heard you last Sunday."

When I resigned as pastor of the Little Brown Church, one woman came up to me and said, "I'm sorry you are leaving. I never knew what sin was, until you came here!"

John O'Brien tried to explain why he left the priesthood. "Were you defrocked?" he was asked.

"No," he replied, "just unsuited."

Mrs. Wanda Watson had asked me to offer the blessing at the women's luncheon being held at her home. But I was delayed by an unforeseen parish emergency. (A snake had appeared in the midst of the pre-school playground.) Mrs. Watson waited as long as she could for me to appear. Finally, she asked her husband Henry to fill in.

Henry hated to speak in public, let alone pray out loud. He was visibly shaken but stood and announced reverently: "As there is no clergyman present, let us thank God."

During his sermon one Sunday morning, Reverend Sam Phillips said, "In each blade of grass there is a sermon."

The following Tuesday one of his flock saw him pushing a lawn mower about the grass in front of the parsonage and paused to say: "Well, Parson, I'm glad to see you engaged in cutting your sermons short."

To his horror, the pastor discovered during the service that he had forgotten his sermon notes, so he said to the congregation, by way of apology, "This morning I shall have to depend upon the Lord for what I might say, but next Sunday I will come better prepared."

Rt. Reverend Charles Francis Hall, Episcopal Bishop of New Hampshire, while attending the 1968 Lambeth Conference in London, was to attend a special service at Westminster Abbey. His wife, out shopping with another bishop's wife, realized it was almost time for the service at the Abbey, jumped into a taxi, directing the driver, "Take us to the cathedral."

Instead of taking them to the Episcopal cathedral, he deposited them at the Roman Catholic cathedral. Not realizing where they were, the woman marched up to an usher, saying, "We're bishops' wives. Where do we sit?"

No one recalls the response of the usher, but the story made the front page of London newspapers the next day.

At Mt. Ebal Baptist Church, Melanie Nelson was in charge of promoting the denominational magazine among the members of the congregation. At the Sunday morning service, she made an appeal to the congregation. "Please, brothers and sisters, if all of us start our subscriptions at the same time, and mail them in before the end of the month, then we'll be able to expire together."

Helen asked Madge, who decorated the altar, what she did with the flowers after the service. Madge replied innocently, "Oh, we take them to the people who are sick after the sermon."

At our congregation's Annual Meeting dinner, my wife and father were seated at the same table as the Conference Minister. Near the end of the meeting, the Conference Minister stood to offer some closing remarks, which became increasingly scattered and disorganized. As he rambled on, he lost his train of thought for the third time. "Now where was I?" he asked.

To the delight of all in attendance, my wife spoke up strongly, saying, "In conclusion!"

A Milwaukee minister, who declared that there are 947 sins, was besieged for copies of the list.

As Father Theodore O'Brien walked down the street one day, he met the Reverend Paul Whittelsey, who was playing "sidewalk superintendent" at the building of his new Congregational church. The priest inquired politely how the church was coming along and how well the contributions were coming in. "Everything is fine, Father," the minister assured him. Then he added, "Perhaps you'd like to make a contribution yourself."

"I'd certainly like to," answered the priest, "but my bishop would never allow me to contribute to a Protestant church."

The next morning, however, when opening his mail, Mr. Whittelsey found a check for fifty dollars with this note from Father O'Brien: "Although my bishop would never consent to a contribution for the erection of a Protestant church, there must be some expense involved in the tearing down of the old church. I'm sure he would never object to my contributing generously to that."

Three men were discussing what they would be, if not what they already were, denominationally.

The Catholic said, "I'd be an Episcopalian."

The Methodist said, "I'd be a Baptist."

The Lutheran said, "I'd be ashamed of myself."

Clara Winslow was attending a meeting of Church Women United. The secretary asked Clara's church affiliation. "I'm a Lutheran," she replied, "but my husband is nondimensional."

When the senior minister knelt at the altar, repeating, "I am nothing, nothing," his assistant was overcome by this show of humility and joined him. The janitor saw them, and moved by it all, did the same. Whereupon the assistant whispered to the minister, "Now look who thinks he's nothing."

Woman complaining to organist: "Your preludes are so loud I can't hear what my friends are saying."

Caitlin Reed noticed that his pastor, Reverend Avery Melton, an overwrought Disciples of Christ minister, went daily to the nearby railway tracks to watch an express train streak by. After observing this several times, Caitlin asked, "Pastor Melton, why do you come here every day and watch the Conrail flyer go by?"

"Because," retorted the pastor, "I like to see something I don't have to push."

Asked to pray, Deacon Weldon said, "Lord, give me patience. And give it to me immediately."

His sermons are sound advice—ninety-nine percent sound, and one percent advice.

Verna Phillips said to her pastor, "Your sermons are so good, they ought to be published."

The pastor, trying to be modest, said, "Posthumously, you mean?"

Nodding enthusiastically, Mrs. Phillips gushed, "Yes, and the sooner the better."

Wally Burns, trying to find a church for the first time, arrived nearly half an hour late. "Is the sermon over yet?" he asked.

The usher at the door replied, "Yes, but the preacher doesn't know it."

Neighbor: "Does your Sunday morning service usually start on time?"

Deacon: "Yes, our service starts at eleven o'clock sharp and ends at twelve o'clock dull."

He doesn't put enough fire into his sermons. It would be better if he put his sermons into the fire.

The preacher who doesn't strike oil in fifteen minutes should stop boring.

Minister (to his wife): "Well, Mrs. Lindy is moving away next week. I'll be sorry to see her go."

Wife: "You'll be sorry to see her go? Why, she's been the worst member of your congregation!"

Minister: "True—but she's given me the material for a lot of great sermons!

He gives a moving sermon. Long before he's finished, his congregation wants to move out of the sanctuary.

One scientist took sixteen years to discover helium. Another took thirty years to find radium. But many preachers take only ten minutes to produce tedium.

Bernard Petrie, a young minister, frequently boasted in public that all the time he needed to prepare his Sunday morning sermon was the few minutes it took him to walk to the church from the parsonage next door.

Soon after, the elders bought him a new parsonage five miles away.

Oliver Mendell, Ph.D., the noted scientist, made a careful study of people who fell asleep in church. His conclusion was that if all the sleeping congregants were laid end to end, they would be a lot more comfortable.

 During a game at the Sunday School's annual picnic, the superintendent was struck on the head by a baseball. He was taken to the local hospital for X-rays.

Sunday morning the assistant superintendent announced, "The superintendent is resting comfortably. The X-rays of his head showed nothing."

Prison Chaplain Larry Swenson said to a soon-to-be ex-convict, "As you make your way in the world, Son, remember the sermons you heard while you were here."

Replied the about-to-be-released prisoner: "Chaplain, no one who's heard you preach would ever want to come back here."

"Mummy," said little Lance, "why does the minister get a whole month's vacation in the summer?"

"Well, son," answered his mother, "if he's a good minister, he needs it. If he isn't, the congregation needs it!"

I know that all of you were saddened to learn this week of the death of one of our church's most valuable members— Someone Else. Someone's passing created a vacancy that will be difficult to fill. Else has been with us for many years, and for every one of those years, Someone did far more than the normal person's share of the work. Whenever leadership was mentioned, this wonderful person was looked to for inspiration as well as results.

Whenever there was a job to do, a class to teach, or a meeting to attend, one name was on everyone's lips, "Let Someone Else do it." It was common knowledge that Someone Else was among the largest givers in the church. Whenever there was a financial need, everyone just assumed that Someone Else would make up the difference. Someone Else was a wonderful person, sometimes appearing super-human, but a person can only do so much. Were the truth known, everyone expected too much of Someone Else. Now Someone Else is gone. We wonder what we are going to do.

Someone Else left a wonderful example to follow, but who is going to follow it? Who is going to do the things Someone Else did? Remember, we can't depend on Someone Else any longer.

—King Duncan

Pastor Tony Jenkins went to see his doctor for advice about his wife's snoring. The doctor asked, "Does her snoring really disturb you?" The pastor replied, "Does it disturb me? Why, it disturbs the entire congregation!"

Noted pastor Henry Ward Beecher said, "If anyone falls asleep in church, I have given the ushers permission to wake up the preacher!"

I asked a group of high school students to write down their favorite hymn.

Jennifer, a sixteen-year-old, wrote, "Charlie Sheen."

Frieda, Henrietta, and Gertrude were Baptist sisters who lived in separate states but always managed to get together for Christmas. One year, they were discussing their respective churches.

Frieda lamented, "Our congregation is sometimes down to thirty or forty on a Sunday."

Henrietta sighed, "That's nothing. Sometimes our congregation is down to six or seven."

Gertrude, a maiden woman in her seventies, topped them all: "Why, it's so bad in our church on Sundays that when the minister says 'dearly beloved,' it makes me blush."

A mission church in an Alaskan town was losing its minister. A pastor-seeking committee was formed, all the proper papers were filled out and many phone calls made to the Board of National Missions in New York City. Months went by without any sign of the church getting a new minister. Finally, in frustration, the committee's chairwoman dashed off one more note to the Board. It read, "Forget the minister. We've found sinning is more fun."

The new minister arrived in two weeks.

When I moved to northern California, I was invited to attend the Rotary Club as a guest. I wanted to become a member but was told that the club already had its quota of ministers. Later they discovered that they had no hog caller in the club and invited me to join in that category.

After some hesitancy I accepted, saying: "When I came here I expected to be the Shepherd of the Flock, but you have lived here longer than I have. I suppose you know the people of this community better than I do."

Father Carl Roth, an Episcopal rector, faxed his bishop asking if it was all right for him to conduct the funeral of a Baptist.

The bishop faxed back, "Bury all the Baptists possible."

John Killinger writes:

My wife, bless her, knows how to do it. We had been in our new pastorate ten months when she found out about a dear lady, well meaning, who was bad-mouthing the pastor because I had not yet called on her mother. (Actually I had, and the poor lady in her senility could never remember it.)

"Tell her to phone me," said my wife. "There are two things I would like to say to her. First, John is not God; and second, stuff it."

I have not heard another word of criticism in the parish.

When a church seeks a pastor, they want the strength of an eagle, the grace of a swan, the gentleness of a dove, the friendliness of a sparrow, the eye of a hawk, and the night hours of an owl. And when they catch this rare bird, they expect him to live on birdseed!

When I was pastor of the Little Brown Church, a visitor asked me, "How many members do you have?"

I replied, "A hundred."

"How many active?"

"All of them are active—fifty for me; fifty against me."

 My friend Gene, who is a traveling revivalist, reports, "Last year in a revival meeting in Iowa they fed me chicken three times a day for two weeks, then called on me to lay the cornerstone for their new Christian Education building. Believe me, I was ready!"

In the neighborhood where I grew up in Chicago, there was a Catholic sister who taught at Our Lady of Angels Parochial School. She gave so many multiple-choice tests that she became known as Nun of the Above!

Todd Rundgren, a Pentecostal pastor who is very popular with his congregation, explains his success as the result of a silent prayer that he offers each time he takes to the pulpit:

"Lord, fill my mouth with worthwhile stuff,
And nudge me when I've said enough."

Rabbi Mordecai Goodman sat in the synagogue all alone, tears streaming down his cheeks. He had just learned that his only son had deserted the ways of his ancestors and had become a Protestant.

The rabbi was sobbing uncontrollably when suddenly he heard the voice of God: "What is troubling you?"

"I'm so ashamed," cried the Rabbi. "My only son gave up being a Jew and became a Christian!"

"Yours, too?" replied the Lord.

A revival meeting was being held in a tent on the outskirts of town, and along the main road was a billboard proclaiming: "If you're weary of sin and want to be saved, turn here, go 100 yards and come into the revival tent."

Below the sign someone had hung another smaller one, "If not weary, call 555-3550."

Agatha Longworth, age seventy-eight and rather deaf, had a tendency to shout when she went to confession. When the priest, Father Leo Dankin, asked her to speak more quietly, since everyone in the church could hear, she shouted, "What did you say?" He carefully told her that she should write down what she had to say in advance.

At her next confession, she knelt and handed a piece of paper to the priest. He looked at it and said, "What is this? It looks like a grocery list."

"Oh dear," said Mrs. Longworth. "I must have left my sins at the Safeway."

After church one Sunday at St. Philip's, two members were critiquing Father Thompson's sermon.

The first one said, "I thought the sermon was divine. It reminded me of the peace of God. It passed all understanding."

The second one observed, "It reminded me of the mercy of God. I thought it would endure forever."

Shirley Sanders came to First Presbyterian Church every Sunday to look for an eligible bachelor. One Sunday her minister, Pastor Larson, asked her, "Why is it that when the rest of the congregation kneels to pray, you just sit there twiddling your thumbs?"

"Oh that," she chuckled. "I figure by this time God knows what I want, and it seems a little silly to keep going over the same old ground."

Pastor Jenkins was well loved by his small town congregation, but his salary was small. When a prosperous congregation in a large city offered to double his salary, the locals could not possibly match the generous financial offer.

"I suppose," a member of the flock worried to the pastor's son, "your father will accept the call to that big city?"

"I really don't know," replied the boy. "Dad's on his knees in the study at this very moment praying for guidance."

"And your ma?"

"She's upstairs packing."

As two priests traveled along a country road, the first complained about the other's habit of constantly interrupting himself. "Tell you what I'll do," said the first priest. "I'll wager you my horse that you won't be able to recite the 'Our Father' through to the end without stopping."

The other agreed to the bet and started the prayer. Halfway through, he looked up and asked, "Do I get the saddle, too?"

—Bishop Fulton J. Sheen

When I saw Lucille Lindy, a congregant of whom I was not particularly fond, coming up my garden path, I scampered upstairs and hid in my study, leaving my wife to handle the situation alone.

A full hour later, I called down to her, "Has that horrible bore gone yet?"

"Yes, dear," answered my wife, cool as a cucumber. "She went long ago. Mrs. Lindy is here now."

I had just completed the baptism of Sandra Anne, the infant daughter of James and Linda Winters. Everything went smoothly. I turned to Linda and said: "I have never seen a child that was so well behaved at a christening. She never as much as whimpered."

Linda replied, "Maybe that's because my husband and I have been practicing on her with a watering can for a week."

Betty Patrick, a member of my congregation, said to me last Sunday, "You sure did preach a powerful sermon today, Pastor. You must live a wonderful life!"

My response: "Betty, I can preach more gospel in fifteen minutes than I can live in fifteen years."

There was a very strict order of monks, and they had a rule that said speaking is permissible only one day a year, one monk at a time.

One year, a monk stood up and said quietly, "I don't like the mashed potatoes here at all. They're too lumpy." And he sat down.

A year later it was another monk's turn. He stood and said, "I rather like the mashed potatoes, I find them very tasty."

The third year came along and it was another monk's turn. He said, "I want to transfer to another monastery. I can't stand this constant bickering."

Following the Vatican's declaration that women cannot become priests because they do not resemble Christ, sources report that Colonel Sanders has declared that he will not employ anyone who doesn't resemble a chicken.   —Jane Curtin

Mark Twain sat through a carefully crafted, dramatically delivered sermon one Sunday morning. Even though he admired the effort, there was something about this minister that had always bothered him. The preacher seemed entirely too proud of his talents. Twain decided to take him down a few pegs.

After the service, Twain walked over to the minister and drawled, "Well, yes, it was a rip snorter, Reverend Wallace, but you know, I have a book at home that has every word of it."

The preacher took the bait at once. "Quite impossible. I would certainly like to see that book, if it exists."

"So you shall. I will mail it to you first thing in the morning."

Eventually, a bulky package arrived from Twain with an enormous postage-due bill attached. The preacher paid the charges and ripped open the wrappings.

Inside was an unabridged dictionary.

Mrs. Reed, who had been a member of the Little Brown Church for more than fifty years, loved to hear a fiery sermon. She would rock back and forth in the front pew in time to the minister's cadences, take a dip of snuff, and cry, "A-a-a-amen," at every ministerial denunciation.

When the minister spoke harshly of sex, drinking, smoking, drug-taking, movie-going, and dancing, she approved heartily, taking snuff at each admonition and shouting her enthusiastic "A-a-a-amen."

One Sunday the minister began, "And now let me talk about another vicious habit that, fortunately, is going increasingly out of fashion. I refer to the deplorable practice of snuff-dipping—"

Whereupon Mrs. Reed sat bolt upright and muttered under her breath, "Wouldn't you know? He's stopped preaching and begun meddling."

I once heard Medwick McGee, an old-fashioned, hell-and-damnation evangelist, berating his audience for their terrible misdeeds. "Remember what it says in the Bible," he thundered. "Jesus tells us in Matthew 22:13 that for those who do evil, there shall be weeping and gnashing of teeth."

"I guess I have nothing to worry about," replied a heckler, pointing to his toothless gums.

"Don't you worry, " the evangelist shot back. "In your case, teeth will be provided!"

In a rural community in Kansas, there was a year-long drought. All the crops were dying. In desperation, Larry Gates, the pastor of the Methodist church, the only church in town, announced that the whole community would assemble at the edge of one of the fields and pray for rain. A large crowd gathered, and Pastor Gates climbed on a tractor and surveyed the flock.

He shouted, "Brothers and sisters! We have come here to pray for rain!"

"Amen!" responded the crowd.

"Well," said the minister, "do you have sufficient faith?"

"Amen! Amen!" shouted the crowd.

"All right, all right," said the minister, "but I have one question to ask you!"

The crowd stood silent, puzzled, expectant.

"Brothers and sisters!" shouted the minister, "Where are your umbrellas?"

Vicar: "I didn't see you in church last Sunday, Nigel. I hear you were out playing football, instead."
Nigel: "That's not true, Vicar. And I've got the fish to prove it!"

There are a number of holy orders in the Catholic Church, among them being the Benedictines, the Dominicans, and the Jesuits—also know as the Society of Jesus, or "S.J." Recently there was a dispute (quite possibly foolish) between some Benedictines and Dominicans as to which order was loved the most by God. After an examination of history, personal experience, and resort to prayer, no agreement could be reached. So the monks decided to send an angel messenger up to God Himself to ask the question.

After a few days the angel returned bearing a message: "I bless both the Benedictines and the Dominicans and envelop you all in my love." The message was signed, "God, S.J."

Then Jesus took his Disciples up the mountain and, gathering them round him, he taught them, saying:

Blessed are the poor in spirit, for theirs is the Kingdom of Heaven.

Blessed are the meek.

Blessed are they who mourn.

Blessed are the merciful.

Blessed are they who thirst for justice.

Blessed are you when persecuted.

Blessed are you when you suffer.

Be glad and rejoice, for your reward is great in Heaven.

Try to remember what I'm telling you!

Then Simon Peter said, "Will this count on our final grade?"

And Andrew said, "Will there be a test on it?"

And James said, "By what date do we have to know it?"

And Philip said, "How many words?"

And Bartholomew said, "Will I have to stand up in front of the others?"

And John said, "The other disciples didn't have to learn this. Why do we have to learn it?"

And Matthew said, "What grade do we get if we learn it? Is this a regular assignment or extra credit?"

And Judas said, "What is it worth? Will it help us to get a better job in the real world?"

And the other disciples questioned him likewise.

Then one of the Pharisees who was present asked to see Jesus' lesson plan and inquired of Jesus, "Good Master, what are your terminal objectives in the cognitive domain?"

And Jesus wept.

Margaret Denton, an elderly church member, was discussing with me an uncle of hers who, after a lifetime of rather wild living, had repented of his sins and joined a Southern Baptist church. "Will my converted uncle's sins be forgiven, Pastor?" she asked.

"Oh, certainly, yes!" I replied. "Remember, the greater the sins, the greater the saint."

Margaret thought silently for a time. Then she said, "I wish I'd known this fifty years ago."

A twenty-seven-year-old minister had been assigned to his first post only a short time when he noticed that one of his parishioners, an old lady, had missed several Sundays in a row. He decided to see her and find out the reason.

"Young man," she answered him firmly, "you aren't old enough to have sinned enough to have repented enough to be able to preach about it!"   —*Funny Funny World*

Over at Holy Ghost Gospel Tabernacle, Pastor Martin Catrell was rather disappointed that things were not "happening" in his church. He asked one of the leading deacons, "What is wrong with our church? Is it ignorance or apathy?"

The deacon responded, "I don't know, and I don't care."

When my late father-in-law ran out of sermon ideas, instead of a sermon, he would have the congregation call out favorite hymn selections. Everyone would sing a verse or two of each. He called such an event a "singspiration." These events got quite popular, and people made a point of checking the Longview, Texas newspaper to see when they were going to happen.

One week, the paper announced that the Longview Cumberland Presbyterian Church would have a "sinspiration" on Sunday evening.

Yes, the crowd was much larger than usual.

—William (Bill) Corbin

From the bulletin of the Church of the Incarnation in Sarasota, Florida: "The Magic of Lassie, a film for the whole family, will be shown Sunday at 5 p.m. in the church hall. Free puppies given to all children not accompanied by parents."

When it comes to church leadership, some members rise to the occasion, while others merely hit the ceiling.

A circus strong man earned his living by displaying astonishing feats of physical strength. His show would normally conclude with a simple but impressive demonstration of his ability to squeeze an orange dry! After completing his act, he would then challenge his audience to produce anyone who could extract even one drop of juice from the crushed fruit.

On one of these occasions, a little man volunteered. He was so diminutive that his very appearance raised a laugh from the spectators. Undaunted, however, the man stepped onto the stage and took from the athlete what appeared to be nothing more than a shriveled-up piece of rind. Then bracing himself, he firmly compressed his right hand. Every eye was on him, and the atmosphere was electric! A moment or two elapsed, and then, to everyone's amazement—and not least the circus strong man—a drop of orange juice formed and dripped to the floor. As the cheers subsided, the strong man invited the little guy to tell the crowd how he had managed to develop such fistic powers.

"Nothing to it," replied the little fellow. With a grin, he added, "I happen to be the treasurer of the local Baptist church!"

As she left church, Peggy Watson shook hands with the minister and said, "Thank you for your sermon. It was like water to a drowning man."

PREACHER-IN-A-BOX

Are you tired of waking up at six in the morning just to drag your family out to hear another of those last-minute, package-mix Church sermons? Are you tired of falling asleep as your minister drones on and on and on about the same thing he rattled on about the month before? Then, friend, you need to meet the latest invention from Theology Technology: Preacher-in-a-Box.

Preacher-in-a-Box is a twenty-one pound lunch-box-size computer system that, when used, will lift the level of spirituality in any church. With the touch of a few buttons anyone can access the three thousand pre-programmed sermons, any of the four hundred song accompaniments, and the fifteen hundred exciting children's stories. With the new voice and sound synthesis systems, Preacher-in-a-Box will perform its tasks with near-perfect accuracy, with much variety, and the expertise of the world's greatest preachers.

Preacher-in-a-Box even does weddings and funerals, and with our new office counseling chip, it will be able to operate on an interactive level with your congregation. In addition, Preacher-in-a-Box mounts easily on any standard-size pulpit when called to speak, and if you act now, we will give you, free of charge, the new extension arm that will enable Preacher-in-a-Box to shake hands with those attending your services. Stop by your local Theology Technology dealer, and see what this amazing new machine can do for you and your church. Oh yeah, in case you were wondering about Preacher-in-a-Box's public relations skills, this entire ad was written and produced by the machine without any outside help.   —Ray McAllister

From a church bulletin:
   "All new sermons every Sunday. No reruns."

You have to get to church pretty early to get a seat in the back row.   —*Funny Funny World*

The minister of a rural church in the Ozarks suggested to his parishioners that they purchase a chandelier. It was put to a vote and all the members voted it down.

"Why do you oppose the purchase of a chandelier?" asked the preacher.

"Well," drawled one of his flock, "first we can't spell it, so how can we order it? Second, even if we did get it, no one can play it, and third, what we really need is more light."

—*Funny Funny World*

Connie: Did you see the new hat Mrs. Smith wore to church this morning?
Lowell: No!
Connie: A lot of good it does you to go to church!

Seymour met a priest on the street. He asked, "How come you wear your collar backwards?

The priest answered, "Because I am a father!"

Rosenberg said, "I have four sons myself!"

The priest smiled and said, "You don't understand. You see, I have thousands of children!"

"Well, then," Rosenberg said, "you should wear your trousers backward!"

During a visit to the big island of Hawaii, my wife and I attended Sunday services at a small Congregational church known for its informality. One Sunday a deacon asked me if I would usher at the morning service. I protested that I was much too casually dressed. "At home," I explained, "the deacons always look for a man wearing a tie when they needed an usher.

"Over here," the deacon laughingly replied, "we look for someone wearing shoes."

I was attending a conference out-of-town with two deacons from my congregation. The first evening's meeting did not finish until rather late, so we decided to have something to eat before going to bed. Unfortunately the only place still open was a seedy bar-and-grill with a questionable reputation. After being served, one of the deacons asked me to say grace. "I'd rather not," I replied. "I don't want Him to know I'm here."

At the Little Brown Church, our music director referred to the choir as "the prison ensemble." When I asked her why, she explained, "Because they're always behind a few bars and trying to find the key."

Father Vazken Movsesian, a Bay Area Catholic priest, recalls:
Uplifted by the Papal Mass at San Francisco's Candlestick Park [a few years back], I gave my congregation a detailed account of how I was escorted to the Forty-Niners' locker room, where I met with representatives of other Christian churches. I expressed the feeling of warmth that was radiating from the seventy thousand faithful that day. Finally, I summarized the inspirational message of Pope John Paul II.
At the conclusion of my remarks, I asked for questions. A young voice piped up eagerly, "Father, did you get to see Joe Montana's locker?"

At the Little Brown Church, I regularly visited shut-ins. Two of my regulars were sisters in their nineties who lived together. I arrived at their home one day to find that Meals on Wheels had just delivered Mexican food, which neither sister liked. "We hate to see food go to waste," said the elder sister. "Won't you please eat it?"
I replied, "I would feel terribly guilty eating the lunch brought to you by Meals on Wheels. Why not give it to the cat?"
"Oh, we tried that," said the younger sister. "He didn't like it, either. It made him throw up."

While I was the new pastor of a church in rural east Tennessee, I assisted a family of parishioners who owned a feed store. It was their busy season, and they needed someone to help fill hundred-pound sacks of corn.

As I pulled my first bag off the scale and started to close it, I noticed a look of concern on the face of the store owner. "When we tie sacks, we use a miller's knot," he said. "I don't suppose you can do that."

He didn't know that I had spent ten years farming before entering the ministry. When I easily tied the knot, he was visibly impressed. "You're the first preacher I ever saw," he told me, "who knew anything at all about working."   —James Huskins

At the Little Brown Church, our Christmas Eve service included a candle-lighting ceremony in which each member of the congregation lit a candle from his neighbor's candle. At the end of the ceremony, the congregation sat hushed, pondering the inspiring beauty of the moment. I rose to announce the concluding hymn and was taken completely by surprise when my invitation evoked laughter: "Now that everyone is lit, let's sing 'Joy to the World.'"

When I first met Father Miles, he had just come from the Catholic church across from his office, where he had been celebrating Mass. He looked odd to me in his cassock and to cover my discomfort I quipped, "I didn't know you wore dresses!"

Without losing a beat, Father Miles replied, "Oh, this old thing."

While I was visiting Father Miles, the UPS guy came by with a large package. He had a very strange look on his face. "I have a package for the Father," he explained.

Miles signed for it. I clearly understood the delivery man's chagrin when I saw what was stamped on the box: "Contents: FULL COLOR MADONNA CALENDARS."

When I received my first call (to be pastor of the St. John's Congregational Church in Philadelphia), I found the first few months at my new job very interesting. One day I'd have ink up to my elbows from repairing a mimeograph machine. The next day, I'd be arranging a rummage sale or a pancake breakfast. The next, I'd be hanging from a tree trying to trim the limbs without getting into the power lines. Then, I'd try to hunt down a carburetor for the church's antique bus. Next, I'd repaint the church nursery. Roofing, plumbing and wiring were also included in my work. One thing's for sure: my instructors were right on target when they said, "The seminary won't teach you all you need to know about being a pastor."

Reverend Mel, a local Baptist minister, liked to slip old proverbs into his sermons, but had trouble getting them right. For example, he would remind the congregation not to "kick a gift horse in the mouth" or that "a stitch in line saves time" or "a fool and his money are soon started" or "you can lead a horse to water, but that's a horse of a different color."

One Sunday, he was describing how easy some task was to perform and said, "It's just like falling off a log." We all thought he had finally mastered one. Then he added, "Once you learn how, you never forget."

2.
KIDS' THEOLOGY

My grandson Jacob once asked me, "Grandpa Lowell, why do so many churches have plus signs on them?"

Elizabeth Peters and her five-year-old grandson Nathaniel were taking a walk in the country just after the first heavy frost of the season had given the foliage a brilliantly colored crazy quilt appearance.

"Just think," the grandmother marveled, gazing at the scarlet and gold hillside, "God painted all that."

"Yes," the grandson agreed, "and He even did it with his left hand."

"What do you mean, 'He did it with his left hand'?" she asked, somewhat puzzled by the remark.

"Well," Nathaniel replied reasonably, "at Sunday School, they told us that Jesus is sitting on the right hand of God!"

During the minister's prayer, there was a loud whistle from the congregation. Gary's mother was horrified. Later she asked, "Gary, whatever made you do that?"

Gary answered soberly, "I asked God to teach me to whistle, and just then he did!" —James Cammack, *Parables Outside Paradise*

Austin Markle, the Sunday School teacher, asked his class: "What are sins of omission?"

After some thought one little fellow said: "They're the sins we should have committed but didn't get around to."

I was helping my grandson Jonathan with his science homework. His assignment was to define the Great Divide. "That's easy, Grandpa," he said. "That's when Moses parted the Red Sea."

Students of a Sunday School class at Brewer's Island United Church were asked to write down what they liked best about Sunday School. One little boy, Harold Winston, who also happened to be the pastor's son, thought for a moment and remembered all the songs the class had sung during the year. His spelling was not as good as his memory for he wrote, "The thing I like best about Sunday School is the sinning."

Dexter Rice, a Sunday School teacher, was telling his class the story of the Prodigal Son. Wishing to emphasize the resentful attitude of the elder brother, he laid stress on this part of the parable.

After describing the rejoicing of the household over the return of the wayward son, Dexter spoke of one who, in the midst of the festivities, failed to share in the jubilant spirit of the occasion. "Can anybody in the class," he asked, "tell me who this was?"

Nine-year-old Olivia had been listening sympathetically to the story. She waved her hand in the air. "I know!" she beamed. "It was the fatted calf!"

One morning, a Sunday School teacher asked her group, "Does somebody know who defeated the Philistines?"

After a few moments one youngster asked, "They're not in the NBA, are they?"

One Sunday late in Lent, a Sunday School teacher decided to ask her class what they knew about Easter.

The first little fellow suggested, "Easter is when all the family comes to the house and we eat a big turkey and watch football." The teacher suggested that perhaps he was thinking of Thanksgiving, not Easter.

Next, a pretty little girl answer said, "Easter is the day when you come down the stairs in the morning and you see all the beautiful presents under the tree." At this point, the teacher was really feeling discouraged. After explaining that the girl was probably thinking about Christmas, she called on a lad with his hand tentatively raised in the air.

Her spirits perked up as the boy said, "Easter is the time when Jesus was crucified and buried." She felt she had gotten through to at least one child, until he added, "And then He comes out of the grave, and if He sees His shadow we have six more weeks of winter."

The Sunday School teacher asked each child to identify a favorite Bible character.

"Mine is King Solomon," declared a little girl.

"And why is that?" asked the teacher.

"Because he was so kind to ladies and animals."

"Who told you that?" asked the startled teacher.

"Nobody told me. I read it myself in the Bible," said the girl. "It says Solomon kept seven hundred wives and three hundred porcupines."

Pastor Denning was talking to the eight-year-olds' Sunday School class about things money can't buy. "It can't buy laughter," he told them. "That comes from the soul. And it can't buy love." Driving this point home, he said, "What would you do if I offered you a thousand dollars not to love your mother and father?"

A few moments of silence ensued while the boys and girls mulled this over. Then a small voice demanded: "How much would you give me not to love my big sister?"

Five-year-old Christopher Walsh excitedly reported to his parents what he had learned in Sunday School. He told the story of Adam and Eve and how Eve was created from one of Adam's ribs. A few days later he told his mother, "My side hurts. I think I'm having a wife."

"Did Moses ever get better in the end?" asked little Sarah when she got home from Sunday school.

"Why," asked her mother, "whatever makes you think he was ill?"

"Well, he must have been," was the reply. "Didn't the Lord have him take two tablets?"

A Sunday School teacher read a passage from the Old Testament Book of Jonah to her class:

"And the Lord appointed a great fish to swallow up Jonah; and Jonah was in the belly of the fish three days and three nights. Then Jonah prayed to the Lord his God from the belly of the fish, saying 'I called to the Lord out of my distress and He answered me.' . . . and the Lord spoke to the fish, and it vomited out Jonah upon the dry land." (Jonah 1:17–2:2, 10)

When she had finished reading, the teacher said, "Now, children, you have heard the Bible story of Jonah and the whale. What does this story teach us?"

Ten-year-old Mark shouted out: "You can't keep a good man down!"

One of my grandsons explained to me that the lions could not eat Daniel because "Daniel was all backbone."

Pastor Ringer asked little Brittany what she thought of her first church service.

"The music was nice," she said, "but the commercial was too long."

At Bayside Baptist, Sandra Alexander, the pastor's wife, asked her Sunday School Class, "What do we learn from the story of Jonah and the whale?"

Ten-year-old Samantha volunteered: "People make whales sick."

Harriett Feneman, the new Sunday school teacher, asked her class, "What do we learn from the story of Jonah?"

Eight-year-old Robert Ashley put up his hand and answered, "Travel by air!"

A little boy asked his father what was the highest number he had ever counted. Replying that he didn't know, the father asked his son his highest number. It was 973.

"Why did you stop there?" asked his father.

"Because church was over."

When I was pastor of a church in Philadelphia, I was busy one afternoon nailing up an errant vine. A neighbor's son stood by watching for a long time. Finally, I asked, "Well, my young friend, are you trying to get a hint or two on gardening?"

"No, sir," said the boy, "I'm just waiting to hear what a minister says when he hammers his thumb."

Reverend Hector Hanks, chaplain at Mills Hospital, was on his way home one evening. Near his house, he saw a group of little boys sitting in a circle with a dog in the middle. He asked them what they were doing with the dog. Little Joey Bateson said, "We ain't doin' nuthin' to the dog, we're just tellin' lies, and the one that tells the biggest one gets to keep the dog."

The chaplain told them, "I am shocked. When I was a little boy, I would never have even thought of telling a lie."

Right away Joey said, "Give him the dog, fellas."

The Alexander family moved from the Methodist Church to the Episcopal Church. The rector asked one of their children, eight-year-old Wendy, why the family had changed churches. "I think," said the Wendy, "that my mother likes the Episcopal lethargy better."

Death and dying are always on the back burners of everyone's mind, from preschoolers to the oldest adult. Some nine-year-old children were asked what they thought of death and dying.

Jim said, "When you die, they bury you in the ground and your soul goes to heaven, but your body can't go to heaven, because it's too crowded up there already."

Judy said, "Only the good people go to heaven. The other people go where it's hot all the time, like in Florida."

John said, "Maybe I'll die someday, but I hope I don't die on my birthday because it's no fun to celebrate it if you're dead."

Marsha commented, "When you die, you don't have to do homework in heaven, unless your teacher is there, too."

—*Good Housekeeping*

"So you attend Sunday school," the reverend asked little Eva.

"Oh, yes, sir," said little Eva.

"And you know your Bible?"

"Oh, yes, sir."

"Could you perhaps tell me something that is in it?"

"I could tell you everything that's in it!"

"Indeed," smiled the reverend. "Do tell me."

"Sister's steady's snapshots are in it," replied little Eva. "And Ma's recipe for Hungarian goulash is in it, and a lock of my hair, cut off when I was a baby is in it, and the hock ticket for Pa's watch is in it." —*Larry Wilde*

A new Sunday school teacher had to iron out some problems with the Lord's Prayer. One child had to be corrected after repeating, "Howard be thy name." Another youngster prayed,

"Lead us not into Penn Station." Still another surprised the teacher with, "Our Father, who art in heaven, how'd you know my name?"

When my daughter Susie was seven, I took her to her first Benediction service. She watched transfixed as the altar boys lit all the candles. "Do you know what happens now?" I whispered.

"Yes," replied Susie sagely, "Liberace's coming."

Once, while affectionately joking with our three-year-old daughter Maria, I asked her, "Where did we get such a nice girl like you?"

She replied, "Jesus gave me to you."

I persisted, "But why did He give you to us, and not to somebody else?"

She thought a moment, then quite confidently blurted, "'Cuz my clothes are here!"   —Karen Lewans in *Catholic Digest*

"Daddy, I want to ask you a question," said little Justin after his first day in Sunday school.

"Yes, Son, what is it?"

"The teacher was reading the Bible to us—all about the children of Israel building the temple, the children of Israel crossing the Red Sea, the children of Israel battling the Philistines, the children of Israel making sacrifices. Didn't the grownups do *anything?*"

"Mommy," said little Wendy, "did you ever see a cross-eyed bear?"

"Why no, Wendy," replied her mother. "But why do you ask?"

"Because we sang about one today in Sunday school. His name is Gladly—'Gladly the cross-eyed bear.'"

(At least they didn't sing that other great animal song, "Just As I Am Without One Flea"!)

Pastor Neville Crutchfield and his wife were quizzing their five-year-old daughter Melanie about what she had learned in Sunday school that morning.

"We learned about fixing things," she said.

"Fixing things? You mean you did crafts."

"No, we learned about fixing things," she insisted. "It's in our memory verse, where Jesus said, 'I go to repair a place for you.'"

My friend, Reverend Victor Sharpe recalls:

"The first time I went to church was when I was seven. I attended with a neighbor. At the service, I heard the minister use the expression, "Ashes to ashes, dust to dust." I asked my mother what it meant.

"It means," she answered, "that we all come from dust and we shall all return to dust."

That night, Mother was startled to hear me call down to her from my bedroom, "Come quick, Mommy—there's someone under the bed either coming or going!"

Irene Davidson, a faithful Sunday school teacher at First Congregational Church, was telling her class the story of Lot. "Lot was warned to take his wife and flee out of the city, but his wife looked back and was turned to salt," she said. She paused dramatically to let this sink in, looked around the class, and saw one little girl, Brittany, tentatively raise her hand.

"Yes?" said the teacher.

"I was wondering," said little Brittany, "what happened to his flea?"

Sylvia Carboni was telling the story of Moses to a class of wild-eyed five-year-olds at Grace Community Tabernacle.

"And who do you suppose," she asked dramatically, "did the beautiful Egyptian princess get to take care of the little boy she had found in the bulrushes?"

Without hesitation, one little girl answered, "A baby sitter!"

A New Testament version goes like this:

A little boy in Sunday School gave the explanation as to why Mary and Joseph took the baby Jesus to Egypt. He claimed, "They couldn't get a sitter."

Miss Evers, the kindergarten teacher, was proud of her class full of extremely bright and articulate children. One day after recess, Miss Evers was presiding over a discussion about the children's fathers and mothers. One child, Beth Cohen, volunteered, "Well, my mother's Catholic and my father's Jewish."

"Wow!" said her playmate, Dalacie. "So what do you believe?"

"I believe in everything!" said Beth.

"What do you mean, everything?" asked Dalacie.

"Well, you know," said Beth, "Jesus, Moses, Snow White—everything."

A Sunday School teacher asked a group of children in her class. "Why do you believe in God?" In reporting some of the answers the teacher confessed that the one she liked best came from a boy who said, "I don't know. I guess it's just something that runs in the family."

During the children's sermon at the First Congregational Church of Klamath Falls, Pastor Jim Hawkins asked, "What is gray, has a bushy tail and gathers nuts in the fall?"

Five-year-old Adam Bronson raised his hand. "I know the answer should be Jesus," he stated, "but it sounds like a squirrel to me."

Father: "Did you learn anything in Sunday School today?"

Son: "We learned that there were cars mentioned in the Bible."

Father: "There are no cars in the Bible, son."

Son: "Then why does it say that God drove Adam and Eve out of Eden and showed them his Fury?"

The following are children's answers to Sunday School questions in a Church of England, as they were reprinted by St. Paul's (Episcopal) Church in Seattle, Washington:

- Noah's wife was called Joan of Ark.
- Henry VIII thought so much of Wolsey that he made him a cardigan.
- The fifth commandment is: Humor thy father and mother.
- Lot's wife was a pillar of salt by day but a ball of fire at night.
- When Mary heard she was to be the mother of Jesus, she went off and sang the Magna Carta.
- Salome was a woman who danced in front of Harrod's (a London department store).
- Holy acrimony is another name for marriage.
- Christians can have only one wife. This is called monotony.
- The Pope lives in a vacuum.
- Next in order after seraphim is paraffin.
- Today, wild beasts are confined to the Theological Gardens.
- The patron saint of travelers is St. Francis of the seasick.
- A Republican is a sinner mentioned in the Bible.
- Abraham begat Isaac and Isaac begat Jacob and Jacob begat twelve partridges.
- The natives of Macedonia did not believe, so Paul got stoned.
- The first commandment: Eve told Adam to eat the apple.
- It is sometimes difficult to hear what is being said in church because the agnostics are so terrible.

A true story told by Anthony Evans:

One of our Sunday School teachers was telling her preschoolers about Jesus' arrest, trial and crucifixion, and had their undivided attention—even Michael was listening. When she finished the lesson and asked for questions, Michael's hand shot into the air; the teacher was thrilled.

"I just want to know one thing," he said. "Where the heck were the State Police when all this was going on?"

Thanksgiving day was approaching, and the family had received a card picturing a Pilgrim family on their way to church. Grandma showed the card to her young grandchildren and remarked, "The Pilgrim children liked going to church with their parents."

"Oh, yeah?" her grandson replied. "Then why is the dad carrying that rifle?"

 The Sunday before Christmas, Melissa James asked her Sunday school students at Holy Trinity Lutheran Church to draw pictures of the Holy Family.

When the pictures were handed in, she saw that some of the youngsters had drawn the conventional pictures—the Holy Family in the manger, the Holy Family riding on the mule, and so forth. But she was confused by the drawing made by little Joshua. She called him up and asked him to explain his picture, which showed an airplane with four heads sticking out of the plane windows.

She said, "I can understand why you draw three of the heads to show Joseph, Mary, and Jesus. But who's the fourth head?"

"Oh," answered Joshua, "that's Pontius the Pilot!"

My six-year-old grandson is inordinately fond of dogs. As Christmas and our church's Nativity pageant approached, I found him in front of the Christmas tree in our living room, down on all fours and barking. When I asked what he was doing, he replied, "I have to practice. I'm going to be one of the shepherds."

When my grandsons came home from Sunday School during one of our weekend visits to their home, I asked if either of them could tell me where to find the Ten Commandments. Blank stares and silence were finally broken when one of them said, "Have you looked it up in the Yellow Pages?"

Young Steve Parker forgot his lines in the Sunday school's Christmas pageant. His mother was in the front row to prompt him. She gestured and formed the words silently with her lips, but it did not help. Her son's memory was blank. Finally she leaned forward and whispered the cue, "I am the light of the world."

The child beamed. With great feeling and a loud, clear voice, he said, "My mother is the light of the world."

After the family sang some carols, four-year-old Kevin Kneeland commented, "Wasn't it good of the shepherds to put on clean clothes when they went to see baby Jesus?"

His mother asked, "What do you mean?"

Johnny explained, "We just sang, 'While Shepherds Washed Their Socks by Night.'"

Nine-year-old Heather quizzed her mother as to her origin, and was given the traditional answer, "God sent you."

"And how did you get here, Mother? Did God send you, too?"

"Yes, dear."

"And Grandma?"

"Yes, dear."

"And Great-grandma?"

"Yes, dear."

"Do you mean to say that there have been no normal births in this family for over a hundred years?"

Maybe I sound like an old fuddy-duddy, but children get confused when we layer the holiest of seasons with fantasy. (No, I don't want to get rid of Santa Claus.) I can appreciate the frustration of the Sunday school teacher who was working with her primary group. "Do you know who Matthew was?" she asked.

When she received no answer she asked, "Do any of you know who Mark was?"

Still no answer.

"I'm sure that somebody knows who Peter was," she said. "Can anyone tell me please? Who was Peter?"

A little boy raised his hand and said, "I think he was a rabbit."

—King Duncan

A letter written to God:

Dear God,

Was there anything special about Bethlehem, or did you just figure that that was as good a place as any to start a franchise?

Your friend,

Jim, age 12

Young George Washington probably did not chop down his father's cherry tree. And he probably did not admit it by saying, "I cannot tell a lie." But many people repeat that story because it features Washington's honesty.

Little Sarah once asked her mother, "Do people who never tell lies go to heaven?"

"Yes," her mother answered. "They are the only ones."

"Gosh, I bet it's lonesome up there with just God and George Washington."

I was baby-sitting my grandson Justin when he was four. I had read him a story, tucked him in, and was downstairs watching television.

A terrible thunderstorm came up, with lightning and fierce noises. Justin shouted down to me, "Grandpa, I'm scared. Come up and help me."

Engrossed in the show, I shouted back, "Don't worry, Justin, you'll be all right. You know God loves you."

"I know God loves me," cried Justin, "but I need something with skin on."

3.
HEAVEN & HELL

If you're not allowed to laugh in heaven, I don't want to go there.
—Martin Luther

As for reincarnation, I have a hard time believing in any religion that says you have to go through puberty again.
—Robert G. Lee

When I told the people of Northern Ireland that I was an atheist, a woman in the audience stood up and said, "Yes, but is it the God of the Catholics or the God of the Protestants in whom you don't believe?"
—Quentin Crisp

Mary Ames died and went to heaven. At the pearly gates, St. Peter was quizzing the new arrivals. "Before you may enter, can you tell me God's first name?" he asked.

After thinking a moment, Mary smiled and said, "Andy!"

"Andy?" St. Peter replied. "Where'd you get Andy?"

"We sang it in church all the time: 'Andy walks with me, Andy talks with me, Andy tells me I am His own.'"

Yiddish proverb: "If triangles had a God, He'd have three sides."

Definitions of heaven and hell:
In heaven . . .
- all the cooks are French
- all the police are English
- all the engineers are German
- all the lovers are Italian
- and everything's organized by the Swiss

In hell . . .
- all the cooks are English
- all the police are German
- all the engineers are French
- all the lovers are Swiss
- and everything's organized by the Italians

Reminds me of two fellows who died recently and were walking the golden streets of God's celestial realm. There was more beauty and more splendor and more joy there than they had ever dreamed imaginable.

One of them turned to the other and said, "Can you believe how wonderful this is?"

The other replied, "Yes, and to think we could have gotten here ten years sooner if we hadn't eaten all that oat bran."

An Episcopalian died and went to Heaven. As St. Peter lead him past Purgatory, he saw some people who were in deep agony. So he asked, "Who are those people, and what have they done to deserve this?"

St. Peter said, "Those are Jews. They are guilty of eating ham."

They went on and passed another group in worse shape, so the man asked who they were and what they had done. St. Peter said, "Those are Catholics, and they are guilty of eating ham on Fridays."

They went on and found a group of people much more despondent than the other two, and so he asked, "Who are these people, and what have they done that was so bad?"

"Those are Episcopalians," said St. Peter, "and they were caught eating ham with their salad forks."

A lawyer dies and finds himself with the devil in a room filled with clocks. Each clock turns at a different speed and is labeled with the name of a different occupation. After examining all of the clocks, the lawyer turns to the devil and says, "I have two questions. First, why does each clock move at a different speed?"

The devil replies, "They turn at the rate at which that occupation sins on the earth. What is your second question?"

The lawyer asks where the attorneys' clock is.

The devil looks puzzled, then his face brightens and he replies, "Oh, we keep that one in the workshop. The workers use it as a fan."

A bus driver and a minister are standing in line to get into Heaven. The bus driver approached the gate and St. Peter said, "Welcome. I understand you were a bus driver. Since I'm in charge of housing, I believe I have found the perfect place for you. See that mansion over the hilltop? It's yours."

The minister heard all this, and begins to stand a little taller. He also thinks to himself, "If a bus driver got a place like that, just think what I'll get." The minister approaches the gate and St. Peter says, "Welcome. I understand you were a minister. See that shack in the valley?"

St. Peter had hardly gotten the words out of his mouth when the irate minister said, "I was a minister, I preached the Gospel, I helped teach people about God. Why does that bus driver get a mansion, and I get a shack?"

Sadly St. Peter responds, "Well, it seems when you preached, people slept. When that bus driver drove, people prayed."

A taxicab driver died and arrived at the Pearly Gates. Just ahead of him was a famous minister, but St. Peter motioned him aside and took the cabbie into heaven at once.

"How come you're making me wait, while that cab driver gets right in? asked the frustrated clergyman. "Haven't I done everything possible to preach the gospel and live a good life?"

"Yes," said St. Peter, "but that cab driver scared hell out of more people than you ever did."

Mistaken identity is one of the oldest and most successful comedy devices. I hope no one is offended by this next one, but it is a classic example of this genre of humor:

St. Peter is getting ready for his annual three-week vacation, and Jesus volunteers to fill in for him at the Pearly Gates. "It's no big deal," St. Peter explains. "Sit at the registration desk, and ask the incoming people a little about their lives. Then tell them to go to housekeeping to pick up their wings."

On the third day, a bewildered old man approaches the registration desk where Jesus is working.

"I'm a simple carpenter," says the man. "Once I had a son, a very special child unlike any other in this whole world. He was born in a very unique way, and he went through an incredible transformation in his lifetime, even though he had holes in his hands and feet. He has been gone a long time, but his spirit lives on forever. His story is told all over the world."

By this time, Jesus is standing with his arms outstretched. Tears well up in his eyes as he embraces the old man.

"Father!" he cries out. "It's been so long!"

The old man squints, stares for a moment, and says, "Pinocchio?"

Four married couples stood at the gates to Heaven. As St. Peter checked their files, he noted that all had pursued dubious paths during their lives.

St. Peter glared at the first man and said, "I can't let you in. You're a notorious drunk—worse than W.C. Fields, I'm told.

All you ever thing about is drink, drink, drink. And I notice that even your wife's name is 'Ginny.'"

St. Peter then looked at the second man and roared, "I can't let you in either, because you're a terrible skinflint—worse than Scrooge, I'm told. All you think about is money, money, money, and I notice that your wife's name is 'Penny.'"

The third man cowered in terror as St. Peter declared, "I'm not going to let you in either. Your record shows that all you value are things that glitter. You make Elizabeth Taylor look unadorned. All you can think about is jewelry, jewelry, jewelry, and I see that your wife's name is 'Ruby.'"

Hearing all of this, the fourth man turned to his wife, and grumbled, "He'll never let us in. Let's get out of here, Fannie!"

—Max Isaackson, *Public Speaking and Other Coronary Threats*

When Fred arrived at the Pearly Gates there was hardly any line and he didn't have to wait more than a minute before his interview. Naturally, he was a little nervous about getting through the gates and into the heavenly city. Very quickly he found himself standing before an impressive Angelic Being with a clipboard who started getting his entry data down. After name, address, and a few other particulars the Angelic Being said, "Fred, it would help the process if you could share with me some experience from your life on earth when you did a purely unselfish, kindly deed."

Well, Fred thought about it for a minute and then said, "Oh, yes. I think I have something you might be interested in. One day I was walking along and I came upon a little old lady who was being mercilessly beaten up by a huge motorcycle-gang type of fellow. He was smacking her back and forth. Well, I stepped right up and first I pushed over his motorcycle —just to distract the biker's attention. And then I kicked him real hard in the shins and told the old lady to run for help. And then I hauled off and gave the guy a great shot right to the gut with my fist."

The angel looked at Fred with a great deal of interest and said, "Wow, that's quite a story. I'm impressed." Then taking his clipboard in hand he said, "Could you tell me just when this happened?"

Fred looked at his watch and said, "Oh, about two or three minutes ago."

A stockbroker appears before the pearly gates and seeks admission.

"Who are you?" says St. Peter.

"I am John Framson, a Wall Street broker."

"What is it that entitles you to admission?"

"Well, for one thing, the other day I saw a homeless, lame woman on Broadway and handed her a nickel."

"Is that in the records, Gabriel?"

"Yes, St. Peter."

"What else have you done?"

"Well, the other night I was crossing the Brooklyn Bridge and I ran into a half-frozen newsboy, and I gave him a nickel."

"Gabriel, is that on the records?"

"Yes, St. Peter."

"What else have you done?"

"That's all I can think of."

"What do you think we ought to do with this guy, Gabriel?"

"Give him back his dime and tell him where he can go."

Brother Hanks was a pillar of his church in Louisiana. He had total faith in God. He lived in a house by a great river. One night there was a terrible flood. He was standing in water up to his knees. Some men came by in a boat to rescue him and said, "Get in."

But he said, "Oh no, I have faith that God will rescue me."

The water kept rising. Pretty soon Brother Hanks had to climb up on the roof of his house to escape being drowned. After a time, some men came by in another boat to rescue him, but he refused. "I have faith that God will rescue me."

A few hours later, he was in water up to his neck. A helicopter flew over and let down a rope ladder, but the man waved them away, shouting, "I have faith that God will rescue me!"

At last, the force of the water broke up the house and Brother Hanks was drowned. He went to Heaven, and when he saw God, he asked, "Oh God, God, I had such faith in you, and you let me drown. Why?"

"What do you mean, let you drown? I sent you two boats and a helicopter, didn't I?"

A tourist wandered too close to the edge of the Grand Canyon, lost his footing and plunged over the side, clawing and scratching to save himself. Just before he fell into space, he encountered a shrubby bush which he desperately grabbed with both hands. Filled with terror he called out towards heaven, "Is there anyone up there?"

A calm, powerful voice came out of the sky, "Yes, there is."

The tourist pleaded "Can you help me?"

The calm voice replied, "Yes, I can. Do you have faith?"

"Yes, yes. I have strong faith."

The calm voice said, "Well, in that case, simply let go of the bush, and everything will turn out fine."

There was a tense pause. Then the tourist yelled, "Is there anyone else up there?"

The golf match of the centuries was played up in Heaven by St. Peter and St. Paul.

St. Peter had the honor on the first tee and promptly made a hole in one.

St. Paul, unfazed, did the same.

Dutifully, St. Peter marked the scores down on his card, then remarked, "What do you say, Paul? Let's cut out the miracles and get down to business."

Three women arrived at the Pearly Gates at the same time. St. Peter came but said he had some pressing business and asked them to please wait. He was gone a long time, but finally he came back and called one of the women in and asked her if she had minded waiting.

"No," she said, "I've looked forward to this for so long. I love God and I can't wait to meet Jesus. I don't mind at all."

St. Peter then said, "Well, I have one question. How do you spell 'God'?"

She said, "Capital-G-o-d."

St. Peter said, "Go right on in."

He went out and got one of the other women, told her to come on inside, said, "Did you mind waiting?"

She said, "Oh, no. I have been a Christian for fifty years, and I'll spend eternity here. I didn't mind at all."

So St. Peter said, "Just one more thing. How do you spell 'God'?"

She said, "G-o-d. No, I mean capital-G."

St. Peter said that was good and sent her on in to Heaven.

He went back out and invited the third woman in and asked her if she had minded waiting.

"Yes, I did," she said. "I've had to stand in line all my life—at the supermarket, when I went to school, when I registered my children for school, when I went to the movies—everywhere. And I resent having to wait in line for Heaven!"

St. Peter said, "Well, that's all right for you to feel that way. It won't be held against you. There is just one more question. How do you spell 'Czechoslovakia'?"

 They have Dial-a-Prayer for atheists now. You call up, and it rings and rings, but nobody answers.

Bob Peabody, our church's resident curmudgeon, underwent an operation at the local hospital. When he came out of the anesthesia, he asked a nurse, "How come all the shades on the windows are pulled down?"

The nurse answered, "The house across the street is on fire, and we didn't want you to wake up thinking that the operation was a failure."

Every Sunday morning, Mike goes to church and prays, "God, please let me win the lottery." Months pass, and although Mike fervently repeats his prayer weekly, it goes unanswered—until one Sunday, when Mike hears a deep voice from above utter his name.

"Is that you, God?" asks Mike.

"Yes, Mike," the voice replies.

"God," Mike implores, "why won't you let me win the lottery?"

"You have to meet me halfway, Mike," God says. "At least buy a ticket."

A man named Harold Bundy was a devoted reader of the obituary column of his local paper. All of Harold's friends knew of this habit, so one day they decided to play a trick on him by placing his name and picture in the obituaries.

The following morning Harold picked up his newspaper, turned to the obituary page, and there he saw his name, his biography and his photo.

Startled, he went to the telephone and rang up his pal, Tom. "Listen," he said. "Do you have the morning paper? You do? Please turn to the obituary page. What do you see in the second column?"

There was a pause on the other end of the line until Tom said, "Holy smokes! It's you, Harold! Wow, that's you, all right! Hey . . . where are you calling from?"

When I was twenty, I prayed for a million dollars. When I was thirty, I prayed for a million dollars. When I was forty, I prayed for a million dollars. Now I'm fifty and I've come to two conclusions: Either I'm praying for the wrong thing—or God isn't picking up His messages.

—Robert Orben

Cardinal Cushing of Boston once said, "Saints are okay in Heaven, but they're Hell on earth."

George, who had lived a wild life on earth, made a deathbed repentance and got through the Pearly Gates by the skin of his teeth. After some time in heaven, George went to Saint Peter and said, "I'm not happy in heaven. The golden streets are hard on my feet. I'm tired of hearing the angels twanging on their harps. Won't you let me go to hell a little while and visit my old friends?"

Saint Peter replied, "Your request is highly irregular. But I don't want anybody in heaven to be unhappy. I'll let you visit your friends in hell, provided you return by six o'clock sharp."

By Saint Peter's grace, George visited his old friends in hell and had such a joyous time with them he forgot the deadline. He didn't return to heaven until nine o'clock—three hours late.

Saint Peter chastised him verbally and declared that he would be compelled to discipline George severely for ignoring the deadline.

"Saint Peter," George replied, "you won't have to do that. I didn't come to stay. I just came to get my clothes."

—Senator Sam J. Ervin, Jr.

An elderly woman was sitting next to me on a plane and getting increasingly nervous about the thunderstorm raging outside. She turned to me and said: "Reverend, you are a man of God. Why can't you do something about this problem?"

"Lady," I replied, "I'm in sales, not management."

Three men, my neighbors, were discussing the proper position and attitude for prayer. One said, "You should be on your knees with your head bowed in reverence to the Almighty."

The second man spoke up and said, "Remember that you were created in God's image. The position in which to pray is to stand up looking into the heavens into the face of God and talk to Him as a child to his father."

The third man spoke up and said, "I know nothing about those positions, but the finest praying I ever did was upside down in a well."

—Saunders Guerrant

Emily Watson goes to a medium in hopes of communicating with the spirit of her late husband, Ben. The medium goes into a deep trance, and after a while a voice says, "Emily, is that you?"

"Ben, I'd know your voice anywhere. How are you?"

"Fine."

"And how is it there—where you are?"

"Wonderful. Today the sky is clear and blue, the temperature is in the seventies, and the grass is deep and high. And there are cows everywhere—beautiful cows of every color."

"Isn't that amazing," says Emily. "I had no idea there'd be cows in heaven."

"Heaven?" says Ben. "Who's talking about heaven? I'm a bull in Wisconsin."

St. Peter and Satan were having an argument one day about baseball. With a beguiling leer, Satan proposed a game to be played on neutral grounds between a select team from the heavenly host and his own hand-picked Hades boys.

"Very well," the gatekeeper of the Celestial City agreed. "But you realize, I hope, that we have all the good players and the best coaches, too."

"Sure," said Satan calmly, "but we have all the umpires!"

—*Keep 'em Laughing*

I don't want to achieve immortality through my work. I want to achieve immortality through not dying. —Woody Allen

Frances Mears, an elderly widow, went to a stonecutter's office to order a tombstone for her husband's grave. After explaining that all she wanted was a small marker with no frills, she told him to put the words "To My Husband" in a suitable place.

When the stone was delivered, she saw, to her horror, this inscription: "To My Husband—in a Suitable Place."

Historian Arnold J. Toynbee at age eighty said, "To be mortal is not by any means wholly disadvantageous. When I catch myself resenting not being immortal, I pull myself up short by asking whether I should really like the prospect of having to make out an annual income tax return for an infinite number of years ahead."

Wilmer Judson's shrewish wife of fifty-three years had died, and as the mourners were on the way to the cemetery, one of the pallbearers tripped over a rock. This shook the casket and revived the woman. She lived another seven years and died again. They were on the way to the cemetery again, and as they approached the same spot, Wilmer shouted out to the pall-bearers, "Watch out for that rock!"

Two men were adrift on a raft in the open sea, and it looked bad for them. Finally one of them, frightened, began to pray: "O Lord, I've broken most of the commandments. I've got some pretty bad habits—I drink, I curse, I steal, I treat people like dirt. But if my life is spared now, I promise you that I'll change, that I'll never again curse, that I—"

Suddenly his friend cried out to him: "Wait, Jack. Don't go too far. I think I see a ship."

—Charles Krieg

I had a dream in which I died and waited at the Pearly Gates for admission into heaven. Another man waited with me. Suddenly St. Peter appeared and said, "We've got room for only one more. Which one of you is more humble?"

Richard Nixon is walking towards heaven and comes to an area with fountains and waterfalls. He sees a gated doorway behind one of the waterfalls with an angel hovering nearby. "Is this Heaven's Gate?" asked Nixon.

"No," replies the angel. "It's Water Gate!"

Reported to be seen on a sign outside a church in Houston, Texas: "The meek shall inherit the earth." Underneath it, a graffiti artist had scrawled (appropriately, perhaps, in oil-rich Texas): "But not the mineral rights."

Prominent surgeon Myron Davis died and went to heaven. The angel at the gate asked, "Is there anything you'd like to get off your conscience before you enter?"

"Yes," said the surgeon. "There is one thing that has been bothering me. In my younger days when I was a junior surgeon at St. Bartholomew's, I used to play for the hospital football team. During a closely fought match, I scored a touchdown which I thought was offside, but the referee allowed it and St. Bartholomew's won the game."

"That's all right," said the angel. "We have a note of that particular incident, and you needn't worry about it at all."

"Well, thank you, St. Peter," said the M.D. "You've set my mind at rest."

"Oh, I'm not St. Peter," said the angel, chuckling. "I'm St. Bartholomew."

If only God would give me a clear sign! Like making a large deposit in my name in a Swiss bank account.   —Woody Allen

W. C. Fields, a lifetime agnostic, was discovered reading a Bible on his deathbed. "I'm looking for a loophole," he explained.

A certain curate in the course of conversation at a dinner party remarked to a friend, "I had a curious dream last night, but as it was about my vicar, I hardly like to tell it." On being pressed, however, he began. "I dreamed I was dead and was on my way to Heaven, which was reached by a very long ladder. At the foot I was met by an angel, who pressed a piece of chalk into my hand and said, 'If you climb long enough you will reach heaven, but for every sin you are conscious of having committed, you must mark a rung of the ladder with the chalk as you go up.' I took the chalk and started.

"I had climbed very, very far and was feeling very tired when I suddenly saw my vicar coming down. 'Hello!' I said. 'What are you going down for?'

"He replied, 'More chalk.'"

Charles Walton, an Oklahoma oil company executive, arrives at the Pearly Gates. St. Peter examines the record of his life and finds it highly commendable. "I'm sorry I can't admit you," he tells Walton. "You see, the quota for oil men has been met," St. Peter tells him.

"But surely something can be done," bleats the startled Walton.

St. Peter replies "Yes, there is one way. I suppose you could enter Heaven if somehow you could get one of the oil men already here to leave."

Walton thinks for a moment. Suddenly his face lights up. "I know what I'll do," he tells St. Peter. "I'll spread the rumor that oil has been discovered in Hell and see if it will cause one of the oilmen in Heaven to go over to the other side." St. Peter thinks it will be a good test, and he allows Walton to plant the rumor.

Within a few hours, there is a stampede through the Pearly Gates, and all of the oil men in Heaven depart. Suddenly an astonished St. Peter notices that even Walton is running in the direction of Hell. "Where are you going?" he calls.

Over his shoulder Walton calls back, "You never know . . . there may be something to this rumor!"

Father Ford and Father Walinski were on their way to a retreat when they were killed in an automobile accident. Upon arriving at the Pearly Gates, St. Peter informs them that the computer is down and that they will have to go back to earth for a week.

"My dear friends," says St. Peter, "don't be disappointed. With the computer out of commission you can go back as anything you'd like and do whatever you want. Because the computer is down, nothing will count against you."

Father Ford tells St. Peter that he had always wanted to be an eagle, soaring over the mountains.

"Go," says St. Peter. "You are an eagle."

Father Walinski first reconfirms that whatever he does will not go into his record, and then says, "Well, I've always wanted to be a stud."

"Go," says St. Peter. "You are a stud."

A week passes and the archangel Gabriel comes to St. Peter to say that the computer has been repaired. "Since you'll be busy here minding the gate, I guess I'll have to fetch those two priests," says Gabriel.

"Well," says St. Peter, "it will be easy to find Father Ford. Right now he's flying over the Grand Tetons in Wyoming. Father Walinsky's another matter, and it's going to be a lot harder to find him. Right now he's in a snow tire somewhere in Minnesota."

I know a guy who has such an ego that when he prays he says, "Dear God, do you need anything?"
—Gene Perret

Father O'Casey, the parish priest, was administering the last rites to a critically ill Billy Flaherty. Before anointing Flaherty the priest asked, "Do you renounce the world, the flesh, and the Devil?"

Flaherty replied: "I think in my condition this is no time to offend anyone."

An economist dreamed that God came to his office. He did not know what to say, and suddenly he remembered that as a little boy, someone had told him that a thousand years was like a minute to the Lord. So he asked the Lord if that was true.

The Lord said, "Yes, that's true."

By this time, the economist had recovered his composure. He said, "Then perhaps it may also be true that what is a million dollars to us is only a penny to you."

And the Lord said, "Yes, that's certainly true."

So the economist said, "Well, Lord, how about giving me one of those pennies?"

The Lord said, "Certainly. I don't happen to have it on me, but I'll go fetch it, if you'll wait a minute."

4.
MEN & WOMEN

One day Adam is talking to God, and he asks, "God, I've been wondering. Why did you make Eve so pretty?"

God replies, "Because I wanted you to like her."

Then Adam asks, "But why did you make her so stupid?"

God answers, "Because I wanted her to like you."

Two of my grandsons were playing marbles when a pretty little girl walked by. "I'll tell you," said Jake to J.D., "when I stop hating girls, that's the one I'm going to stop hating first."

Tony attended the men's prayer breakfast and heard a visiting psychologist speak on the topic of showing appreciation to the important people in one's life. Tony decided to start with his wife, so after work that night, he went to the shopping mall, where he bought a dozen long-stemmed roses, a box of chocolates, and a pair of earrings. He chortled with self-satisfaction as he contemplated surprising his wife, showing her how much he appreciated her.

He stood at the front door with the roses in his right hand, the gaily wrapped box of candy under his arm, and an open jewelry box displaying the earrings in his left hand. With an elbow he rang the doorbell. His wife came to the door, opened it, and stared at him for a long minute. Suddenly she burst into tears.

"Sweetheart, what's wrong?" asked the bewildered husband.

"It's been the worst day of my life," she answered. "First, Jimmy tried to flush his diaper down the toilet. Then Eric melted his plastic airplane in the oven. Then the dishwasher got clogged and overflowed all over the kitchen floor. Then Brittany came home from school with a note from the teacher saying that she beat up a boy in her class. And now you come home drunk!"

Helen Marbury, an elderly woman, tottered into a lawyer's office and asked for help in arranging for a divorce. The lawyer just did not believe it. "Tell me," he said, "how old are you?"

"Eighty-four," she said. "And my husband is eighty-seven."

"How long have you been married?"

"Almost sixty-two years."

The lawyer slapped his forehead. "Married sixty-two years? Why do you want a divorce now?"

"Because," she said, "enough is enough."   —Ray Ortlund

My wife rushed into the supermarket to pick up a few items. She headed for the express line, where the clerk was talking on the phone with his back turned to her. "Excuse me," she said, "I'm in a hurry. Could you check me out, please?"

The clerk turned, stared at her for a second, looked her up and down, smiled and said, "Not bad."

The wit and charm of Adlai E. Stevenson II made him a constant target for autograph seekers. Once, as he left the United Nations Building in New York City and was surrounded by admirers, a small elderly woman in the crowd finally succeeded in approaching him.

"Please Mr. Ambassador," she said, holding out a piece of paper, "your autograph for a very, very old lady."

"Delighted!" Stevenson replied, smiling. "But where is she?"

A famous author was autographing copies of his new novel in a department store. One gentleman pleased him by bringing up not only his new book for signature, but two of his previous ones, as well.

"My wife likes your stuff," he remarked apologetically, "so I thought I'd give her these signed copies for a birthday present."

"A surprise, eh?" hazarded the author.

"I'll say," agreed the customer. "She's expecting a Mercedes."

A lecturer asked her audience, "Who is wiser than Ann Landers, more controversial than Geraldo Rivera, wittier than Robin Williams and handsomer than Mel Gibson?"

From the audience came a forlorn voice: "My wife's first husband!"

The farm couple was driving through town one hot summer afternoon. As it got hotter and hotter, the farmer's wife appealed to her husband, "John, dear, it must be two hundred degrees in here. Could we please roll down the windows?"

"Are you out of your mind?" he replied. "And let all the town folks know our car isn't air-conditioned?"

Mr. and Mrs. Ivers were pushing their cart down the aisle at the supermarket when they spotted an elderly pair walking hand in hand. Said Mrs. Ivers: "Now, that looks like a happy married couple."

"Don't be too sure, dear," replied Mr. Ivers. "They're probably saying the same thing about us."

When Barbara and Jim were dating, Barbara became concerned over the lavish amount of money Jim was spending on her. After an expensive dinner date, she asked her mother, "What can I do to stop Jim from spending so much money on me?"

Her mother replied simply, "Marry him."

 **A** despondent woman was walking along the beach when she saw a bottle on the sand. She picked it up and pulled out the cork. *Whoosh!* A big puff of smoke appeared.

"You have released me from my prison," the genie told her. "To show my thanks, I grant you three wishes. But take care, for with each wish, your mate will receive double of whatever you request."

"Why?" the woman asked. "That bum left me for another woman."

"That is how it is written," replied the genie.

The woman shrugged and then asked for a million dollars. There was a flash of light, and a million dollars appeared at her feet. At the same instant, in a far-off place, her wayward husband looked down to see twice that amount at his feet.

"And your second wish?"

"Genie, I want the world's most expensive diamond necklace." Another flash of light, and the woman was holding the precious treasure. And, in that distant place, her husband was looking for a gem broker to buy his latest bonanza.

"Genie, is it really true that my husband has two million dollars and more jewels that I do, and that he gets double of whatever I wish for?"

The genie said it was indeed true.

"OK, genie, I'm ready for my last wish," the woman said. "Scare me half to death."

Fire swept the plains and burned down the farmer's barn. While he surveyed the wreckage, his wife called the insurance company and asked them to send a check for fifty thousand dollars, the amount of insurance on the barn.

"We don't give you the money," a company official explained. "We replace the barn and all the equipment that was in it."

"In that case," replied the wife, "cancel the policy I have on my husband."

A friend of Mr. and Mrs. George Bernard Shaw's tells of an evening he spent with them. While Mr. Shaw. told stories, Mrs. Shaw busied herself knitting.

"What are you knitting?" asked the guest in an aside.

"Oh, nothing, nothing at all," whispered Mrs. Shaw. "It's just that I've heard these stories of his two thousand times, and if I didn't do something with my hands, I'd choke him."

Louise, a young Catholic woman, fell head over heels in love with Keith, who returned her love with equal passion. But there was one serious problem, for, as Louise explained to her mother, "Keith is a Baptist, and he's opposed to the idea of marrying a Catholic. And you know that I could never give up my faith—even for love!" As she told her mother of her dilemma, the young woman began to weep uncontrollably.

"Now, wait, honey," said her mother, who was a district manager for Mary Kay Cosmetics. "Don't give up. Why not try some real salesmanship? Tell him how wonderful our church is. We're the first Christian church. Or tell him of our great beliefs, our martyrs, our saints, our cathedrals and chapels, and the wonderful inspiration our priests give us through their words of comfort and forgiveness. You know all this. Go out and sell Keith on the Catholic Church!"

Louise dried her eyes and agreed to try. She spent the next few evenings with Keith and for a while was looking happier. But one morning after a date her mother heard her sobbing again. "What's the matter, darling?" asked Louise's mother. "Didn't your sales campaign work?"

"No, Mother!" sobbed Louise. "I oversold him. Now he wants to become a priest!"

In *The New York Times:* Man who drives in from New Rochelle every day would like to meet woman who lives in Midtown Manhattan with vacant garage.

Cessna Aircraft ran this ad to publicize its fixed-price pilot training program: "Cessna will make you a pilot for $2990. Guaranteed."

Shortly thereafter, the company received a letter from seven Kansas women. "Dear Cessna," it read. "In response to your ad in the latest *Popular Mechanics,* we would like to order a pilot. The following particulars should be built into your design: male—quick learner; height 6'2"–6'5"; weight 190 pounds; chest forty-six inches; waist thirty-four inches; shoe size eleven (optional); hairy chest and muscular; dark blue eyes; wavy brown hair.

"We see by your ad that this pilot is guaranteed, but we would prefer to take him on approval. We have several other people also interested in your pilot program. Could we get a discount on case lots?"   —*Flying Magazine*

A young school teacher ran into a friend she hadn't seen since they were teenagers. With eyes aglow, the school teacher said to her friend, "Guess what? Since last we saw one another, I've gotten married."

Her friend said, "That's good."

The school teacher said, "But my husband is homely. He's not very handsome."

Her friend said, "That's bad."

The teacher said, "But he is a millionaire."

Her friend said, "That's very good."

The teacher said, "He is also very stingy."

Her friend said, "That's very bad."

The teacher said, "In his stinginess he did manage to build me a palatial mansion."

Her friend said, "That's good."

"But," the teacher said, "it burned down."

Her friend said, "That's bad."

The school teacher said, "When it burned down, he was in it."

Her friend didn't know what to say.   —King Duncan

Seth, the self-proclaimed "world's greatest lover," struck up a conversation with an attractive woman seated beside him on a transcontinental flight. He asked her, "What kind of man most attracts you?"

"I've always been drawn to Native American men," she replied. "They're in harmony with nature and have such a great sense of inner peace."

"I see," said Seth.

"But, then," she added, "I really am fond of Jewish men who put women on a pedestal, and I can really be swept away by the way Southern gentlemen treat their ladies with such respect."

"Please allow me to introduce myself," said Seth. "My name is Tecumseh Goldstein, but all my friends call me Bubba."

A week after I married a young couple at my church, I received the following thank you note from the bridegroom: "Dear Reverend, I want to thank you for the beautiful way you brought my happiness to a conclusion."

Mona Reston was on trial for the murder of her third husband. The district attorney asked her, "What happened to your first husband?"

"He died of mushroom poisoning," said Mrs. Reston.

"How about your second husband?" asked the D.A.

"He died of mushroom poisoning, too," replied Mrs. Reston.

"Well," asked the D.A., "what about your third husband?"

Mrs. Reston replied, "He died of a fractured skull."

The prosecutor asked, "Why did that happen?"

Mrs. Reston hesitated, then answered, "He didn't particularly like mushrooms."

FOR SALE—Complete twenty-five volume set of *Encyclopedia Britannica.* Latest edition, never used. Wife knows everything.

"She told me," a woman complained to a friend, "that you told her the secret I told you not to tell her."

"Well," replied her friend in a hurt tone, "I told her not to tell you I told her."

"Oh, dear," sighed the first woman. "Don't tell her I told you that she told me."

A certain church held a Sunday service patterned after those in colonial America. The pastor dressed in long coat and knickers, and the congregation was divided by gender: men on the left side of the aisle and women on the right.

At collection time, the pastor announced that this, too, would be done in the old way. He asked the "head of the household" to come forward and place the money on the altar. The men instantly rose. To the amusement of the entire congregation, many of them crossed the aisle to get money from their wives.

—Billy D. Strayhorn

A new group of applicants had just arrived in heaven. St. Peter instructed them, "All men who were henpecked on earth, please line up on the left; all those who were bosses in their own homes, line up on the right."

The line quickly formed on the left. Only one man, a Caspar Milquetoast type, stepped to the right. St. Peter saw the frail fellow standing by himself and inquired, "What makes you think you belong on that side?"

"Well," said the meek little man, "this is where my wife told me to stand."

In announcing the church's new public address system, Pastor Melankamp told the congregation that the microphone and wiring had been paid with church funds.

Then he added, "The loudspeaker has been donated by a member of the congregation, in memory of his wife."

The bridegroom, who was in a horribly nervous condition, asked to the minister in a loud stage whisper, at the close of the ceremony, "Is it kisstomary to cuss the bride?"

The minister replied, "Not yet, but soon enough!"

Tommy Lee asked Pastor Parkes, "Reverend, am I right in assuming that the Bible says it's wrong to profit from other people's mistakes?"

Pastor Parkes replied, "That is substantially correct."

Tommy Lee demanded, "In that case, how about refunding the twenty dollars I paid you for marrying us last year?"

In the Garden of Eden one morning, Eve asked Adam, "What's wrong with eating this apple?"

"I'll bite," smiled Adam.

Mrs. Bettis had an attack of laryngitis and lost her voice for nearly a week. The doctor told her not even to whisper.

Mr. Bettis, trying to help his wife communicate with him, devised a system of taps. He explained his system to her: "One tap means 'yes.' Two taps means 'no.' Three taps means 'give me a kiss,' and one hundred forty-nine taps means 'take out the garbage.'"

Kevin and Sarah, a young couple, were sitting out on a porch swing. Sarah asked, "Kevin, do you think my eyes are beautiful?"

Kevin answered, "Yep."

In a few moments: "Kevin, do you think my hair is attractive?"

Again Kevin answered, "Yep."

In a while: "Would you say that I have a gorgeous figure?"

Once again Kevin answered, "Yep."

"Oh, Kevin," she said, "You say the nicest things."

My wife isn't jealous. She doesn't care how good looking my secretary is, as long as he's efficient.

I wonder if the rumor is true that Adam began staying out late and sneaking back into the Garden of Eden in the wee hours?

I understand that Eve watched these goings on suspiciously for a while and then one morning, after Adam had crept in and fallen into a heavy sleep, Eve stole silently to his side and carefully counted his ribs.

Seven houses down from ours is an attractive little park with several citrus trees and a nice sandy beach. It's also heavily infested with snails.

A few years ago, my wife and I were having a dinner party for the major movers and shakers in our church. My wife was very excited about this and wanted everything to be perfect. At the very last minute, she realized that she did not have any escargot for hors d'oeuvres for the dinner party. She instructed me to run down to the beach with a bucket to gather some snails. "And do not dawdle," she warned.

Very grudgingly I agreed, took the bucket, walked out the door, down the steps, through the park, and down to the beach. As I was collecting the snails, I noticed a neighbor, whom I had not seen in some time, strolling just a little farther down the beach. I greeted her, we got into a long and pleasant conversation, and I lost track of time. As the sun began to set, I realized that it was nearly time for my wife's dinner party! So I scooped up as many snails as I could find and ran through the park and toward my house.

I ran up the front stairs of my house, but I was in such a hurry that when I got to the top stair, I dropped the bucket of snails. Snails scattered all down the stairs. The door opened just then, and there was a very angry wife standing in the door way wondering where I had been all this time.

I looked at the snails spread down the steps, then looked at her, then back at the snails. "Come on, guys," I said; "we're almost there!"

Benton Farbish, the rector of a wealthy parish in Boston, advertised for a manservant. The next morning a nicely dressed young man rang the bell.

Before the young man could say a word, the rector began interrogating him: "Can you start the fire and get breakfast by seven o'clock?" asked the minister.

"I guess so," answered the young man.

"Well, can you polish all the silver, wash the dishes, and keep the house neat and tidy?"

"Say, Parson," said the young man, "I came here to see about getting married—but if it's going to be as much work as all that you can count me out right now."

"I'm lonely," Adam told God in the Garden of Eden. "I need to have someone around for company."

"OK," replied God. "I'm going to give you the perfect woman. Beautiful, intelligent and gracious—she'll cook and clean for you and never say a cross word."

"Sounds good," Adam said. "But what's she going to cost?"

"An arm and a leg."

"That's pretty steep," countered Adam. "What can I get for just a rib?"

—*Talkin' Texan*

On their honeymoon, Eric took Louise by the hand and said, "Now that we're married, dear, I hope you won't mind if I mention a few little defects that I've noticed about you."

"Not at all," Louise replied sweetly. "It was those little defects that kept me from getting a better husband."

I asked my friend Brian why he resigned as a pastor of his church. He answered, "Because there were fifteen single women there, all trying to marry me."

"But don't you know there's safety in numbers?" I asked.

"Not for me," Brian guffawed, pointing to a door. "I found mine in Exodus."

A woman went to the police station with her next door neighbor to report that her husband was missing. The police officer asked for a description. She said, "He's thirty-five years old, six foot two, has dark eyes, dark wavy hair, an athletic build, weighs 185 pounds, is soft-spoken, and is good to the children."

The next-door neighbor protested, "Wait a minute! Your husband is five foot four, chubby, bald, has a big mouth, and is mean to your children."

The wife replied, "Sure, but who wants him back?"

Aunt Harriet once explained to me the secret of a lasting marriage: "Your Uncle Albert and I have managed to be happy together for forty years. I guess this is because we're both in love with the same man."

My Uncle Marty explains his long-term marriage in this way:

My wife and I have very little in common. I'm a big city boy; she's a small town girl. I like spicy food; she doesn't. I enjoy action and suspense movies; she goes for romance and comedy. Nothing in common. Yet we are deeply in love. It just goes to show that you don't get harmony when everybody sings the same note.

After five years of marriage, Amber and Ed began having problems. They argued so bitterly that Ed decided to seek out a divorce lawyer.

At their first session, the lawyer asked Ed, "What first attracted you to this woman?"

Ed replied, "Her forthrightness, straightforwardness and frankness."

The counselor asked, "Then why are you now telling me you want to end the relationship?"

Ed answered, "Her forthrightness, straightforwardness and frankness."

When my parents were first married, fifty-seven years ago, my mother dutifully prepared a substantial lunch for my dad to take with him to work. However, no matter what she prepared, he always complained that after eating lunch he was still hungry.

I remember one particular week. On Monday, Mother prepared a generous roast beef sandwich as the main item, and when Dad returned, she asked him what he thought of his lunch. Sourly Dad replied, "Pretty good, what there was of it."

On Tuesday, she made two large sandwiches and added sliced carrots and apples on the side, but on his return, Dad said once more, in response to her query, "Pretty good, what there was of it."

More than a little upset, Mother took a whole loaf of French bread, sliced it lengthwise, and stuffed the entire thing with a variety of cold cuts, cheeses, hard boiled eggs, sardines, anchovies, lettuce, tomato, pickles, and hot peppers.

This time, when Dad returned, he did not want to be questioned. He fixed a cold eye on Mother and said, "Back to one sandwich again, eh?"

Ricky was telling his father about his new girlfriend. He said, "Since I met her I can't eat, drink, or sleep."

"Why's that?" asked his father.

"Because," he said, "I'm broke."

One husband knew that every year on the family's way to their vacation spot, just as they would get about eighty miles out of town, his wife would cry out, "Oh, no! I'm sure I left the iron on." Each year they would return home only to find it unplugged.

One year, however, was different. The man had anticipated what was coming. When his wife gasped, "We must go back, I just know I left the iron on," he stopped the car, reached under his seat, and handed his wife the iron.

—Allen Klein, *The Healing Power of Humor*

Sid was a non-stop talker. When his wife became ill, the doctor said, "I prescribe absolute quiet for your wife. Here's a bottle of sleeping pills."

"When do I give them to her?" asked Sid.

"You don't give them to her," said the doctor. "You take them yourself."

—Bennett Cerf

My daughter lives in Los Angeles. A few years ago she was dining out with a friend after work. Suddenly she interrupted her conversation and summoned the headwaiter.

"That's Tom Selleck at the bar, isn't it?" she asked. He assured her that it was. "He's annoying me," she said.

"Annoying you?" The headwaiter raised an eyebrow. "Why, he hasn't even looked at you!"

"That," said my daughter, "is what's annoying me."

My dad says, "The cooing stops with the honeymoon. The billing goes on forever."

My wife and I have an agreement that works. She's responsible for the small decisions, and I'm responsible for the big ones.

This means that she decides things like where to take our next vacation, the make of our next car, and the construction budget for adding on the new family room.

I decide whether or not the President should extend most-favored-nation trading status to China, how high the Federal Reserve should raise short term interest rates, and the timetable for eliminating CFCs from automobile air conditioners.

My Aunt Marlene had a troubled marriage. She sought the advice of one of those phone-in psychics. The psychic told her, "Prepare yourself for widowhood. Your husband is about to die a violent death."

Marlene sighed deeply and asked, "Will I be acquitted?"

Thomas Wheeler, chief executive officer of the Massachusetts Mutual Life Insurance Company, tells a good story on himself.

He says that while he and his wife were out driving he noticed they were low on gas, so he pulled off at the first exit. He came to a dumpy little gas station with one pump. There was only one man working the place, so he asked the man to fill it up while he checked the oil. He added a quart of oil and closed the hood.

Wheeler noticed his wife talking and smiling at the gas station attendant. When they saw him looking at them, the attendant walked away and pretended as though nothing had happened.

As they drove down the road, he asked his wife if she knew the attendant. She admitted she did know him. In fact, she had known him very well. It seems that they not only had gone to high school together, but they dated seriously for about a year.

Wheeler couldn't help bragging a little. "Boy, were you lucky I came along," he said. "If you had married him, you'd be the wife of a gas station attendant instead of the wife of a chief executive officer."

His wife replied, "Dear, if I had married him, he'd be the chief executive officer and you'd be the gas station attendant."

—*Vital Speeches*

Census-takers have found that one third of all married couples aren't.

My wife's Aunt Aggie is looking for an older man with a strong will—made out to her.

Several years ago, someone wrote to Abigail Van Buren, "Dear Abby, I'm single; I'm forty years old; I'd like to meet a man about the same age who has no bad habits."

Abby replied, "So would I!"

Taking a dime from his pocket, John said to Mary, "I'll bet you ten cents I can kiss you on the lips without touching them."

"You're crazy," said Mary. "That's impossible. Here's a dime that says you can't."

The two dimes were placed on the mantelpiece and John then enfolded Mary and for ten minutes kissed her passionately and intimately.

She broke away at last, panting and disheveled, and said, "You did nothing but touch my lips."

John pushed the dimes toward her and smiled as he said, "I guess I lose."

Maybe this will give you an idea how difficult my wife can be. She bought me two ties for my birthday. To please her, I wore one. When she saw me in it, she said sadly, "What's the matter, don't you like the other one?"

When his wife died, old Sam Kleinbell, the distinguished jurist, decided to retire and join his friends, Mike and Kathy O'Connor, in Key Biscayne. Taking Kleinbell under their wing, the O'Connors were pleased with his rapid adjustment to life in the sun. Years went by.

One day Kleinbell announced to his old friends that he was going to marry a twenty-one-year-old waitress.

"Sam, you've only known her a few weeks," cautioned Mike, "and consider the risks. You're almost eighty-five. At this point sex could be fatal!"

Kleinbell shrugged philosophically. "If she dies, she dies."

While my wife and I were shopping at the mall, a shapely young woman in a short, form-fitting dress strolled by. My eyes followed her.

Without looking up from the item she was examining, my wife asked, "Was it worth the trouble you're in?"

During World War II, my uncle Ed, a naval aviator, went into a barber shop to get a shave, and since the manicurist was really beautiful, he asked for a manicure at the same time. He kept looking at her, really taken with her, and finally said, "How about going out with me tonight?"

She said, "No, I'm married."

He said, "Well, just tell your husband you're busy tonight."

"Tell him yourself," she said, "He's shaving you."

One year my Aunt Aurelia told Uncle Floyd, "Honey, I've bought you an unusual birthday present."

"What did you buy me?" he asked her.

"A cemetery plot."

He agreed with her that it was indeed unusual but thanked her anyway.

The next year, when she didn't buy him a gift at all, he asked her why.

She said, "You didn't use the gift I bought you last year."

If you want to be sure you'll always remember your wife's birthday, just try forgetting it once.

A couple got married and spent their first night at the bride's home. She was very religious, so she told her husband they would have to pray before going to bed. "Not me," he said. "I've never prayed a single prayer in my whole life."

"I don't care," she said. "You will tonight."

So he did pray.

Next morning at breakfast he said, "I did something last night I never did before." That got everybody's attention.

Then his wife said, "Yes, and if you're not good today, I'll tell everybody how awkward you were in doing it."

—*Hometown Humor, USA,*

Two neighbors met after not having seen one another for some months. "And how are things with you?" asked one of the women.

"Oh," said the other, "I'm managing all right, although I lost my husband several months back."

"What happened?" asked the friend.

"Well," explained the widow, "I was making dinner and asked him to go out to the garden and pick some corn. After he had been gone a long time, I went to see what the trouble was. There he was, dead—a heart attack."

"How awful! What did you do?"

"Oh," said the widow, "I had a can of corn in the house, so I just used that."

My Aunt Edna tells me:

As we were preparing for a fishing trip, I noticed my husband looking at me lovingly. "What's on your mind?" I asked.

"Oh," he replied, "I was just thinking what great lures your earrings would make."

There are two times when a man doesn't understand a woman—before marriage and after marriage.

Our pastor was preaching on Proverbs 16:24: "Pleasant words are as a honeycomb, sweet to the soul, and health to the bones." The minister then added, "You know, you catch more flies with honey than you do with vinegar."

My wife leaned over, put her head on my shoulder and whispered in my ear, "I just love to watch your muscles ripple when you take out the garbage."

One teen-age boy to another: "My Dad had a long talk with me about girls last night. He doesn't know anything about them, either."

My three grandsons were thinking of going to the movies to see a cowboy picture, but one objected to it because he'd heard it had too many kissing scenes. His younger brother said, "That's okay. When the kissing starts, we can close our eyes and pretend he's choking her."

As the crowded elevator descended, Mrs. Meltzer became increasingly furious with her man, who enjoyed being pressed against a gorgeous blond. As the elevator stopped at the main floor, the blonde suddenly turned, slapped Mr. Meltzer, and told him, "That will teach you to pinch!"

Puzzled, Mr. Meltzer was halfway to the parking lot with his wife when he stammered, "I . . . I didn't pinch that girl!"

"Of course you didn't," said his wife, consolingly. "I did."

Driving along a lonely road a man saw a women looking helplessly at a flat tire. He stopped and changed the tire. As he picked up the tools the lady said: "Please let the jack down easy. My husband is asleep in the back seat."

Two husbands were talking about their married lives. Although happily married, both confessed to the occasional argument. Then Joel said, "I've made one great discovery. I now know how to always have the last word."

"Really!" said Harry, "How did you manage that?"

"It's simple," replied Joel. "My last word is always 'Yes, Dear.'"

Rob: My wife is very touchy. The smallest thing will set her off.
Stan: You're fortunate. Mine is a self-starter.

If a woman has to choose between catching a fly ball and saving an infant's life, she will choose to save the infant's life without even considering if there are men on base.　　—Dave Barry

"My wife is always asking for money," complained a guy to his friend. "Last week she wanted three hundred dollars. The day before yesterday she asked me for a hundred and fifty. This morning she wanted two hundred bucks."

"That's crazy," said the friend. "What does she do with it all?"

"I don't know," said the guy, "I never give her any."

 The only time a woman really succeeds in changing a man is when he's a baby. —Natalie Wood

When I first dated the woman who would later become my wife, I thought that her kisses left something to be desired—the rest of her.

My wife thinks I'm too nosy. At least that's what she keeps scribbling in her diary. —Drake Sather

The sure way to tell if a man is a bachelor is to check his silverware. If it's full of nicks from going through the garbage disposal a couple of dozen times, he's for real. —Nick Arnette

I don't think of myself as single. I'm romantically challenged. —Stephanie Piro

To attract men, I wear a perfume called "New Car Interior." —Rita Rudner

Explain weddings to me. A bride will make her best friends in the whole world wear the ugliest dresses known to mankind. And she will lie to them by saying "I'm sure you can wear it again!" To which every bridesmaid is thinking, Sure I will, if the Polka Festival ever comes to town. —Robert G. Lee

THE FIVE TOUGHEST QUESTIONS WOMEN ASK MEN
(and How to Answer Them)

The five questions are:

- What are you thinking?
- Do you love me?
- Do I look too heavy?
- Do you think she is prettier than me?
- What would you do if I died?

What makes these questions so bad is that every one of them is guaranteed to explode into a major argument and/or divorce if the man does not answer properly, which is to say, dishonestly. For example:

WHAT ARE YOU THINKING?

The proper answer to this question, of course, is, "I'm sorry if I've been pensive, dear. I was just reflecting on what a warm, wonderful, caring, thoughtful, intelligent, beautiful woman you are and what a lucky guy I am to have met you."

Obviously, this statement bears no resemblance whatsoever to what the guy was really thinking at the time, which was most likely one of five things:

a. Baseball
b. Football
c. How much weight you have put on
d. How much prettier someone else is
e. How I would spend the insurance money if you died.

The other questions also have only one right answer but many wrong answers:

DO YOU LOVE ME?

The correct answer to this question is, "Yes." For those guys who feel the need to be more elaborate, you may answer, "Yes, dear!"

Wrong answers include:

a. I suppose so.
b. Would it make you feel better if I said yes?
c. That depends on what you mean by "love."
d. Does it matter?
e. Who, me?

DO I LOOK TOO HEAVY?

The correct male response to this question is to confidently and emphatically state, "No, of course not," and then quickly leave the room.

Wrong answers include:
a. I wouldn't call you heavy, but I wouldn't call you thin, either.
b. Compared to what?
c. A little extra weight looks good on you.
d. Lots of pople are heavier than you.
e. Could you repeat the question? I was thinking about your insurance policy.

DO YOU THINK SHE'S PRETTIER THAN ME?

The "she" in the question could be an ex-girlfriend, a passer-by you were staring at so hard that you almost caused a traffic accident, or an actress in a movie you just saw. In any case, the correct response is, "No, you are much prettier."

Wrong answers include:
a. Not prettier, just pretty in a different way.
b. I don't know how one goes about rating such things.
c. Yes, but you have a better personality.
d. Only in the sense that she's younger and thinner.
e. Could you repeat the question? I was thinking about your insurance policy.

WHAT WOULD YOU DO IF I DIED?

Correct answer: "Dearest love, in the event of your untimely demise, life would cease to have meaning for me and I would perforce hurl myself under the front tires of the first Domino's Pizza truck that came my way."

This might be the worst question of the lot, as is illustrated by the following stupid joke:

"Dear," said the wife. "What would you do if I died?"

"Why, dear, I would be extremely upset," said the husband. "Why do you ask such a question?"

"Would you remarry?" persevered the wife.

"No, of course not, dear, " said the husband.

"Don't you like being married?" asked the wife.

"Of course I do, dear," he said.

"Then why wouldn't you remarry?"

"All right," said the husband, "I'd remarry."

"You would?" said the wife, looking vaguely hurt.

"Yes," said the husband.

After a long pause the wife asked, "Would you sleep with her in our bed?"

"Well, yes, I suppose I would," replied the husband.

"I see," said the wife indignantly. "And would you let her wear my old clothes?"

"I suppose, if she wanted to," said the husband.

"Really," said the wife icily. "And would you take down the pictures of me and replace them with pictures of her?"

"Yes. I think that would be the correct thing to do."

"Is that so?" said the wife, leaping to her feet. "And I suppose you'd let her play with my golf clubs, too!"

"Of course not, dear," said the husband. "She's left-handed."

When an admiring lady fan wrote to ask Richard Brinsley Sheridan the essential difference between man and woman, the famous British playwright replied:

> Dear Madam,
>
> I cannot conceive.
>
> Sincerely yours,
> Richard Brinsley Sheridan

When a man says, "Honey, there are only two minutes left in the football game," it is the same amount of time as when his wife says, "Honey, I'll be ready in two minutes."   —Ann Landers

Confirmed bachelor: One who thinks that the only thoroughly justified marriage was the one that produced him.

—Harlan Miller

Uncle Irv was convinced that Aunt Harriet had a hearing problem. So one night, he stood behind her while she was sitting in her lounge chair, reading a novel.

He spoke softly to her, "Honey, can you hear me?"

There was no response.

He moved a little closer and said again, "Honey, can you hear me?"

Still, there was no response.

Finally he moved right behind her and said, "Honey, can you hear me?"

She replied, "For the third time, YES!"

I'm thirty-three, single . . . Don't you think it's a generalization you should be married at thirty-three? That's like looking at somebody who's seventy and saying, "Hey, when are you gonna break your hip? All your friends are breaking their hip—what are you waiting for?"

—Sue Kolinsky

A bachelor is a man dedicated to life, liberty, and the happiness of pursuit.

Wife to husband as he pays bills: "Living beyond our means sounds so ordinary, Gerald. Why not live beyond our wildest dreams?"

—Schwadron, *Extra Newspaper Features*

Bigamy: The only crime on the books where two rites make a wrong.

—Bob Hope

A man seldom makes the same mistake twice. Generally it's three times or more.

—Perry Griswold

The biggest difference between men and boys is the cost of their toys.
—Dr. Joyce Brothers

A man was griping to his friend about how he hated to go home after a late card game.

"You wouldn't believe what I go through to avoid waking my wife," he said. "First, I kill the engine a block from the house and coast into the garage. Then I open the door slowly. Next I take off my shoes and tiptoe to our room. But just as I'm about to slide into bed, she always wakes up and gives me grief."

"I make a big racket when I go home," his friend said.

"You do?"

"Sure. I honk the horn, slam the door, turn on all the lights, stomp up to the bedroom and give my wife a big kiss. 'Hi, Alice,' I say. 'How about a little smooch for your old man?'"

"And what does she say?" his friend asked in disbelief.

"She doesn't say anything," his buddy replied. "She always pretends she's asleep."

After Aunt Harriet woke up, she told Uncle Irv, "I just dreamed you gave me a pearl necklace for Valentine's Day. What do you think it means?"

"You'll know tonight," he said.

That evening, Uncle Irv came home with a package and gave it to this wife. Delighted, she opened it—to find a book entitled, *The Meaning of Dreams.*

A porter loaded down with suitcases followed the couple to the airline check-in counter. As they approached the line, the husband glanced at the pile of luggage and said to his wife, "Why didn't you bring the piano, too?"

"Are you trying to be funny?" she replied.

"No," he sighed. "I left the tickets on it." —Phil Hartman

The plumber asked the lady of the house, "Where's the drip?"
She answered, "He's in the basement, trying to fix the leak!"

A man took his wife to a psychiatrist and said, "What's-her-name here complains that I don't give her enough attention!"

My dad complains, "Your mother must think she's Teddy Roosevelt. She runs from store to store yelling, "Charge."

Tom: My wife makes me feel like a god.
Bob: Why do you say that?
Tom: She feeds me burnt offerings at meals.

The Song of Solomon is the one book of the Bible dedicated solely to romantic love. Isn't it ironic that its initials are SOS?
—Paul McGinty

What's the first thing a little girl wants when she gets a new bike? A basket—she's prepared to shop.
What's the first thing a boy wants on his bike? A bell or horn—he's prepared for traffic.
What's the first toy a little girl wants? A doll—she's prepared to shop with friends.
What's the first toy a little boy wants? A gun—he's prepared for traffic.
—Jason Chase

Caterina Rando, my colleague in the Northern California chapter of the National Speakers Association, has collected thousands of sage citations from numerous sources in her electronic book, *Words of Women: Quotations for Success*. Here are some choice things women have to say about men:

- Next to hot chicken soup, a tattoo of an anchor on your chest, and penicillin, I consider a honeymoon one of the most overrated events in the world. —Erma Bombeck

- Why does a woman work ten years to change a man's habits and then complain that he's not the man she married?
  —Barbra Streisand

- American men are obsessed with money, American women are obsessed with weight. The men talk of gain, the women talk of loss, and I do not know which is the more boring.
  —Marya Mannes

- If a man watches three football games in a row, he should be declared legally dead. —Erma Bombeck

- Never go to a doctor whose office plants have died.
  —Erma Bombeck

- An archeologist is the best husband a woman can have; the older she gets, the more interested he is in her.
  —Agatha Christie

- I never married because I have three pets at home that answer the same purpose as a husband. I have a dog that growls every morning, a parrot that swears all afternoon, and a cat that comes home late at night. —Marie Corelli

- If men can run the world, why can't they stop wearing neckties? How intelligent is it to start the day by tying a little noose around your neck? —Linda Ellerbee

- When he's late for dinner, I know he's either having an affair or is lying dead in the street. I always hope it's the street.
  —Jessica Tandy

- Women's liberation is just a lot of foolishness. It's men who are discriminated against. They can't bear children. And no one's likely to do anything about that.
  —Golda Meir

- When men reach their sixties and retire, they go to pieces. Women just go right on cooking.
  —Gail Sheehy

- Whatever women do, they must do twice as well as men to be thought half as good. Luckily, this is not difficult.
  —Charlotte Whitton

- Personally, I think if a woman hasn't met the right man by the time she's twenty-four, she may be lucky.
  —Deborah Kerr

- Women complain about sex more often than men. Their gripes fall into two major categories: (1) Not enough (2) Too much.
  —Ann Landers

- Sometimes I wonder if men and women really suit each other. Perhaps they should live next door and just visit now and then.
  —Katharine Hepburn

5.
FAMILY & HOME

Fond as we are of our loved ones, there comes a time during their absence of unexplainable peace.

—Ann Shaw

Happiness is having a large, loving, caring, close-knit family in another city.

—George Burns

A funeral service was being held for a rather unsavory character who had never been near a place of worship in his life. The services were being conducted by a minister who had never heard of him. Carried away by the occasion, he poured on praise for the departed man.

After ten minutes of hearing the late lamented described as an ideal father, husband, and boss, the widow nudged her son and whispered, "Go up there and make sure it's Papa."

A woman drove a mini-van filled with a dozen screaming kids through the mall parking lot, looking for a space. Obviously frazzled, she coasted through a stop sign.

"Hey, lady, did you forget how to stop?" yelled an irate man.

She rolled down her window and said, "What makes you think these kids are all mine?"

Any kid will run an errand for you, if you ask him at bedtime.

—Red Skelton

There's one thing about children—they never go around showing snapshots of their grandparents.   —Bessie and Beulah

My friend has a baby. I'm recording all the noises he makes, so later I can ask him what he meant.   —Steven Wright

I was born by cesarean section . . . but not so you'd notice. It's just that when I leave a house, I go out through the window.

—Steven Wright

Wealthy man making his will: "To my cousin, Osgood, I leave my stock portfolio and properties on the Outer Cape. . . .To my faithful cook, Minnie, I leave my Palm Beach estate. . . .To my nephew, Brutus, who always argued that health is more important than wealth, I leave my sweat socks and jogging shoes."

—Art Swanson, Newspaper Enterprise Association

A four-year-old boy accompanied his pregnant mother to the gynecologist's office. When mother heaved a sigh and clutched her stomach, her son looked alarmed. "Mommy, what is it?" he asked.

"The baby brother you're going to have is kicking," his mother explained.

"He's probably getting restless," the youngster decided. "Why don't you swallow a toy?"

A husband who says he is boss in his own house is probably a liar about other things, too.   —Will Rogers

My neighbor is mighty slow returning tools and commodities he borrows from me, but when it comes to bringing back my small children from his own little boys' birthday parties, golly, is he on time.   —Rod Cavanaugh

The mother of three notoriously unruly youngsters was asked whether or not she'd have children if she had it to do over again.

"Sure," she replied, "but not the same ones."

The bride brought her new husband up to meet Granny at the family picnic. The old woman looked the young man over carefully and then said to him, "Young man, do you desire to have children?"

He was a bit startled by her candid approach. "Well, yes, as a matter of fact, I do," he managed to say.

She looked at him scornfully and then surveyed the very large clan gathered around a dozen picnic tables and said, "Well, try to control it."

School days are the happiest days of your life—providing, of course, your youngsters are old enough to go.   —Paul Selden

If you've given up on getting a bottle or jar opened, just forbid your four-year-old to touch it.   —Victor Borge

Fatherhood is pretending that the present you love most is soap-on-a-rope.   —Bill Cosby

I never got along with my dad. Kids used to come up to me and say, "My dad can beat up your dad." I'd say, "Yeah? When?"
                                                      —Bill Hicks

A baby is God's opinion that the world should go on.

—Carl Sandburg

The daughter of a wealthy movie producer was asked at school to write a story about a poor family. Her essay began: "Once upon a time there was a poor family. The mother was poor. The daddy was poor. The children were poor. The butler was poor. The chauffeur was poor. The maid was poor. The gardener was poor. Everybody was poor."

Arriving for a visit, Joan Ludwig asked her small granddaughter, "Angela, how do you like your new baby brother?"

"Oh, he's all right," the child shrugged. "But there were a lot of things we needed worse."

"**G**randpa," the little boy asked as he returned from Sunday School, "were you and Grandma in Noah's Ark?"

"Of course not," replied his grandfather huffily.

"Why weren't you drowned, then?"

A young usher, who had never before participated in a wedding, asked an arriving guest, "Are you a friend of the bride or groom?"

"I'm a friend of both," came the reply.

"I'm sorry, Madam," the youthful usher replied. "I'm afraid you'll have to choose a side. I haven't been told where to seat the neutrals."

A family is a unit composed not only of children, but of men, women, an occasional animal, and the common cold.

—Ogden Nash

In our area, there are a lot of football addicts. I was seated next to one—a lady—at a football game not too long ago. There was an empty seat beside her.

"It was my husband's, but he died," she explained. "Oh, I'm sorry," I said. Then as an afterthought I asked, "Isn't there someone else in the family who could use the ticket?"

"No," she replied, "They're all at the funeral."

Motorists along a busy highway are getting an unusual reminder to slow down in Lancaster, Pennsylvania.

"Caution: Nudist Crossing" declares a sign erected by Danny and La Vonna Scheurich on their property on Stroudsburg Pike in East Lampeter Township.

The Scheurichs say they were concerned about the safety of their two sons and two daughters, ages seven through thirteen. "It's more or less a joke, but there is seriousness behind it," Mrs. Scheurich said. "But believe it or not, they are slowing down." —*Funny Funny World*

A little boy answered the home telephone. The caller was a salesman, and the following conversation took place:

"Is your mother at home?"

"No."

"Is your father at home?"

"No."

"Is there anyone else at home I can speak to?"

"Yes, my sister."

"Would you mind getting her to the telephone?"

"OK." There was a long pause. Finally, the little boy returned. "I'm back."

"Where's your sister?"

"I can't lift her out of the playpen."

They say kids bring warmth into a home, and I tend to believe it. I get hot every time I see the phone bill!

When her daughters were very young, Mrs. Dwight Morrow gave a high tea at which one of the guests was to be the senior J. P. Morgan. The girls were to be brought in, introduced and ushered out. Mrs. Morrow's great fear was the possibility that Anne, the most outspoken of them, might comment audibly upon Mr. Morgan's celebrated and conspicuous nose. She therefore took pains beforehand to explain to Anne that personal observations were impolite and cautioned her especially against making any comment upon Mr. Morgan's nose, no matter what she might think of it.

When the moment came and the children were brought in, Mrs. Morrow held her breath as she saw Anne's gaze fix upon the banker's most prominent facial feature and remain there. Nonetheless, the introduction was made without incident. The little girls curtsied politely and were sent on their way.

With a sigh of relief, Mrs. Morrow turned back to her duties as hostess and inquired of her guest, "And now, Mr. Morgan, will you have cream or lemon in your nose?"

"Honey," scolded the mom, "you shouldn't always keep everything for yourself. I've told you so many times that you should let your brother play with your toys half of the time."

"I've been doing it," the boy said, "I take the sled going downhill, and he takes it going up."

Mother: Cindy, what have you been doing this morning while I was working in the den?
Cindy: I was playing postman, Mom.
Mother: How could you play postman, without any letters?
Cindy: I was looking through your trunk in the attic and I found a packet of letters tied with a nice ribbon. So, I posted one in everyone's mailbox on our street.

I've noticed that the one thing about parents is that no matter what stage your child is in, the parents who have older children always tell you the next stage is worse.
—Dave Barry

A little girl in southern California was having her first glimpse of snow. "Oh, mama, what is it?" she asked excitedly.

"Why, that's snow, Penny. What did you think it was?"

"It looks like popped rain."

Words are so important. I was telling our six-year-old, "When you talk to the neighbors, just say your aunt likes to crochet. Don't call her the happy hooker."

Helga Anderson, mother of twelve, was asked how in the world she could take care of all her children. "Well," she replied, "when I had only one, it took all my time, so how could eleven more make any difference?"

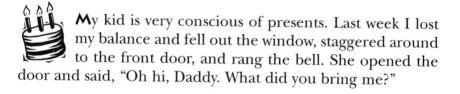 **My** kid is very conscious of presents. Last week I lost my balance and fell out the window, staggered around to the front door, and rang the bell. She opened the door and said, "Oh hi, Daddy. What did you bring me?"

All kids need warm, sincere, enlightened reassurance. Just yesterday one of my kids came up to me and I said, "Stephen, of course I'm concerned and interested in what you're doing— huh? Sorry. *Matthew*, of course I'm concerned and interested in what you're doing. . . ."

Mother's Day is when the kids say she's the greatest cook in the whole world—and then make her a dinner that proves it!

A golfer was walking around the fairway with four caddies. "Why so many?" a friend asked.

"It's my wife's idea," the golfer answered. "She thinks I should spend more time with the kids."

"Mommy, we want a hamster," the children wailed.

"You can't have a hamster. You won't take care of it. It will end up being my responsibility," Mom replied.

"We'll take care of it," they protested. "We promise."

So Mom relented. She bought them a hamster, and they named it "Danny." Two months later, though, when Mom found herself responsible for cleaning and feeding the creature, she located a prospective new home for Danny the hamster.

When she told the children the news of Danny's imminent departure, they took the news quite well, which somewhat surprised her. One of the children remarked, "He's been around here a long time. We'll miss him."

Mom agreed, saying, "Yes, but he's too much work for one person, and since I'm that one person, I say he goes."

Another child offered, "Well, maybe if he wouldn't eat so much and wouldn't be so messy, we could keep him."

But Mom was firm. "It's time to take Danny to his new home now," she insisted. "Go and get his cage."

In tearful outrage the children shouted, "Danny? We thought you said, 'Daddy!'"

A woman was speaking to her friend about her two beaus. "If I could combine their qualities, I'd be the happiest person in the world. Ronald is rich, handsome, and witty. Tony wants to marry me."

"Well, Ted, how does it feel to be a grandfather?"

"Oh, it's wonderful, of course, but I'll tell you, it's hard to get used to the idea of being married to a grandmother."

A father complaining to a friend: "Things were a lot different when I was a boy. In his room my son has a color TV, a computer, VCR, a refrigerator, a stereo, several radios and his telephone. When I want to punish him, I have to send him to my room!"

In his book *How to Use Humor for Business Success,* Malcolm Kushner reports that there are three ways to get things done:
- do it yourself
- ask someone else to do it
- ask your kids not to do it

"Mr. Jones," began the timid-looking man, "er . . . ah, that is, can . . . er I, will you—"

"Why, yes, my boy, you may have her," Jones cheerfully replied.

The young man gasped. "What's that? Have whom?" he nervously asked.

"My daughter, of course," answered Jones. "You want to marry her, don't you?"

"Not really," stammered the young man. "I just want to know if you could lend me twenty-five dollars."

"Certainly not!" Jones exclaimed. "I hardly know you!"

Mark and Teresa, teenage sweethearts, were on the sofa in one another's arms when there came the sound of a key in the front door of the luxurious apartment.

Teresa bolted upright. Her eyes were wide with alarm.

"Oh, no!" she cried. "It's my father! Quick, jump out the window."

Mark, equally alarmed, raced toward the window, then protested. "Are you crazy? I can't jump," he said; "we're on the thirteenth floor."

"For heaven's sake!" cried Teresa in exasperation, "This is no time to be superstitious!"

Art Sansom notes: "My great-grandfather rode a horse, but he wouldn't go near a train. Grandpa rode on trains, but he was afraid of automobiles. Pop drove a car, but he was afraid to fly. I love to fly, but I'm afraid to ride a horse."

We're all familiar with Murphy's Law, "If anything can go wrong, it will." In his book *The Official Rules at Home*, Paul Dickson adds a few new corollaries. Here's a sample of Dickson's laws, rules, observations and maxims:

- *Ballweg's Discovery.* Whenever there is a flat surface, someone will find something to put on it.
- *Rabbe's Rule of the Bedroom.* The spouse who snores louder always falls asleep first.
- *Rosenbaum's Rule.* The easiest way to find something lost around the house is to buy a replacement.
- *Smith's Fourth Law of Inertia.* A body at rest tends to watch television.

When my niece Muriel was expecting her first baby, she told her doctor, "Look, I'm willing to try Lamaze for childbirth if you are willing to give it a try for root canal."

A woman with fourteen children, ages one through fourteen, sued her husband for divorce on the grounds of desertion.

"When did he desert you?" the judge asked.

"Thirteen years ago," she replied.

"If he left thirteen years ago, where did all these children come from?"

"Oh," said the woman, "he kept coming back to say he was sorry."

Alice and Mildred, two sisters kept up a feud for thirty years. On Mildred's seventieth birthday, Alice, who was seventy-five, felt a pang of remorse, but it passed. Yet later, when she heard Mildred was ill, she felt compelled to visit.

From her sickbed, Mildred looked sternly at her sister. At last she said in a faint voice, "The doctors say I'm seriously ill, Alice. If I pass away, I want you to know you're forgiven. But if I pull through, things stay as they are!"

Mr. and Mrs. Johnson's blissful marriage was almost derailed by the presence in the household of old Aunt Virginia. For twelve long years she lived with the Johnsons, always crotchety, always demanding, always critical, never satisfied. Finally, the old woman had a stroke and died. On the way back from the funeral, Mr. Johnson sadly confessed to his wife, "Darling, if I didn't love you so much, I don't think I ever could have stood having your Aunt Virginia in the house all these years."

His wife looked at him, aghast. "My Aunt Virginia!" she cried. "I thought she was *your* Aunt Virginia!"

During World War II, my Uncle Phil was saved by an Italian woman, who hid him in her apartment for two years. She lived in Youngstown, Ohio.

The phrases that best sum up the Christmas season? "Peace on Earth," "Good will to all," and "Batteries not included."

When the fellow called a motel and asked how much they charged for a room, the clerk told him that the rates depended on room size and number of people. "Do you take children?" the man asked.

"No, sir," replied the clerk. "Only cash and credit cards."

—*Successful Meetings Magazine*

My Uncle Joe's Immutable Law of Love: People always fall in love with and marry someone having the opposite body temperature.

I come from a big family. As a matter of fact, I never got to sleep alone until I was married.

—Lewis Grizzard

Helga and Johann Andersen and their twelve children visited the zoo. Upon arriving, they found the admission was one dollar per family. Johann guided his twelve kids through a gate and handed the ticket collector a dollar bill. "Are all these your kids?" he asked.

"Sure are," answered the proud father.

"Then here's your dollar back. It's worth more for the animals to see your family then for your family to see the animals."

Auntie Norma: Go on, Jason dear, eat your spinach. It's good for growing children.
Jason: I don't want to grow any children.

Lowell: Oh, no! Beans again!
Connie: I don't get it. You liked beans on Monday, Tuesday, and Wednesday, and now suddenly you don't like beans.

Imagination is something that sits up with Dad and Mom the first time their teenager stays out late.

Weary of the constant disorder in her two sons' room, a mother laid down the law: For every item she had to pick up off the floor, they would have to pay her a nickel.

At the end of a week, the boys owed her sixty-five cents. She received the money promptly—along with a fifty-cent tip and a note that read, "Thanks, Mom. Keep up the good work!"

Sign by the entrance to a maternity shop:
Clothes for the Wait Conscious

Sign in an obstetrician's office:
Pay as You Grow

One of the great mysteries of life is how the idiot that your daughter married can be the father of the smartest grandchildren in the whole wide world.

Before I got married I had six theories about bringing up children. Now I have six children and no theories. —Lord Rochester

Two explorers, camped in the heart of the African jungle, were discussing their expedition. "I came here," said one, "because the urge to travel is in my blood. City life bored me, and the smell of exhaust fumes on the highways made me sick. I wanted to see the sun rise over new horizons and hear the flutter of birds that never had been seen by man. I wanted to leave my footprints on sand unmarked before I came. In short, I wanted to see nature in the raw. What about you?"

"I came," the second man replied, "because my son was taking saxophone lessons."

Hamlet is the tragedy of tackling a family problem too soon after college.
                                        —Tom Masson

When a schoolboy went home with a pain in his stomach, his mom said, "Well, sit down and drink your tea. Your stomach hurts because it's empty. It'll be all right when you've got something in it."

Afterward Dad came home from the office, complaining of a headache. "That's because it's empty," said the bright son. "You'd be all right if you had something in it."

Five-year-old: Do you know what thumbs are for?
Seven-year-old: They're to hold up bottoms of sandwiches.

An alarm clock is an instrument used to wake up people who have no kids.

Teacher: Did you do your homework?
Matt: No, Teacher.
Teacher: Do you have an excuse:
Matt: Yes. It's all my mother's fault.
Teacher: She kept you from doing it?
Matt: No, she didn't nag me enough.

Two Dutch boys and their mom were standing on the dike looking at the rough ocean, when suddenly the mother slipped, fell into the ocean, and disappeared. One boy turned to the other and said, "Look, Hans, no Ma."

If you ask me, mothers are the greatest actresses of our time. Who else can show such delight at getting a sixty-four-ounce bottle of perfume—with a twenty-five cents label still on it?

The kids next door told their mother she wasn't to lift a finger on Mother's Day. They were going to do all the cooking. So they took out three pots, two frying pans, a double boiler, three mixing bowls, a chopping board, six measuring spoons, eight serving dishes—and Mom was delighted. She said it was the best Jell-O she ever tasted.

The greatest Mother's Day tribute I ever heard came from a very successful businessman. He said: "Yes, I am a self-made man—but the blueprints came from my mother."

The minister was visiting the home of his parishioners, and in one he asked several questions about the family. A grubby but cheerful little boy caught the kindly cleric's attention. He asked him his name, and the lad replied, "Bolivar Reginald Shagnasty, the Third, Sir."

The minister turned to the boy's dad and asked, "Why did you give the boy a name like that?"

"'Cause I want 'em to be a professional boxer," replied the parent, "and with a name like that, he'll get plenty of practice at school."

Did you hear about the very well-behaved little boy? Whenever he was especially good his dad would give him a penny and a pat on the head. By the time he was sixteen he had twenty-five dollars in the bank and a flat head.

Todd came thundering down the stairs, much to his father's annoyance. "Todd," he called, "how many more times do I have to tell you to come down those stairs quietly! Now, go back upstairs and come down like a civilized human being."

There was a silence, and Todd reappeared in the front room. "That's better," said his father. "Now in the future will you always come down the stairs like that."

"Suits me," said Todd. "I slid down the banister."

Mom: Tiffany, was that the stepladder I heard falling over?
Tiffany: Yes, Mom.
Mom: Has your dad fallen down?
Tiffany: No, Mom, he's still hanging on the curtain rod.

Baby sitter: A teenager who must behave like an adult so that the adults who are out can behave like teenagers.   —John R. Fox

Adults are always asking kids what they want to be when they grow up, because they are looking for ideas.   —Paula Poundstone

First mother: I just returned from a pleasure trip.
Second mother: Where did you come from?
First mother: I took my children to camp.

My brother just got his ear pierced. Now he's got my father's looks and my mother's jewelry.   —Scott Wood

An usher was passing the collection plate at a large church wedding. One of those attending looked up, confused. Without waiting to be asked the usher nodded his head and murmured, "I know it's unusual, but the father of the bride requested it."

Teacher: Justin, your poem is the worst in the class. It's not
    only ungrammatical, it's rude and in bad taste. I'm going to
    send your father a note about it.
Justin: I don't think that would help, Ma'am. He wrote it.

A young mother requested her husband to take their two-year-old baby for a walk. The husband was busy with a project, but with a deep sigh, he got the baby carriage and started walking around the block in the hot sun.
    "Honey," called his wife from the second-story window.
    "Leave me alone!" he shouted back. "We're fine."
    After an hour his wife once again shouted, "Honey."
    "Well, what is it this time?" he answered gruffly. "Is there any problem in the house?"
    "Nothing, honey," replied his wife. "But you've been wheeling little Jennifer's doll the whole afternoon. Don't you think it's time for the baby to have a turn?"

The head of the house was reading a newspaper article carefully. Presently he said to his wife, "You know, darling, I think there's something in what this article says—that the cleverness of the father often proves a stumbling block to the boy."

The wife heaved a sigh of relief. "Thank goodness," she replied, "our Dustin won't have anything to fall over."

Human beings are the only creatures that allow their children to come home.

—Bill Cosby

Two businessmen were having lunch and they started talking about world problems, high taxes, the cost of living, their families. One of them said proudly, "I have six boys."

So the other guy said, "That's a nice family. I wish to heaven I had six children."

And the proud father said with a touch of sympathy in his voice, "Don't you have any children?"

And the other guy said, "Yeah, ten!"

—Soupy Sales

Parents can't be more content than when their children are in bed, safe and soundless.

Shopper: I'd like a pair of stockings for my wife.
Clerk: Sheer?
Shopper: No, she's at home.

The police woman watched as a young man backed his car around the block. He circled again, and again. Finally she stopped him and asked why he was driving backward. At first the youth wouldn't explain his strange behavior. Eventually he admitted to her that he had borrowed his father's car for the evening and had driven farther than he had promised. He was backing up to take some of the miles off the odometer.

Mrs. Moore apologized to her unexpected ministerial guest for serving the apple pie without cheese. Her son slipped quietly away from the table for a moment, then returned with a small piece of cheese, which he laid on the guest's plate.

The visitor smiled thankfully at the lad. Putting the cheese in his mouth, he remarked, "You must have sharper eyes than your mother, sonny. Where did you find it?"

The boy replied with a flush of pride, "In the mousetrap."

Six-year-old Beth Marsh was asked what she was going to give her brother for Christmas. "I don't know," she answered.

"What did you give him last year?"

"The chicken pox."

Wanting to take his wife out for the evening, Marty Schell dropped off his ten-year-old son Woody at Grandma's house. As Marty went out the door, Grandma Schell asked, "When do you want him back?"

"When he's nineteen!" replied the father.

"My kid said, 'Daddy, Mommy said you should take me to the zoo.' I said, 'If the zoo wants you, let them come and get you.'"

—Slappy White

Adolescence is . . .

- the awkward stage in the life of a youngster when they're too old for an allowance and too young for a credit card.
- a period of rapid changes. Between the ages of twelve and seventeen, a parent ages as much as twenty years.
- the period when a teenager acts like a baby if you don't treat him like an adult.
- the age at which children stop asking questions because they know all the answers.
- the awkward age when a child is too old to say something cute and too young to say something sensible.

A child is growing up when he stops asking where he came from and starts refusing to tell you where he's going.

Adolescent: One who is well informed about anything he doesn't have to study.

If you want to recapture your youth, just cut off his allowance.

The trouble with the 1990s as compared with the 1970s is that teenagers no longer leave home.

There ought to be an FAA requirement that crying babies have to go into the overhead compartment.
—Bobby Slayton

Every baby resembles the relative who has the most money.
—Luke McLuke, a.k.a. James Syme Hastings

People are giving birth underwater now. They say it's less traumatic for the baby because it's in water. Then it comes out into water. I guess it probably would be less traumatic for the baby, but certainly it's more traumatic for the other people in the pool.
—Elayne Boosler

George: Rich, me? No, I'm a pauper.
Gracie: Congratulations. Boy or girl?
—Burns and Allen

Giving birth is like pushing a flaming log through your nostril.

The child had every toy his father wanted.
—Robert E. Whitten

Parents who are afraid to put their feet down usually have children who step on their toes.

My crazy brother-in-law, I wish he would learn a trade. That way we'd know what kind of work he's out of.   —Henny Youngman

When I was a boy, my family took great care with our snapshots. We really planned them. We made compositions. We posed in front of expensive cars, homes that weren't ours. We borrowed dogs. Almost every family picture taken of us when I was young had a different borrowed dog in it.   —Richard Avedon

The main purpose of children's parties is to remind you that there are children more awful than your own.
—Katharine E. Whitehorn

Who of us is mature enough for offspring before the offspring themselves arrive? The value of marriage is not that adults produce children but that children produce adults.   —Peter de Vries

Children are unpredictable. You never know what inconsistency they're going to catch you in next.   —Franklin P. Jones

Many a man wishes he were strong enough to tear a telephone book in half—especially if he has a teenage daughter.
—Guy Lombardo

The most beautiful sight from the pulpit is a whole family seated together in a pew. The church service is not a convention to which a family should send one delegate.   —Charles Myers

Announcement from the proud parents of a baby daughter: "We have skirted the issue."
—Earl Wilson

I came from a family where gravy was a beverage and ketchup was a vegetable.
—Erma Bombeck

As a child my family's menu consisted of two choices—take it or leave it.
—Buddy Hackett

We never talked, my family. We communicated by putting Ann Landers articles on the refrigerator.
—Judy Gold

I came from a family of pioneers. My mother invented guilt in 1936.
—Erma Bombeck

God gives us relatives; thank God we can choose our friends.
—A. Mizner

Teenagers were put on earth to keep adults from wasting time on the telephone.

A young girl watched her mother prepare a ham and noticed that her mother cut the ends of the ham before placing it in the baking pan. "Why do you do that?" the child asked. The mother could only say, "That's the way your grandmother always did it."

So the little girl asked her grandmother, who responded, "Well, that's the way my mother always did it."

Visiting Great-grandmother, the girl asked her the same question. The old woman replied, "All I had was a small pan, so I had to cut off the ends to make it fit."

The young couple met with their pastor to set a date for their wedding. When he asked whether they preferred a contemporary or a traditional service, they opted for contemporary.

On the big day, a major storm forced the groom to take an alternate route to the church. The streets were flooded, so he rolled up his pants legs to keep his trousers dry.

When he finally reached the church, his best man rushed him into the sanctuary and up to the altar, just as the ceremony was starting.

"Pull down your pants," whispered the pastor.

"Uh, Reverend, I've changed my mind," the groom responded. "I think I want the traditional service."

A Catholic priest, a Baptist minister, a Jewish rabbi, and an Episcopalian vestryman are discussing the question of when life begins.

The Catholic priest states, "Life begins at the moment of conception when the sperm and the egg unite."

The Baptist minister declares, "No, it begins when the fetus is viable, when if it should be born, it would be able to live."

The rabbi insists, "Life does not begin until the very moment of birth."

The Episcopalian vestryman argues, "In my opinion, life begins when the children go off to college and the dog dies."

Three mothers were bragging about their sons. "My son is a wealthy lawyer," said one. "For my birthday he gave me this fur coat."

Said the second: "My son is a medical doctor. Last winter he gave me a vacation in Miami Beach."

The third thought for a moment, then blurted, "My son sees a fancy psychiatrist each week. He pays the psychiatrist a hundred fifty dollars an hour. And guess who he spends his time talking about? Me!"

When I first met my wife, she was a schoolteacher. I used to write her passionate love letters—and she'd send them back corrected.

I must be the only man in the world who returned from his honeymoon and received a report card.

It said, "Dick is neat and friendly and shows a keen interest in fun and games."

—Dick Lord

A disconcerted minister to his congregation: "Crying babies and disruptive children, like good intentions, should be carried out immediately."

The attorney gathered the entire family for the reading of the will. Relatives came from near and far, to see if they were included in the bequests. The lawyer somberly opened the will and began to read:

"To my cousin Ed, I leave my ranch.

"To my brother Jim, I leave my money market accounts.

"To my neighbor and good friend, Fred, I leave my stocks.

"And finally, to my cousin George, who always sat around and never did anything, but wanted to be remembered in my will, I say, 'Hi, George.'"

—King Duncan

When I was pastor of the Little Brown Church, our wealthiest member died. He bequeathed half a million to our denomination's "Make a Difference" campaign and another half a million to each of his relatives. At the cemetery, I noticed that among the well-dressed mourners was a shabby young stranger who cried as though his heart were breaking. After the service, I walked over to the young man. "I noticed you crying," I said. "Were you related to the deceased?"

"No," the young man responded, "I wasn't related at all."

"Then, why are you crying?" I asked.

The man replied, "I just told you—because I wasn't related."

CHRISTMAS, UPDATED

'Tis the day after Christmas and inside and out,
The holiday carnage lies scattered about.

And Ma, with a wet towel atop of her head
And aspirin tablets, has crawled into bed.

The kiddies, God bless 'em, are raising a din,
With thundering drums and shrill trumpets of tin.

While Pa, like a schoolboy, forgetting his years,
Is all tangled up in the bicycle gears.

Old Duffer, the dachshund, delightfully smug,
Lies gnawing a carcass upon the new rug.

And Muffet, the kitten, despaired of a lap,
On the dining room table is taking her nap.

Plaid neckties and pink socks and what-nots galore
Await their exchange at the five-and-ten store.

While tidbits and knickknacks of leftover sweets
Must furnish the menu for future-day eats.

'Tis the day after Christmas, and once every year
Folks willingly pay for their holiday cheer.

With toothaches from candy and headaches from bills,
They call up the doctor and order more pills.

—Marguerite Gode, *Fertile Imagination*

During his freshman year, my son Steve couldn't get home for Christmas, so he sent me a set of inexpensive cuff links and a note reading "Dear Dad: This isn't much, but it's all you could afford."

'Twas the night before Christmas, when all through our house
Not a creature was sleeping, not even my spouse.
The stockings were hung by the chimney with screws.
(If you can't find the nails, what else do you use?)
The children were restless, awake in their beds,
While visions of spanking them danced in our heads.

I worked in my bathrobe. My husband, in jeans,
Had gone down to the den with directions and dreams
To assemble a bike that came in small pieces
With deflated tires and fenders with creases.
Soon down in the den there arose such a clatter,
I sprang from my task to see what was the matter.

Away to my husband I flew like a flash;
He was shuffling through cardboard; his actions were rash.
The bike on the rug by this now-flustered dad
Soon gave me a hint as to why he was mad.
He needed a kickstand. It had to be near.
I shuffled some papers—he saw it appear!

We twisted the screws; we were lively and quick,
And we soon knew assembly would be quite a trick.
Fast as eagles in flight the pieces were found,
And he whistled and shouted for parts all around:
"Now socket! Now pedal! Now tires! Now brakes!
On handles! On kickstand! On horn! . . .Oh . . .But wait!"

In the top of the toolbox, he fumbled around;
"I need two more screws!" he said with a frown.
And like all good parents determined to please
When they meet with an obstacle late Christmas Eve,
We shouted and yelled some complaints to each other.
There was never more frustrated father and mother!

And then, in a panic, we heard on the stairs
The prancing and hopping of feet . . .'bout two pairs!
I opened the door and was turning around,
When kids burst from the hall with a leap and a bound.
They were dressed all in flannel, from their necks to their knees,
And their nightgowns were soiled with sugar and cheese!

Excuses poured forth from each pair of lips;
They stood in defiance with hands on their hips.
Their eyes were wide open, and each little child
Jumped when I yelled with a voice hardly mild.
They were frightened but cute, though much bigger than elves,
And we laughed when we saw them, in spite of ourselves.

A wink of the eye and a pat on the head
Soon let them both know they had nothing to dread
They saw not a thing but went straight to their beds,
And we finished the bike and put bows on the sleds.
Then wheeling the bike by the tree (out of sight),
My hubby announced we should call it a night.

He sprang to his bed, to the clock gave a whistle,
As the time had flown by like a large Titan missile.
And I heard him exclaim as he turned out the light,
"Merry Christmas, my dear . . . but next year, NO BIKE!"

—P. R. Van Buskirk, *Ask the Theologians*

We got the kids something nice for Christmas—their own apartment.

In a cartoon by Guindon, a weary woman shopper is shown resting for a moment with her arms filled with packages. She is in the middle of a very busy department store filled with other Christmas shoppers, and she is explaining the whole Christmas scene to her small son as follows: "No one is quite sure how Christmas worked out like this, dear. Theologians are working very, very hard on that question right now."

A woman testified to the transformation in her life that had resulted through her experience in conversion. She declared, "I'm so glad I got religion. I have an uncle I used to hate so much, I vowed I'd never go to his funeral. But now, why, I'd be happy to go to it any time."

—Norton Mockridge

Daughter: "Is it true that Santa Claus brings us our Christmas presents?"

Mother: "Yes, that's true."

Daughter: "And the stork brings us babies?"

Mother: "Yes, that's true."

Daughter: "And the Police Department protects us?"

Mother: "That's right."

Daughter: "Then what do we need Daddy for?"

Behind every great man is . . . his mother:

Mrs. Washington: "Oh George, you never did have a head for money."

Mrs. Morse: "Sam, stop tapping your fingers on the table, it's driving me crazy!"

Mrs. Lindbergh: "Charles, can't you do anything by yourself?"

Mrs. Armstrong: "Neil has no more business taking flying lessons than the man in the moon." —*Modern Maturity*

Folks today are in love with love. One fellow bought up every book he saw on the physical art of love. One day in a used book shop at an airport, he saw a book with the intriguing title, *How to Hug*. He was in such a hurry to catch his plane, he didn't have time to examine it before he paid for it. It wasn't until he was in the air that he had a chance to see what he had bought: the fifth volume of an encyclopedia.

When the power failed at the elementary school, the cook couldn't serve a hot meal in the cafeteria, so at the last minute she whipped up huge stacks of peanut butter and jelly sandwiches. As one little boy filled his plate, he said, "It's about time. Finally, a home-cooked meal."

I was concerned that my daughter was growing up too quickly, until I saw her wetting her hair rollers with a water pistol.

PREPARATION FOR PARENTHOOD

Preparation for parenthood is not just a matter of reading books and decorating the nursery. Here are twelve simple tests for expectant parents to take to prepare themselves for the real-life experience of being a mother or father.

Women: to prepare for maternity, put on a dressing gown and stick a pillow-sized beanbag down the front. Leave it there for nine months. After nine months, take out ten percent of the beans.

Men: to prepare for paternity, go to the local pharmacy, tip the contents of your wallet on the counter, and tell the pharmacist to help himself. Then go to the supermarket. Arrange to have your salary paid directly to their head office. Go home. Pick up the paper. Read it for the last time.

Before you finally go ahead and have children, find a couple of people who are already parents and berate them about their methods of discipline, lack of patience, appallingly low tolerance levels, and how they have allowed their children to run rampant. Suggest ways in which they might improve their child's sleeping habits, toilet training, table manners and overall behavior. Enjoy it; it'll be the last time in your life that you will have all the answers.

To discover how the nights will feel, walk around the living room from 5:00 PM to 10:00 PM carrying a wet bag weighing approximately eight to twelve pounds. At 10:00 PM put the bag down, set the alarm for midnight, and go to sleep. Get up at midnight and walk around the living room again with the bag till 1:00 AM. Put the alarm on for 3:00 AM. As you can't get back to sleep, get up at 2:00 AM and make a drink. Go to bed at 2:45 AM. Get up again at 3:00 AM when the alarm goes off. Sing songs in the dark until 4:00 AM. Put the alarm on for 5:00 AM. Get up. Make breakfast. Keep this up for five years. Look cheerful.

Can you stand the mess children make? To find out, smear peanut butter onto the sofa and jam onto the curtains. Hide a fish finger behind the stereo and leave it there all summer. Stick your fingers in the flowerbeds then rub them on the clean walls. Cover the stains with crayons. How does that look?

Dressing small children is not as easy as it seems. First, buy an octopus and a string bag. Attempt to put the octopus into the string bag so that none of the arms hang out. Time allowed for this: all morning.

Take an egg carton. Using a pair of scissors and a pot of paint, turn it into an alligator. Now take a toilet tube. Using only scotch tape and a piece of foil, turn it into a Christmas cracker. Last, take a milk container, a ping pong ball, and an empty packet of Cocoa Pops and make an exact replica of the Eiffel Tower. Congratulations. You have just qualified for a place on the Playgroup Committee.

Forget the Miata and buy a Taurus. And don't think you can leave it out in the driveway spotless and shining. Family cars don't look like that. Buy a chocolate ice cream. bar and put it in the glove compartment. Leave it there. Get a quarter. Stick it in the cassette player. Take a family-size packet of chocolate cookies. Mash them down the back seats. Run a garden rake along both sides of the car. There. Perfect.

Get ready to go out. Wait outside the bathroom for half an hour. Go out the front door. Come in again. Go out. Come back in. Go out again. Walk down the front path. Walk back up it. Walk down it again. Walk very slowly down the road for five minutes. Stop to inspect minutely every cigarette end, piece of used chewing gum, dirty tissue and dead insect along the way. Retrace your steps. Scream that you've had as much as you can stand, until the neighbors come out and stare at you. Give up and go back into the house. You are now just about ready to try taking a small child for a walk.

Repeat everything you say five times.

Go to your local supermarket. Take with you the nearest thing you can find to a pre-school child—a fully grown goat is excellent. If you intend to have more than one child, take more than one goat. Buy your week's groceries without letting the goats out of your sight. Pay for everything the goats eat or destroy. Until you can easily accomplish this, do not even contemplate having children.

Hollow out a melon. Make a small hole in the side. Suspend it from the ceiling and swing it from side to side. Now get a bowl of soggy oatmeal and attempt to spoon it into the swaying melon by pretending to be an airplane. Continue until half the oatmeal is gone. Tip the rest into your lap, making sure that a lot of it falls on the floor. You are now ready to feed a twelve-month-old baby.

Learn the names of every character from Postman Pat and Fireman Sam to Teenage Mutant Ninja Turtles and Power Rangers. When you find yourself singing "Postman Pat" at work, you finally qualify as a parent.   —Source Unknown

In trying to get her son to behave, Mom commented one day, "Every time you're naughty I get another gray hair."

To which the son replied, "Mom, you must have been a terror when you were young. Just look at Grandma."

A grandmother got a note from her son and daughter-in-law that her grandchildren would be coming to spend a week with her. She loved her lively little granddaughter and precious little grandson, and when she thought about the pleasures that awaited her with them in her home, she went to church and, as a token of anticipation, put five dollars in the offering plate.

She kept her granddaughter and grandson for that week, and what a week it was. When they went home, she went back to church. As a token of thanksgiving, she put a twenty dollar bill in the offering plate.

The other day my daughter came home from school and asked a question of my wife. My wife said, "Why not wait until your dad comes home and ask him?"

To which my daughter replied, "But, Mom, I don't want to know that much about it!"

A super-cautious mother always wore a gauze mask when coming near her baby and insisted that all visitors do likewise. Several older and wiser women tried to tell her tactfully that she was carrying things too far, but the young mother insisted that most parents were absolutely criminal in their carelessness about a child's health.

One day the mother mentioned that she thought the baby was beginning to cut a tooth and she wished she could find out about it in some way. A friend with more experience said, "Why, just put your finger in his mouth and . . ."

There was such a horrified expression on the mother's face that the friend quickly added, "Of course, you should boil your finger first."

Helen Broderick phoned her insurance company and said she wanted to change the beneficiaries of her insurance policy. "I've just had twins," she informed her agent.

The agent had difficulty in hearing her, and asked: "Will you repeat that, please?"

She shot back emphatically: "Not if I can help it!"

Grandma Betty was saying good-night to her granddaughters when six-year-old Beth remarked, "Mommy and Daddy are entertaining some very important people downstairs."

Grandma said, "Yes, I know they have guests. But what makes you think they are important?"

The little girl responded, "Just listen. Mommy is laughing at all of Daddy's jokes."

"I'm really worried," said one teenager to another. "Dad slaves away at his job so I'll never need anything, and so I can go to college. Mom spends every day washing and ironing and cleaning up after me, and she takes care of me when I'm sick."

"So what are you worried about?"

"I'm afraid they might try to escape."

—Jack Moore, Universal Press Syndicate

My parents used to put us to sleep every night by tossing us up in the air. Of course, for this method to work, you have to have very low ceilings.

Agnes and Beverly were discussing their respective grown-up children. "Do you mean to tell me that your son and daughter-in-law were married six months ago and you haven't visited them yet?" exclaimed Agnes. "I'm shocked!"

"What's there to be shocked about?" demanded Beverly. "I'm waiting until they have their first baby. Everybody knows that a grandma is always more welcome than a mother-in-law."

Once when I was baby-sitting, my six-year-old grandson refused to eat anything set before him. In exasperation I asked, "Jonathan, you tell me you don't like beef, you don't like chicken, you don't like fish, you don't like fruit, you don't like vegetables, you don't like milk, and you don't like juice. Tell me, what do you like?"

Turning his innocent blue eyes on me, he answered, "I like you, Grampa!"

Little Ted was told not to go swimming in a nearby pond. Nonetheless, he came home with his hair wet. He told his mother he had fallen into the water.

"Then why aren't your clothes wet, too?" she asked.

"Well," he replied, "I had a hunch I might fall in, so I took off my clothes and hung them on a tree."

It's not easy being a father. One cynic, speaking from his own experience, noted that children go through four fascinating stages. First they call you Da-Da. Then they call you Daddy. As they mature they call you Dad. Finally they call you collect.

—King Duncan

My parents seldom drank, but when they did, they made up for lost time. Following one particularly festive party, my folks decided to leave the assorted bottles and dregs until the next morning. As they staggered downstairs next day, they found my sister, brother, and me finishing off all we could find and, needless to say, looking quite a bit the worse for wear. Not knowing what to do, my mother suggested to my father that he take us out in the car for some fresh air.

A traffic policeman, seeing our car going repeatedly round the block for no apparent reason, pulled my father over and gave him a breathalyzer test. As you might imagine, the meter showed positive.

While matters were being sorted out, my eight-year-old sister asked the officer if she could try the breathalyzer. When she did, the meter again showed positive!

"Oh, well," said the policeman, "Another faulty meter!" He then apologized to my dad for stopping him, and drove off without another word.

I just heard this on the radio, purportedly factual:

A West Virginia man, considering getting a vasectomy, decided to discuss it with his priest.

The priest gave him various bits of advice, and suggested that he discuss it with his doctor.

The doctor likewise advised him on various aspects, but on discovering that he hadn't talked to his family about it yet, urged him to do so.

His family voted in favor, fourteen to four.

I heard about one poor man who had a very difficult mother, but he felt obligated to take care of her. He had a basement apartment built in his home just for her. One day a friend of his paid a visit. They were chatting in the living room. "I remember," said his friend, "what a difficult time your mother gave you. Where is the old girl now?"

Fearing that the conversation would be overheard, the poor man simply pointed downward in the direction of the basement apartment. "Oh, I'm sorry," said his friend. "I didn't even know she had died."

—King Duncan

Even though children are deductible, they can also be very taxing.

Taking care of your baby is easy, as long as you don't have anything else to do.   —King Duncan

Bill Cell and Ed Woodward, two professors of theology, were walking across the campus of United Theological Seminary when Bill asked Ed, "Do you believe in Original Sin?"

Ed answered, "Yes, I do. We have a child."

"Do you believe in Total Depravity?" asked Bill.

"No, I don't. That's an excess of Calvinistic theology," replied Ed.

Bill looked at his friend and replied, "Well, just wait till you have more children."

There was once a man who was trying to read the evening newspaper after coming home from a rough day at the office. As he attempted to read, his children constantly interrupted him.

One child came and asked for money for an ice cream cone, and his father gently reached into his pocket and gave him the necessary coins.

Another child arrived in tears. Her leg was hurt, and she wanted her daddy to kiss the hurt away.

An older son came with an algebra problem, and they eventually arrived at the right answer.

Finally, the last and youngest of them all burst into the room looking for good old Dad. The father said cynically, "What do you want?"

The little youngster said, "Oh, Daddy, I don't want anything. I just want to sit on your lap."

—Ben and Karen Lewans in *Catholic Digest*

After the kids leave home, some parents suffer from the empty-nest syndrome. Others change the locks.   —King Duncan

When my son Stephen was seven years old, he asked his mother, "Mom, what's sex?"

Visibly flustered, his mother answered, "Well, that's whether you're a girl or a boy. You know, like when we signed you up for swimming lessons, and the form asked what your sex was, that's what they wanted to know."

Looking satisfied by this answer, Stephen said, "Thanks, Mom," and left the room.

His mother wiped her brow: "Whew!"

The next day Stephen cornered his mother while she was making dinner and exclaimed, "Mom, my friend Robby says that sex is when you take off your clothes and rub against each other. Is that true?"

His mother said, "Well, yes, that's another meaning of 'sex.'"

Stephen asked again, "*All* your clothes?"

His mother nodded in assent.

Stephen's response: "*Yuck!* That's *gross!*"

Struggling to regain control of the situation, his mother added, "Well, Stevie, I'm real glad you asked me about this. If you have any more questions, please ask."

Stephen said, "Well, I do have one more."

Breaking into a sweat, Mom asked, "Yes, dear?"

"Where does plastic come from?" he asked.

One of Mark Twain's best known remarks is worth repeating:

"When I was a boy of fourteen, my father was so ignorant I could hardly stand to have the old man around. But when I got to be twenty-one, I was astonished at how much the old man had learned in seven years."

I never liked hide-and-seek ever since the time I hid in the closet and my family moved.

You show me a child who doesn't play with toys, and I'll show you a father who's not done with them yet.

A local Romeo's face appeared in the window of his beloved's bedroom. "Get a move on," he hollered, "and let's get this eloping business over with."

"Be quiet," cautioned his Juliet. "Daddy will hear us and spoil our plans."

"I wouldn't worry about that," said Romeo. "He's down on the ground holding the ladder."

I went to visit my friend Father Miles at his office in the city. As I entered his office, he instructed his secretary, "Unless it's the archbishop or the pope, don't put any calls through."

In the middle of our meeting, the phone rang. Annoyed, Father Miles answered it. Then his eyes widened. "Yes," he said, "that's right. I told her not to let any calls through unless they came from the archbishop, the pope or you, Mom."

This sounds a lot like an urban myth, but my brother-in-law tells me that this happened to the wife of someone he works with. I must admit that I'm a bit skeptical, but it's certainly good for a chuckle.

It seems that this lady didn't quite make it to the hospital for the birth of her child. In fact, the baby was born on the lawn just outside the main entrance. The poor woman was dreadfully embarrassed and was being consoled by one of the nurses, who said; "Don't worry about it. It could have been worse. Why, two years ago we had a woman who gave birth in the elevator."

The woman cried out, "That was me!" and burst into tears.

My Uncle Will was an angry man. In his will, he instructed my Aunt Celia to put on his tombstone: "What are you lookin' at?"

How come it takes so little time for a child who is afraid of the dark to become a teenager who wants to stay out all night?

While critiquing a survey intended for mothers of infants less than one year old, I came across the following multiple-choice question.

Have you ever breast fed your baby? Select one answer from the following:

- Yes
- No
- Don't know

My uncle Irv thinks he's just a little better than everybody else. When he spells his name, he capitalizes the first two letters.

We knew they were too young to get married when they insisted on going to summer camp for their honeymoon. —Gene Perret

It's a good idea to have children while your parents are still young enough to take care of them. —Rita Rudner

 The harried housewife sprang to the telephone when it rang and listened with relief to the kindly voice in her ear. "How are you, darling?" it said. "What kind of a day are you having?"

"Oh, Mother," said the housewife, breaking into bitter tears, "I've had such a bad day. The baby won't eat, the washing machine broke down, I haven't had a chance to go shopping, and besides, I've just sprained my ankle and I have to hobble around. On top of that, the house is a mess and I'm supposed to have two couples to dinner tonight."

The mother was shocked and was full of sympathy. "Oh, darling," she said, "sit down, relax, and close your eyes. I'll be over in half an hour. I'll do your shopping, clean up the house, and cook your dinner for you. I'll feed the baby, and I'll call a repairman I know who'll be at your house to fix the washing machine promptly. Now stop crying. I'll do everything. In fact,

I'll even call George at the office and tell him he ought to come home and help out for once."

"George?" said the housewife. "Who's George?"

"Why, George! Your husband! . . . Is this 284-1373?"

"No, it's 284-1376."

"Oh, I'm sorry. I guess I have the wrong number."

There was a short pause. Then the young woman asked, "Does this mean you're not coming over?"

When my grandson Jonathan was five, he was looking at his parents' wedding pictures in the family album. Matt, his father, described the ceremony and tried to explain its meaning.

In a flash, Jonathan understood (or thought he did). "I think I've got it," he exclaimed. "That's when Mom came to work for us, right?"

At a dinner party, several doting mothers were discussing their children's illnesses with the guest of honor, a noted pediatrician. One mother asked, "Doctor, what do you find to be the principal ailment of children?"

The doctor considered the questions, then answered gravely, "Parents, madam."

A mother had just brought her newborn triplets home from the hospital. Her older boy, a four-year-old, took his first doubtful look at the new babies and said, "We'd better start calling folks. They're going to be a lot harder to get rid of than kittens."

I was trying to help my grandson with his arithmetic homework. I said to him, "Suppose you reached in your right pocket and found a ten dollar bill, and you reached in your left pocket and found another one, what would you have?"

My practical grandson's answer: "Somebody else's pants."

Hospitality is making your guests feel at home, even if you wish they were.

I once heard my Aunt Lou pray:

"Lord, help me to believe and accept the truth about myself, no matter how beautiful it is."

Two brothers had grown up in the country. One day, one of them announced he was going to the city to seek his fortune. The other one said he'd stay home and look after the farm and their parents.

The brother in the city became a salesman. He worked hard and soon was made sales manager, then vice president, and eventually president of the company. His business was bought by a larger corporation. After a little while, he became president of the conglomerate.

One day he got a call from his brother on the farm, who said, "Daddy died, and the funeral is Friday."

He said, "Oh, my goodness. I have to leave Thursday for a big merger meeting in Japan. I just can't come, but I want you to give Daddy the best funeral you can get and send the bill to me. It's the least I can do."

The brother did that, and in a few weeks, the successful brother received a bill for sixteen thousand dollars, and he paid it. The following month, a bill for four hundred dollars came. Thinking they had forgotten something, he paid it. The next month, another bill for four hundred dollars came, and he paid that one, too. When another bill for four hundred arrived the third month, he called his brother and asked if he knew why he was getting these bills.

"Oh, yes, " the brother said, "I think I do. See, when we got Daddy all dressed up in his old serge suit in that new casket with that polished wood and satin lining, he just didn't look right. Since you said you wanted the best, we rented him a tuxedo."

—J. Richard Carleton in *Hometown Humor, USA*, edited by Jones and Wheeler

Miss Swenson's fifth grade class was assigned to write a short essay on parents. Samantha Peters' essay read: "The trouble with parents is that when we get them, they are so old that it is very hard to change their habits."

After several years of marriage, Thelma and Bob Robson finally had their first baby, a healthy boy whom they named Barnaby. When the child was one year old, he hadn't said a word; one and a half years, still not a word. The parents took the baby to a pediatrician, who said, "Everything's perfectly normal. Just be patient."

And so it went until Barnaby's fourth birthday. The Robsons were all having breakfast, when Barnaby turned to his mother and said, "This oatmeal is too lumpy."

The parents were amazed. They said, "Why haven't you talked before?"

Young Barnaby shrugged and replied, "Up till now, everything's been great!"

Helen Aberg used to give generous Christmas presents to her several grandchildren, but the kids never sent thank-you notes, despite the urgings of their respective parents. But then one year, things changed. Grandma sent a hundred dollar Christmas check to each grandchild. The very next day, each child came over in person to thank her. She was telling this to a friend of hers, who said, "How wonderful! What do you think caused them to become so polite?"

"Oh," said Helen, "it was easy. This year I didn't sign the checks."

Love is staying awake all night with a sick child . . . or a healthy adult.
—David Frost

"Good grief," cried Whistler, when he saw his mother on her hands and knees scrubbing the floor. "Are you off your rocker?"

Remember that as a teenager you are at the last stage in your life when you will be happy to hear that the phone is for you.

—Fran Lebowitz

Abigail Van Buren once printed the following letter:

Dear Abby,

I couldn't believe the letter from the wife who complained about her husband leaving the toilet seat up. She admitted she couldn't "count the number of times" she had fallen in. And then she said, "He still hasn't learned."

Abby, tell me, who hasn't learned?

Five-year-old Mo was amazed by grandfather's false teeth. He watched as Gramps removed his dentures, washed them and put them back in. Mo asked to see it done again and again. "OK," said the grandfather, humoring the child. "Anything else?"

"Yeah," said the child. "Now take off your nose."

 Having a family is like having a bowling alley installed in your brain.

—Martin Mull

A family spent the night in a motel and the wife awoke early. She packed the bags and carried them to the car. Returning after one load, she accidentally went into the wrong room. Seeing a sleeping man and assuming it was her husband, she shouted as loud as she could, "Get out of that bed!" Suddenly she realized her mistake, turned, and ran out. As she did, she heard the man exclaim, "Boy, that sure is some wake-up service."

Motherhood is full of frustrations and challenges. Eventually, though, they move out.

My eight-year-old grandson Jonathan was waiting in line at an ice cream stand and hanging on to the hand of his three-year-old cousin Mark. "I want vanilla!" Mark yelled impatiently. "Vanilla!"

The stand was out of vanilla, but the older boy handled the situation with all the skill of a child psychologist. He bought two strawberry cones and handed one to his cousin, saying, "Here you are—pink vanilla!"

Having a baby is like taking your lower lip and forcing it over your head.

—Carol Burnett

Aunt Frieda asked her five-year-old daughter Heather, "Why can't you behave like Tracy next door?"

"Because she's a doctor's kid," Heather protested.

"What's that got to do with it?" her mother demanded.

"The doctor always keeps the best babies for himself," Heather replied.

My son Stephen was always very businesslike. I was told about the way that he answered the telephone one day when he was five years old. "I'm very sorry," he said, "but my mother and father have gone shopping. Would you like to leave a message?"

"Yes," said the caller. "Tell them Mr. Whitney called about the television set."

"OK," said Stephen. "How do you spell Whitney?"

"W-H-I-T-N-E-Y," said the caller.

"OK," said Stephen. "How do you make a 'W'?"

One day in 1962, my five-year-old came home from a birthday party and told his mother, "I'm never going to believe another word you say. I was the only kid at the party who didn't know that babies are brought by the stork."

A woman came to ask the doctor if a woman should have children after thirty-five. I say thirty-five children is enough for any woman.

—Gracie Allen

When you're a parent you become an idiot. It's not our fault. It's the television shows we watch. I used to watch the news. Now I watch *Sesame Street* and Mr. Rogers.

He read in the paper that it takes ten dollars a year to support a kid in India. So he sent his kids there.

—Red Buttons

Mother: Do you love me, Albert?
Albert: Yes.
Mother: Yes what?
Albert: Yes, please.

—Tom Stoppard

I was recently informed by a five-year-old kid that Disney had to re-release *Snow White* because of all the publicity her daughter, Vanna, was getting.

While I was on a shopping spree in a department store, I heard a little five-year-old talking to his mother on the down escalator. He asked, "Mommy, what do they do when the basement gets full of steps?"

—Hal Linden

Our three-year-old daughter looked at a calendar and asked, "How many be-good days until Christmas?"

—John Hokel

I once asked my four-year-old grandson how he liked his Thanksgiving dinner. "I didn't like the turkey much," he replied, "but I sure loved the bread it ate."

When my son Stephen was a first-grader, he demonstrated how really practical school children can be. He slipped in the hall at school and skinned his knee. A gym teacher attempted psychological first aid: "Remember, big boys don't cry, Sonny."

"I'm not going to cry," Steve replied. "I'm going to sue!"

When my daughter Susan was in kindergarten, the teacher displayed several flags. "What flag is this?" asked the teacher.

"That is the flag of our country," answered Susie.

"And what is the name of our country?"

Susie's quick reply: "'Tis of thee!"

A little four-year-old brought his puppy to visit his grandmother. She was busy fixing dinner and paid no attention to the pup. After a while the boy, his eyes filling with tears, asked her reproachfully: "Aren't you even going to speak to your granddog?"

A three-year-old boy went with his dad to see a new litter of kittens. On returning home, he breathlessly informed his mom, "There were two boy kittens and two girl kittens."

"How did you know that?" his mother asked.

"Daddy picked them up and looked underneath," he replied. "I think it's printed on the bottom."

My Aunt Marie was standing at our front door after Thanksgiving dinner, ready to go home. Her four little children stood at her side, and her arms were full of coats.

Her husband, coming down the stairs, asked why she was standing there.

She replied, handing him the coats, "This time, you put the children's coats on and I'll go honk the horn."

Husband to wife: "I'll say this for television. The more unsuitable the program, the quieter it keeps the children!"

And do you know what the most dangerous time in any American household is? Thirty-five minutes before visitors are supposed to arrive. If you're a husband, suddenly the whole house is off limits!

The Vatican came down with a new ruling. No surrogate mothers. It's a good thing they didn't make this rule before Jesus was born.
—Elayne Boosler

Boy to playmate at door: "Sorry, but I'm going to be tied up for six or seven hours—I promised to teach my folks how to work the VCR again."

A MAN'S HOME IS HIS HASSLE

My wife and I recently bought a new home near the Pacific Ocean. When my father learned the price, he asked me how I had come up with the down payment.

My reply: "I owe my success to keen investments in the stock market, my wife's thrift, and Mom's failure to throw away my comic book collection."

Cleaning your house before the kids have stopped growing is like shoveling the walk before it stops snowing. —Phyllis Diller

My young daughter's favorite food is strawberry jam and chocolate syrup on white: white walls and white sofas.
—Joan Rivers

To spare others from dashed hopes, shattered dreams and tired feet, here is a guide to familiar real estate ad phrases:

- *Charming.* Tiny. Snow White might fit but five of the dwarfs would have to find their own place. See "Cute," "Enchanting," and "Good Starter Home."
- *Much potential.* Grim. Steer clear unless you have a lot of money and believe your blind dates really did have nice personalities. See "Ready to Rehab."
- *Unique city home.* Used to be a warehouse.
- *High-Tech/Contemporary.* Lots of steel shelving with little holes—the kind your dad used to store his tools in the basement.
- *Daring design.* Still a warehouse.
- *Completely updated.* Avocado dishwasher and harvest-gold carpeting. Or vice versa.
- *You'll love it.* No, you won't.
- *Sophisticated.* Black walls and no windows. See "Architects Delight."
- *One-of-a-kind.* Ugly as sin.
- *Brilliant concept.* Do you really need a two-story live oak in your thirty-foot sky dome? See "Makes A Dramatic Statement."
- *Upper bracket.* If you have to ask . . .
- *Must see to believe.* An absolutely accurate statement.
- *Reduced to move.* Been on market for years.
- *Close to school.* Backs up on basketball court.
- *Extra storage.* Four hooks.
- *Luxury living.* Overpriced.
- *Cozy.* Smaller than a phone booth.
- *Fixer-upper.* Resembles Berlin after World War II.
- *Lovely water view.* Underwater during heavy rains.
- *Country charm.* Cows processing food next door.
- *Hidden away.* Eight miles of dirt road to nearest blacktop.
- *Close to everything.* A holdout in center of busy commercial district.
- *Cute as a bug's ear.* And only slightly larger.
- *Has real potential.* Enter at your own risk.

I sure am glad a realtor didn't write Abe Lincoln's life story. The tiny log cabin of his childhood would have become a "rustic country estate."

—Bill Jones

Real estate agent to prospective home buyers: "Yes, we have a house in your price range. Its present owner is a German shepherd named Prince."

When I was a college student, I rented this terrible little apartment. I once complained to the landlord: "My roof is leaking, rain is coming in through a broken window, and the floors are flooded. How long is this going to continue?"

"How should I know?" responded the landlord. "What do I look like—a weatherman?"

Comedian Steven Wright offers these unique comments on his home:
- My friend Winny and I lived in a house that ran on static electricity. . . . If you wanted to run the blender, you had to rub balloons on your head. If you wanted to cook, you had to pull off a sweater real quick.
- For my birthday I got a humidifier and a de-humidifier. . . . I put them in the same room and let them fight it out.
- I have a switch in my apartment. It doesn't do anything. Every once in a while, I turn it on and off. . . . One day I got a call. It was from a woman in France. She said, "Cut it out!"
- In my house on the ceilings I have paintings of the rooms above . . . so I never have to go upstairs.
- I installed a skylight in my apartment. . . . The people who live above me are furious!
- Ever notice how irons have a setting for *permanent* press? I don't get it.

6.
BLOOPERS, BUMPER SNICKERS, & ZINGERS

The trouble with doing nothing is that you never know when you are finished.

Always remember: "Beauty is skin deep, but ugly goes all the way to the bone. Beauty fades, but ugly holds its own."

Douglas Fairbanks, Jr. began a speech with one of the all time best opening lines: "I feel like a mosquito in a nudist colony. I look around and I know it's wonderful to be here, but I don't know where to begin."

A story in the *Chicago Press* quoted a new state representative who supports crime prevention: "We don't want residents to start looking at elected officials and asking, "Why can't we keep those people in jail?"

Tattoo: Permanent proof of temporary insanity.

—Wise & Aldrich

HEADLINE HOWLERS

These classics all really appeared in newspapers:

- Survivor of Siamese Twins joins parents
- Two sisters reunited after 18 years in checkout counter
- Juvenile court to try shooting defendant
- Officers' wives to select new officers
- Jury gets drunk driving case here
- Man is fatally slain
- Night school to hear pest talk
- Prisoners escape from prison farm after execution
- Hotel burns. Two hundred guests escape half glad
- Santa Rosa man denies he commited suicide in South San Francisco
- Enraged cow injures farmer with ax
- Senate passes death penalty. Measure provides for electrocution for all persons over 17
- Thugs eat then rob proprietor
- Toilet seats stolen. Police have nothing to go on
- Wild wife league will meet tonight
- Local man has longest horns in all Texas
- Officer convicted of accepting bride
- Staten Island Ferry Hits Pie, 18 Injured

MANGLED MAXIMS

Here are a few I heard from my grandchildren:

- If you can't stand the heat, get out of the oven.
- A bird in the hand is . . . messy.
- Don't count your chickens; eat them.
- You can't teach an old dog new math.
- When in Rome, do your math in Roman numerals.
- A fool and his money are my best friends.
- A penny saved is one cent.
- Look before you run into a pole.
- A watched pot never disappears.
- A rolling stone makes you flat.
- Every cloud has a wet spot.

In 1989, Michael J. Irvin distributed the following brief collection of cute sayings:

- A closed mouth gathers no feet.
- A journey of a thousand miles begins with a cash advance.
- A penny saved is ridiculous.
- All that glitters has a high refractive index.
- Any small object when dropped will hide under a larger object.
- Of the choice of two evils, I pick the one I've never tried before.
- Death is Nature's way of saying, "Slow down."
- Don't force it; get a larger hammer.
- Don't hate yourself in the morning—sleep till noon.
- Drive defensively—buy a tank.
- Entropy isn't what it used to be.
- Fairy tales: horror stories for children, to get them used to reality.
- Familiarity breeds children.
- History does not repeat itself; historians merely repeat each other.
- It's not hard to meet expenses; they're everywhere.
- Lynch's Law: When the going gets tough, everyone leaves.
- Mediocrity thrives on standardization.
- Never lick a gift horse in the mouth.
- Old MacDonald had an agricultural real estate tax abatement.
- "Reality"—the only obstacle to happiness.
- The only difference between a rut and a grave is the depth.
- The road to success is always under construction.
- Those who can't write, write Help files.
- To err is human; to really foul things up requires a computer.
- Today is the last day of your life so far.
- When all else fails, read the instructions.
- When in doubt, don't bother.

I have been told that freeways were first mentioned in Genesis: "The Lord made every creeping thing. . . ."

BUMPER STICKER SNICKERS

On a Buick in Nashville:
> God bless America . . . and please hurry!

Seen on a Chevy:
> On a quiet night, you can hear the old Fords rust.

Seen on a Ford:
> Friends don't let friends drive Chevys.

On a real estate agent's car:
> Site-seeing bus

MORE "BUMPER WISDOM"

- Honk if you hate bumper stickers that say "Honk if . . ."
- I don't care what you love, what your other car is, who you brake for and what you'd rather be doing.
- Illiterate? Write for help.
- I don't have a solution, but I certainly admire the problem.
- Every time I think I know where it's at, they move it.
- To err is human, to forgive is not Company Policy.
- Confidence is the feeling you have before you understand the situation.
- All things are possible, except skiing through a revolving door.
- Never hit a man with glasses. Hit him with a baseball bat.
- They told me I was gullible . . . and I believed them.
- Honesty is the best policy, but insanity is a better defense.
- If at first you don't succeed, redefine success.
- Never put off till tomorrow what you can avoid all together.
- Your lucky number has been disconnected.
- A professor is one who talks in someone else's sleep.
- Amnesia used to be my favorite word, but then I forgot it.
- I haven't lost my mind—it's backed up on disk somewhere.
- The shortest distance between two points is under construction.
- It is impossible to make anything foolproof, because fools are so ingenious.

- Anytime things appear to be going better, you have over-looked something.
- No matter what goes wrong, it will probably look right.
- Once a job is fouled up, anything done to improve it only makes it worse.
- Too much of a good thing is wonderful.
- It's not an optical illusion; it just looks like one.
- You are only young once, but you can stay immature indefinitely.
- If God intended men to smoke, He would have set them on fire.
- Never eat more than you can lift.
- Until you walk a mile in another man's moccasins, you can't imagine the smell.
- It was such a lovely day I thought it was a pity to get up.
- I talk to myself because I like dealing with a better class of people.
- I have a new philosophy. I'm only going to dread one day at a time.
- The only reason people get lost in thought is because it's unfamiliar territory.
- If you drink, don't drive. Don't even putt.
- You've been leading a dog's life. Stay off the furniture.
- The whole purpose of your life is to serve as a warning to others.
- Laugh at your problems; everyone else does.
- If Murphy's Law can go wrong, it will.
- I'm prepared for all emergencies. But I'm totally unpre-pared for everyday life.
- He had never seen the Catskill Mountains, but had seen them kill mice.
- The pants were very sad. They were depressed.
- The former ruler of Russia and his wife were called Tsar and Tsarina, so clearly their children were Tsardines.
- He thought the formula for water was H-I-J-K-L-M-N-O, H-to-O.
- Did you hear about the two peanuts walking down the road? One of them was assaulted.

- It's bad luck to be superstitious.
- Radioactive cats have eighteen half-lives.
- Support bacteria; it's the only culture some people have.
- Don't let people drive you crazy when you know it's within walking distance.
- When does summertime come to Minnesota, you ask? Well, last year I think it was a Tuesday.
- According to my best recollection, I don't remember.
- Anything worth doing is worth overdoing.
- If you don't care where you are, then you ain't lost.
- Everybody is somebody else's weirdo.
- Honk if you like peace and quiet.
- Slogan of 105.9, the classic rock radio station in Chicago: "Of all the radio stations in Chicago . . . we're one of them."
- If money can't buy happiness, I guess you'll just have to rent it.
- I used to think I was indecisive, but now I'm not too sure.
- Famous last words: Don't unplug it; it will just take a moment to fix.
- Famous last words: Don't worry, it's not loaded.
- Famous last words: What happens if you touch these two wires tog—
- Everything I need to know I got from watching *Gilligan's Island*.
- It doesn't matter how hard you've studied; the material won't be on the exam anyway.
- If it doesn't fit, force it; if it breaks, it needed replacement anyway.
- Reality is a figment of your imagination.
- Life is just one of those things.
- I can handle pain until it hurts.
- It's not what you say in your argument, it's how loud you say it.
- The ultimate reason is "because."
- I'm objective; I object to everything.
- You cannot achieve the impossible without attempting the absurd.
- Kiss me twice. I'm schizophrenic.
- If you cannot convince them, confuse them.

- A day for firm decisions! Or is it?
- If you can't learn to do it well, learn to enjoy doing it badly.
- It's only a game until you lose.
- If God had intended man to watch TV, he would have given him rabbit ears.
- Overdrawn? But I still have checks left!
- No matter where you go, you're there.
- I'd love to go out with you, but it's my parakeet's bowling night.
- If you knew what you were doing, you'd be bored.
- Save the whales; collect the whole set.
- Oh well, I guess this is just going to be one of those lifetimes.
- No one is perfect, but some of us are closer than others.
- If you understand something today, it must be obsolete.
- Since when is talking a sign of thinking?
- The light at the end of the tunnel is the headlight of the oncoming train.
- Repetition is always better the second time.
- Life without bears would be unbearable.
- Lead me not into temptation; I can find it myself.
- I've no time to prepare a profound message.
- Optimism: Waiting for a ship to come in when you haven't sent one out.
- It's been Monday all week.
- When all else fails, lower your standards.
- I don't know, I don't care, and it doesn't make any difference.
- I'm only a hypochondriac when I'm feeling sick.
- Never trust a nun with a gun.
- If there were no such thing as bears, what kind of hugs would we give?
- It's your right to be stupid, but it doesn't mean you should be.
- Life's a trip, and then you run out of Travelers' Checks.
- Wouldn't it be nice if there were an Escape key for all of our problems?
- Be fruit fly and multiple.
- Gravity always gets me down.
- Hairy Kiwi: Death by fruit.
- If we're going to have fun, we've got to be serious about it.

- For him to get an idea, it would be a surgical process.
- Being good at being stupid doesn't count.
- Madness takes its toll. Please have exact change.
- On a Rabbit convertible: "I'm not a brat. Am not, am not, am not!"

My Aunt Laura is such a snob that her automobile sports the following sign:

> Private Bumper Sticker—Do Not Read.

A truck in California displays this personalized license plate:

> EIEIOH

I suspect it belongs to a farmer named MacDonald.

LORD, GIVE US A SIGN

Sign in store window:

> Any faulty merchandise will be cheerfully replaced
> with merchandise of equal quality.

In a Seattle barber shop window:

> Four barbers to serve you!
> Come in and have a panel discussion about anything.

At a mechanic's shop:

> Let me brake you, muffle you, and shock you.

On a tree in the middle of the roadway near Seville, Spain:

> This tree hits cars only in self-defense.

In a cemetery:

> Persons are prohibited from picking flowers
> from any but their own graves.

On a tombstone near Pigeon Forge, Tennessee:
Once I wuzn't, then I wuz, now I ain't agin!

In a Miami Beach restaurant:
Checks accepted only if you are over eighty years old
and accompanied by your parents.

The sign on the desk of an airline executive in Chicago reads:
Don't bother to agree with me,
I've already changed my mind.

On the sales lot for mobile homes:
Wheel Estate

In a public utilities office:
We're Pleased to Meter You!

In a TV repair shop:
Do it yourself—then call us.

In a doctor's office:
The doctor is very busy—please have your symptoms ready.

On the front door of a spiritualist:
Please ring bell. Knocking on door only causes confusion.

On the rest room wall at my doctor's office:
Don't take life too seriously, you'll never get out of it alive.

From a card in a Moroccan hotel room:
Males and snacks may be served in your room
at any time. Please call room service.

In a Minneapolis toy store:
No eating, drinking, or whining.

In a science-fiction bookstore:
Warning—shoplifters will be disintegrated.

On a hotel marquee in Commerce, Calif.:
Our towels are so fluffy,
it'll be hard to put them in your suitcase.

Posted for the All Seasons Resorts in Lake Delton, Wisconsin:
Closed for the winter.

In the window of a clothing store in Miami Beach:
Grand opening clearance sale!

In an elevator:
Button for 8th floor out of order. Push 5 and 3.

In a tailor shop:
As you rip, so shall we sew.

On the signboard in front of a church:
THE WORST THING IN THE WORLD
Singing by our quartet morning and evening.

In a Los Angeles taxi during the early 1990s:
Driver does not wish to have a conversation about
Haiti, Clinton, or the baseball strike.

On the door of a dress shop being remodeled:
Pardon us while we change into something more comfortable.

On a college bulletin board:
Books for sale. Like new. Hardly used.

In a supermarket in Westchester:
THIS IS THE EXPRESS LANE.
Your are limited to 15 items or less.
The number 15 is NOT subject to negotiation.

On the desk of a plumbing supply manufacturer:
Don't tell me what I mean.
Let me figure it out myself.

In a grocery store in Northampton, Massachusetts:
>Please do not fondle our fruit. Wait for clerk.

In a watchmaker's window:
>There's no present like the time.

On a display of "I love only you " Valentine's Day cards:
>Now available in multi-packs!

In a Maine restaurant:
>Open seven days a week and weekends.

Outside a Philadelphia business:
>Open most days about 9 or 10, occasionally as early as 7,
>but some days as late as 12 or 1. We close about 4 or 5, but
>sometimes as late as 11 or 12. Some days we aren't here at all,
>and lately I've been here just about all the time,
>except when I'm someplace else.

On a bookstore going out of business in Chicago:
>Words failed us.

Psychologist James Dobson reports seeing a sign on a convent in Southern California reading:

>ABSOLUTELY NO TRESPASSING
>Violators Will Be Prosecuted
>to the Full Extent of the Law.

It was signed, "The Sisters of Mercy."

My office at the Little Brown Church, had a full-length mirror. So, for my first wedding service, I let the bride use the office as her dressing room. To protect her privacy, I posted this sign on the door: "Caution—do not enter—bride under construction."

This notice on a photography studio in Maryland may be the sign to end them all:

OPEN NIGHTS
    Except Tuesday
    Except during Christmas week.
Friday
    See summer schedule, April to
    September only.
Thursday
    Except during total eclipse.
Sunday
    Never Usually

Note: When Halloween falls on Tuesday, add one day to each item above.

—Funny Funny World

There is nothing more horrifying than stupidity in action.

—Adlai Stevenson

You have to question any period in history in which people are saying that God is dead and Elvis is alive.

—Robert Orben

If you keep your head while all about you are losing theirs, you're probably not paying attention.

You know you're going to have a bad day when you buy a tube of Krazy Glue and the label falls off.

The slogan "Come alive with Pepsi!" was rendered too literally in the Taiwan market. In Chinese, it read, "Pepsi brings your ancestors back from the grave."

—Australian Sun-Herald

FORM FUMBLES

Some people who had automobile accidents were asked to summarize exactly what happened on their insurance form. The following quotes were taken from those forms:

- Coming home, I drove into the wrong house and collided with a tree I don't have.
- I collided with a stationary truck coming the other way. The guy was all over the road; I had to swerve a number of times before I hit him.
- I had been driving my car for forty years when I fell asleep at the wheel and had an accident.
- My car was legally parked as it backed into the other vehicle.
- An invisible car came out of nowhere, struck my vehicle and vanished. I told the police that I was not injured, but on removing my hat, I found that I had a skull fracture.
- The pedestrian had no idea of which way to go, so I ran over him.
- The indirect cause of this accident was a little guy in a small car with a big mouth.
- The telephone pole was approaching fast. I was attempting to swerve out of its path when it struck my front.

—*Toronto Sun*, July 20, 1977

Critics are people who are quick on the flaw, as evidenced by these harsh words in theater, film, and TV reviews:

- Several of the characters are psychic, which puts them in the unique position of being able to understand what goes on in this movie.
- Its leading man gives a performance so wooden you could make a coffee table out of it.
- There's nothing better than a really good British spy story. Too bad this isn't one of them.
- The play is one big piece of Swiss cheese, minus the cheese.

Brooke Shields, on why she wanted to become spokesperson for a federal anti-smoking campaign: "Smoking kills. If you're killed, you've lost a very important part of your life."

CLASSIC CLASSIFIEDS (REAL ADS FROM REAL NEWSPAPERS)

- In the Lake Zurich, Ill., *Advertiser:* Braille dictionary for sale. Must see to appreciate.
- Help-wanted ad in the Camdenton, Mo, *Reveille/Lake Sun:* Singer for new rock band. Must be male or female.
- For Sale ad in the Roanoke, Illinois, Review: Hope chest: Brand new, half price, long story.
- Help Wanted ad in a Michigan paper: Adult or mature teenager to baby-sit. One dollar an hour, plus fridge benefits.
- Notice in the Los Altos, California, *Town Crier.* Lost: Gray and white female cat. Answers to electric can opener.
- Lost: small apricot poodle. Reward. Neutered. Like one of the family.
- For sale: an antique desk suitable for lady with thick legs and large drawers.
- For sale: a quilted high chair that can be made into a table, potty chair, rocking horse, refrigerator, spring coat, size 8 and fur collar.
- Four-poster bed, 101 years old. Perfect for antique lover.
- Have several very old dresses from grandmother in beautiful condition.
- For Rent: 6-room hated apartment.
- Man, honest. Will take anything.
- Wanted: Part-time married girls for soda fountain in sandwich shop.
- Man wanted to work in dynamite factory. Must be willing to travel.
- Christmas sale. Handmade gifts for the hard-to-find person.
- Wanted: Hair-cutter. Excellent growth potential.
- Wanted. Man to take care of cow that does not smoke or drink.
- Three-year-old teacher needed for pre-school. Experience preferred.
- Our experienced Mom will care for your child. Fenced yard, meals, and smacks included.
- Mixing bowl set designed to please a cook with round bottom for efficient beating.
- Girl wanted to assist magician in cutting-off-head illusion. Blue Cross and salary.

- Wanted. Widower with school-age children requires person to assume general housekeeping duties. Must be capable of contributing to growth of family.
- Mother's helper—peasant working conditions.

MARKETING MISHAPS

- A superb and inexpensive restaurant. Fine food expertly served by waitresses in appetizing forms.
- Dinner Special—Turkey $2.35; Chicken or Beef $2.25; Children $2.00.
- Now is your chance to have your ears pierced and get an extra pair to take home, too.
- We do not tear your clothing with machinery. We do it carefully by hand.
- No matter what your topcoat is made of, this miracle spray will make it really repellent.
- Creative daily specials, including select offerings of beef, foul, fresh vegetables, salads, quiche.
- Tired of cleaning yourself? Let me do it.
- Vacation Special: have your home exterminated.
- Mt. Kilimanjaro, the breathtaking backdrop for the Serena Lodge. Swim in the lovely pool while you drink it all in.
- Get rid of aunts: Zap does the job in twenty-four hours.
- Toaster: A gift that every member of the family appreciates. Automatically burns toast.
- Stock up and save. Limit: one.
- Save regularly in our bank. You'll never reget it.
- We build bodies that last a lifetime. Offer expires Dec. 31 or while supplies last.
- This is the model home for your future. It was panned by *Better Homes and Gardens.*
- Used Cars: Why go elsewhere to be cheated? Come here first!
- Auto Repair Service. Free pick-up and delivery. Try us once, you'll never go anywhere again.
- Semi-Annual After-Christmas Sale.
- And now, the Superstore—unequaled in size, unmatched in variety, unrivaled inconvenience.

- We will oil your sewing machine and adjust tension in your home for $1.00.
- For sale at reduced prices—shirts for men with minor flaws.
- A coupon for a Wooster, Ohio car wash: "Absolutely nothing touches your car except soup and water."
- An ad for Morrison's Family Dining in the *Miami Herald*: "Home Baked Pies & Breads to Go. Entire Menu Made from Scotch Daily."
- An ad in a Hong Kong newspaper: Teeth extracted by the latest Methodists.

PRICELESS PRESS

In a Religious News Service press release: "*Eternity Magazine* will cease publishing with the January issue."

Letter to a weekly magazine:

Dear Sir: When I subscribed a year ago you stated that if I was not satisfied at the end of the year I could have my money back. Well, I would like to have it back.

On second thought, to save you trouble, please apply it to my next year's subscription.

From the Cincinnati Post: "Representatives of teachers' organizations appeared before the board to ask for a further cost-of-loving adjustment in wages."

From the Prescott, Ariz., *Daily Courier:* "Arizona's fifth-largest bank is seeking experienced bankers to stuff a downtown office."

The Peoria, Ill., *Journal Star* reported that after an accident a man "was ticketed for driving while expired."

Gadget: Any mechanical device that performs a kitchen task in one-twentieth the time it takes to find it.

You know you're in a small town when . . .

- The airport runway is terraced.
- Third Street is on the edge of town.
- Every sport is played on dirt.
- You don't use your turn signal, because everyone knows where you're going.
- You dial a wrong number and talk for fifteen minutes anyway.
- You drive into the ditch five miles out of town, and the word gets back into town before you do.
- The pickups on main street outnumber the cars three to one.
- You miss a Sunday at church and receive a get-well card.
- Someone asks you how you feel, then listens to what you say.

There is nothing busier than an idle rumor.

Security is knowing what tomorrow will bring. Boredom is knowing what the day after tomorrow will bring.

 Comedian Gary Shandling says, "They should put expiration dates on clothes, so people would know when they go out of style."

It is much easier to love humanity as a whole than to love one's neighbor.
—Eric Hoffer

My wife tells me that in this day and age, nothing is impossible . . . except some people.

The three least credible sentences in the English language:
1. "The check is in the mail."
2. "Of course I'll respect you in the morning."
3. "I'm from the government, and I'm here to help you."

THE BIGGEST LIES IN THE WORLD

- It's a good thing you came in today. We have only two more of those items in stock.
- I promise to pay you back out of my next paycheck.
- Five pounds is nothing on a person with your height.
- But Officer, I only had two beers.
- You made it yourself? I never would have guessed.
- It's delicious, but I can't eat another bite.
- Your hair looks just fine.
- The river never gets high enough to flood this property.
- The delivery is on the truck.
- Go ahead and tell me, I promise I won't get mad.
- This car is just like new. It was owned by two retired school teachers who never went anywhere.
- The doctor will call you right back.
- So glad you dropped by. I wasn't doing a thing.
- You don't look a day over forty.
- Dad, I need to move out of the dorm into an apartment of my own, so I can have some peace and quiet when I study.
- The baby is just beautiful.
- The new ownership won't affect you. The company will remain the same.
- I gave at the office.
- You can tell me. I won't breathe a word to a soul.
- The puppy won't be any trouble, Mom. I promise I'll take care of it myself.
- I'm a social drinker, and I can quit anytime I want to.
- Put the map away. I know exactly how to get there.
- You don't need it in writing. You have my personal guarantee.
- Sorry the work isn't ready. The computer broke down.
- Our children never caused us a minute's trouble.
- This is a very safe building. There is no way you will ever be burglarized.
- Having a great time. Wish you were here.
- And of course, the three biggest lies: I did it. I didn't do it. I can't remember.

BULLETIN BLOOPERS

Each of these really appeared in some church's bulletin:

- The ushers will eat all latecomers.
- A cookbook is being compiled by the ladies of the church. Please submit your favorite recipe, also a short antidote for it.
- The senior pastor will be away for two weeks. The staff members in charge during his absence can be found pinned to the church notice board.
- Visitors are asked to sing their names at the church entrance.
- Our young people are preparing the pizza dinner. It will be held in the perish hall.
- Hymn No. 58, "Gold Will Take Care of You."
- The pastor will preach, and there will be special sinning by the congregation.
- Ushers will swat late comers at these points in the service.
- The concert was a great success. Special thanks are due the vicar's daughter who labored the whole evening at the piano, which as usual fell upon her.
- Do you know what Hell is like? Come in and hear our organist.
- Don't let worry kill you—let the church help.
- Thursday night—Potluck supper. Prayer and medication to follow.
- For those of you who have children and don't know it, we have a nursery downstairs.
- The rosebud on the alter this morning is to announce the birth of David Allan Belzer, the sin of Rev. and Mrs. Julius Belzer.
- Weight Watchers will meet Tuesday at 7 P.M. at the First Presbyterian Church. Please use the large double door at the side entrance.
- The ladies of the church have cast off clothes of every kind and they may be seen in the church basement on Friday afternoon.
- As the maintenance of the churchyard is becoming increasingly costly, it would be appreciated if those who are willing would clip the grass around their own graves.

- "Change Your Wife Through Prayer" will be the sermon subject Sunday.
- A note from the pastor: I shall be away from the parish attending the Diocesan Clergy School from April 21-24. It will be convenient if parishioners will abstain from arranging to be buried, or from making other calls on me during this time.
- The choir will sing, "I Heard the Bills On Christmas Day."
- Wednesday at 7:30 PM there will be a meeting of the Little Mothers Club. All wishing to become Little Mothers, please meet with the minister in his study.
- A bean supper will be held Saturday evening in the church basement. Music will follow.
- This being Easter, we will ask Mrs. Johnson to come forward and lay an egg on the altar.
- This afternoon there will be a meeting in the south and north sides of the church. Children will be baptized at both ends.
- On Sunday, a special collection will be taken to defray the expenses of the new carpet. All those wishing to do something on the carpet please come forward and get a piece of paper.
- A song fest was hell at the Methodist Church Wednesday.
- Eight new choir robes are currently needed due to the addition of several new members and the deterioration of some older ones.
- Due to the Rector's illness, Wednesday's healing services will be discontinued until further notice.
- The eighth-graders will be presenting Shakespeare's *Hamlet* in the church basement. The congregation is invited to attend this tragedy.
- Twenty-two members were present at the church meeting held at the home of Mrs. Marsha Crutchfield last evening. Mrs. Crutchfield and Mrs. Ranking sang a duet, The Lord Knows Why.
- The choir invites any member of the congregation who enjoys sinning to join the choir.
- Today's sermon: "How Much Can a Man Drink?" with hymns from a full choir.

- Offertory: "Jesus Paid It All"
- Remember in prayer the many who are sick of our church and community.

Among the graffiti on the wall of a Purdue University building: "If God had wanted us to use the metric system, he would have chosen ten disciples."

If the metric system ever takes over we may have to change some popular sayings to the following:
- A miss is as good as 1.6 kilometers.
- Put your best 0.3 of a meter forward.
- Spare the 5.03 meters and spoil the child.
- Twenty-eight grams of prevention is worth 453 grams of cure.
- Give a man 2.5 centimeters and he'll take 1.6 kilometers.
- Peter Piper picked 8.8 liters of pickled peppers.

MUSIC EDUCATION

These are stories and test questions accumulated by music teachers in the state of Missouri.
- Agnus Dei was a woman composer famous for her church music.
- Refrain means don't do it. A refrain in music is the part you better not try to sing.
- A virtuoso is a musician with real high morals.
- John Sebastian Bach died from 1750 to the present.
- Beethoven wrote music even though he was deaf. He was so deaf he wrote loud music. He took long walks in the forest even when everyone was calling him. I guess he could not hear so good. Beethoven expired in 1827 and later died from this.
- Henry Purcell is a well known composer few people have ever heard of.
- Most authorities agree that music of antiquity was written long ago.

- Aaron Copland is one of your most famous contemporary composers. It is unusual to be contemporary. Most composers do not live until they are dead.
- An opera is a song of bigly size.
- In the last scene of Pagliacci, Canio stabs Nedda who is the one he really loves. Pretty soon Silvio also gets stabbed, and they all live happily ever after.
- Music sung by two people at the same time is called a duel.
- Caruso was at first an Italian. Then someone heard his voice and said he would go a long way. And so he came to America.
- Probably the most marvelous fugue was the one between the Hatfields and McCoys.
- My very best liked piece of music is the Bronze Lullaby.
- My favorite composer is Opus.
- A harp is a nude piano.
- A trumpet is an instrument when it is not an elephant sound.
- While trombones have tubes, trumpets prefer to wear valves.
- The double bass is also called the bass viol, string bass, and bass fiddle. It has so many names because it is so huge.
- When electric currents go through them, guitars start making sounds. So would anybody.
- Question: What are kettle drums called? Answer: Kettle drums.
- Last month I found out how a clarinet works by taking it apart. I both found out and got in trouble.
- For some reason, they always put a treble clef in front of every line of flute music. You just watch.
- I can't reach the brakes on this piano!
- Anyone who can read all the instrument notes at the same time gets to be the conductor.
- The flute is a skinny-high shape-sounded instrument.
- Music instrument has a plural known as orchestra.
- I would like for you to teach me to play the cello. Would tomorrow or Friday be best?
- It is easy to teach anyone to play the maracas. Just grip the neck and shake him in rhythm.
- Just about any animal skin can be stretched over a frame to make a pleasant sound once the animal is removed.

— *Missouri School Music Newsletter*, collected by Harold Dunn

A COLLECTION OF T-SHIRT SAYINGS
SEEN AROUND THE SAN FRANCISCO BAY AREA

- What's good for Ugoose is good for Uganda.
- We have them just where they want us.
- I'd rather have Lockheed deliver the mail than ride around in a plane built by the post office.
- Just because you're not paranoid doesn't mean they're not out to get you.
- The knack of flying is learning how to throw yourself at the ground and miss.
- Love is blind but like is just too freaked out to see straight.
- Great spirits have always encountered violent opposition from mediocre minds. —Albert Einstein
- Time flies when you don't know what you're doing.
- Age and treachery will always overcome youth and skill.
- We are the people our parents warned us about.
- There is intelligent life on Earth, but I'm just visiting.
- Power means not having to respond.
- Everything you know is wrong, but you can be straightened out.
- The secret of success is sincerity. Once you can fake that you've got it made.
- I'm not as dumb as you look.
- I'd like to help you out. Which way did you come in?
- When in charge, ponder. When in doubt, mumble. When in trouble, delegate.
- To err is human. To forgive is unusual.
- Only those who attempt the absurd can achieve the impossible.
- I'm not going deaf. I'm ignoring you.
- Our parents were never our age.
- Never underestimate the power of human stupidity.
- In the country of the blind, the one-eyed man is king.
- It's hard to soar like an eagle when you're surrounded by turkeys.
- I'm really enjoying not talking to you, so let's not talk again real soon, okay?
- He who laughs last didn't get the joke.
- I'm not prejudiced. I hate everyone equally.
- I used to be lost in the shuffle. Now I just shuffle along with the lost.

- Yesterday was the deadline on all complaints.
- Work fascinates me. I could sit and watch it for hours.
- The future isn't what it used to be.
- Love your enemies. It'll make 'em crazy.
- I refuse to have a battle of wits with an unarmed opponent.
- Why be difficult, when with a bit of effort you can be impossible?
- Perfect paranoia is perfect awareness.
- If I follow you home, will you keep me?
- Bureaucrats do not change the course of the ship of state. They merely adjust the compass.
- The number of people watching you is directly proportional to the stupidity of your action.
- Don't think of organ donation as giving up part of yourself to keep a total stranger alive. It's really a total stranger giving up almost all of themselves to keep part of you alive.
- If you don't know what you're doing, do it neatly.
- An easily-understood, workable falsehood is more useful than a complex, incomprehensible truth.
- You have a right to your opinions. I just don't want to hear them.
- Eat a live toad in the morning, and nothing worse will happen to you for the rest of the day.
- It's not that you and I are so clever. It's just that the others are such fools.
- I'm not cynical. Just experienced.
- I know you think you understood what I said, but what you heard was not what I meant.

MORE OF THE BIGGEST LIES
- You get this one; I'll pay next time.
- My wife doesn't understand me.
- Trust me, I'll take care of everything.
- Of course I love you.
- I never inhaled.
- It's not the money; it's the principle of the thing.
- I never watch television except for PBS.

- . . . but we can still be good friends.
- She means nothing to me.
- Don't worry, I can go another twenty miles when the gauge is on "empty."
- Don't worry, he's never bitten anyone.
- I'll call you later.
- We'll release the upgrade by the end of the year.
- Read my lips: no new taxes.
- I've never done anything like this before.
- Now, I'm going to tell you the truth.
- It's supposed to make that noise.
- . . . then take a left. You can't miss it.
- Senator, I don't remember.

ELEMENTARY ERRORS

Grade school teachers like to keep journals of amusing things their students have written in papers. Here are a few examples:

- The future of "I give" is "I take."
- The parts of speech are lungs and air.
- The inhabitants of Moscow are called Mosquitoes.
- A census taker is a man who goes from house to house increasing the population.
- Water is composed of two gins. Oxygin and hydrogin. Oxygin is pure gin. Hydrogin is gin and water.
- H_2O is hot water and CO_2 is cold water.
- A virgin forest is a forest where the hand of man has never set foot.
- The general direction of the Alps is straight up.
- Most of the houses in France are made of plaster of Paris.
- The people who followed the Lord were called the twelve opossums.
- The spinal column is a long bunch of bones. The head sits on the top and you sit on the bottom.
- We do not raise silk worms in the United States, because we get our silk from rayon. He is a larger worm and gives more silk.
- One of the main causes of dust is janitors.

- A scout obeys all to whom obedience is due and respects all duly constipated authorities.
- One by-product of raising cattle is calves.
- To prevent head colds, use an agonizer to spray into the nose until it drips into the throat.
- The four seasons are salt, pepper, mustard and vinegar.
- The climate is hottest next to the Creator.
- Oliver Cromwell had a large red nose, but under it were deeply religious feelings.
- The word "trousers" is an uncommon noun because it is singular at the top and plural at the bottom.
- Syntax is all the money collected at the church from sinners.
- The blood circulates through the body by flowing down one leg and up the other.
- In spring, the salmon swim upstream to spoon.
- A person should take a bath once in the summer, not so often in the winter.

If we had our way, more of us would choose the front of the bus, the back of the church and the center of attention.

USA *Today* has come out with a new survey: three out of four people make up seventy-five percent of the population.

—David Letterman

Is it true that Gideon wrote a special version of the Bible for use in motel rooms?

The world is full of people who want to live forever but don't know how to spend a rainy Sunday afternoon.

Proofs of a new hymn book contained this typo: "Praised is the Lord by day and praised by night; praised is he when we lie down and praised when we wise up."

ALL-TIME WORST COUNTRY-WESTERN SONG TITLES

- I've Been Roped and Thrown by Jesus in the Holy Ghost Corral
- Does Your Chewing Gum Lose Its Flavor on the Bedpost Overnight?
- Don't Cry on My Shoulders 'Cause You're Rustin' My Spurs
- Drop-kick Me, Jesus, Through the Goalposts of Life
- How Can I Miss You If You Won't Go Away?
- I Changed Her Oil, She Changed My Life
- I Don't Know Whether to Kill Myself or Go Bowling
- I Keep Forgettin' I Forgot About You
- I Would Have Writ You a Letter, But I Couldn't Spell Yecch!
- I Wouldn't Take Her to a Dawg Fight, 'Cause I'm Afraid She'd Win
- I'd Rather Have a Bottle in Front of Me than a Frontal Lobotomy
- If Love Were Oil, I'd Be a Quart Low
- If the Phone Don't Ring, Baby, You'll Know It's Me
- If You Don't Leave Me Alone, I'll Go and Find Someone Else Who Will
- I'm Just a Bug on the Windshield of Life
- I'm So Miserable Without You, It's Like Having You Here
- I've Got Four on the Floor and a Fifth Under the Seat
- I've Got Tears in My Ears from Lying on My Back in My Bed 'n' Cryin' Over You
- Learning to Live Again Is Killing Me.
- Mama Get the Hammer (There's a Fly on Papa's Head)
- May the Bird of Paradise Fly Up Your Nose
- My Every-day Silver Is Plastic
- My John Deere Was Breaking Your Field, While Your Dear John Was Breaking My Heart
- My Wife Ran Off with My Best Friend, and I Sure Do Miss Him
- I've Got Hair Oil on My Ears and My Glasses Are Slipping Down, but Baby, I Can See Through You
- Oh, Lord! It's Hard to be Humble When You're Perfect in Every Way
- Please Bypass This Heart
- She Got the Gold Mine, and I Got the Shaft
- She Made Toothpicks Out of the Timber of My Heart

- Thank the Lord and Greyhound She's Gone
- They May Put Me in Prison, but They Can't Stop My Face from Breakin' Out
- Velcro Arms, Teflon Heart
- When You Leave, Walk Out Backwards, So I'll Think You're Walking In
- You Can't Deal Me All the Aces and Expect Me Not to Play
- You Can't Have Your Kate and Edith Too
- You Can't Roller Skate in a Buffalo Herd
- You Done Tore Out My Heart and Stomped That Sucker Flat
- You're Ruining My Bad Reputation

There are so many twelve-steps today. For example, you have AA, or Alcoholics Anonymous. Then there's ACA—Adult Children of Alcoholics. These are not inclusive enough. Here is a recovery program that covers all the bases:

ABCDEFGHIJKLMNOPQRSTUVWXYZ

Or, Adult Bad Children of Dysfunctional Evil Families Getting Hooked Into Just Keeping Little Mean Nasty Old People Quiet, Requiring Specialized Treatment Using Valium With eX-treme unYielding Zeal.
—Guy Owen

Finally, a great bumper sticker to flash at cellular phone users:
"HANG UP AND DRIVE!"

7.
SPORTS & LEISURE

As Plato remarked, "You can discover more about a person in an hour of play than in a year of conversation."

You know that you are watching too much TV if . . .

- You can name all the characters on *As the World Turns* but can't remember the names of the Twelve Disciples.
- You can anticipate in advance the outcome of an *ER* episode but can't remember how the New Testament ends.
- You can recognize the local TV News reporter on the street but wouldn't know your next-door neighbor if you saw her standing on the porch.
- Your cable TV bill is more each month than your contribution to your local church. —Harold Bales

Some people's idea of "roughing it" is not having cable.
—Nick Arnette

I have a hobby. . . . I have the world's largest collection of sea shells. I keep it scattered on beaches all over the world. Maybe you've seen some of it. . . . —Steven Wright

You know you're going to have a bad day when you hit a hole-in-one, but you're playing alone.

Woman to spouse as he leaves to play golf in rainstorm: "Perhaps you're right, Walter. As the eye of the hurricane passes over, you can probably get in nine holes."   —Franklin Folger

Wife: Henry, you promised you'd be home by five o'clock. Now its *nine* o'clock.

Husband: Honey, listen to me. Poor ol' Roger is dead. He just dropped over on the seventh green.

Wife: Oh, that's terrible!

Husband: It really was. For the rest of the game it was hit the ball, drag Roger, hit the ball, drag Roger . . .

A dignified English lawyer with a considerable income had long dreamed of playing Sandringham, one of Great Britain's most exclusive golf courses. One day he made up his mind to chance it when he was traveling in the area. Entering the clubhouse, he asked at the desk if he might play the course. The club secretary inquired, "Member?"

To which he replied, "No, sir."

"Guest of a member?"

"No, sir."

The answer came back, "Sorry."

As he turned to leave, the lawyer spotted a slightly-familiar figure seated in the lounge, reading the London Times. It was the distinguished Lord Parham. He approached and, bowing low, said, "I beg your pardon, your Lordship, but my name is Higginbotham of the London solicitors Higginbotham, Willinby and Barclay. I should like to crave your Lordship's indulgence. Might I play this beautiful course as your guest?"

His Lordship gave Higginbotham a long look, put down his paper and asked, "Church?"

"Church of England, sir, as was my late wife."

"Education?"

"Eton, sir, and Oxford."

"Sport?"

"Rugby, sir, a spot of tennis and No. 4 on the crew that beat Cambridge."

"Service?"

"Brigadier, sir, Coldstream Guards. Victoria Cross and Knight of the Garter."

"Campaigns?"

"Dunkirk, El Alamein, and Normandy."

"Languages?"

"Private tutor in French, fluent German, and a bit of Greek."

His Lordship considered this briefly, then nodded to the club secretary and said, "Nine holes."

There was once a golf match between an eminent Supreme Court Justice and an equally-distinguished Virginia bishop. The bishop missed four straight short putts without saying a single word. The Justice watched him with growing amusement and remarked, "Bishop, that is the most profane silence I have ever heard."

Malcolm George, a man with a terrible temper, was playing a round of golf with his pastor, Rev. Jack Pardee. After leaving three straight putts on the edge of the cup, Mr. George exploded. "I missed!" he screamed. "How could I miss?" With that he heaved his putter into a nearby lake, kicked a wheel on the golf cart and drove his fist into a nearby tree.

Pastor Pardee was shocked. "I have never seen such a terrible display of anger," he said to the poor man. "Don't you know that God doesn't like us when we are angry? I have heard that there are angels whose one assignment is to search out people who express their anger so ferociously and to send lightning bolts from heaven to burn them to a crisp."

George was embarrassed. Heeding the warning of Pastor Pardee, on the next few holes, he managed to control himself. However, on the last three holes his putting failed him again. When the last putt veered off to the right just in front of the hole, George went crazy. "I missed!" he screamed in despair. "How could I miss?" He broke his club across his knee and threw it as far as he could, he kicked up several large clumps of dirt on the edge of the green, and once more drove his fist into a nearby tree.

Suddenly the sky grew dark as an ominous cloud passed over. There was a clap of thunder and an awesome burst of lightning—and the pastor was burned to a crisp!

An eerie silence filled the golf course. All that could be heard was a quiet voice from heaven: "I missed! How could I miss?"

Our local Catholic priest took up golf as a way of relaxing. Unfortunately, the frustrations of the game had the opposite effect on him. One day while he was playing, he splashed ball after ball into the water hazard. Resisting the temptation to throw his golf clubs in after his five balls, he took a deep breath, recited song lyrics, and finally regained his composure.

"Aha," he said to his caddy, "I've finally figured out what I've been doing wrong. I just forgot to pray before each shot; that was all." He uttered a brief prayer, then swung at the ball—and, just as before, it sailed right into the water.

"Father," asked the caddy, "might I make a suggestion?"

"Certainly, my son," the priest said.

"Well, Father," the caddy said, "the next time you pray, keep your head down."

After a long day on the course, the exasperated golfer turned to his caddie and said, "You must be the absolute worst caddie in the world."

"No, I don't think so," said the caddie. "That would be too much of a coincidence."

Al: Why aren't you playing golf with the colonel any more?

Bob: What! Would you play with a man who swears and curses with every shot, who cheats in the bunkers, and who enters false scores on his cards?

Al: Certainly not!

Bob: Well, neither will the colonel. —Freddie Oliver

As the golfer approached the first tee, a hazardous hole with a green surrounded by water, he debated whether he should use his new golf ball. Deciding that the hole was too treacherous, he pulled out an old ball and placed it on the tee.

Just then he heard a voice from above say loudly: "USE THE NEW BALL!"

Frightened, he replaced the old ball with the new one and approached the tee.

Now the voice from above shouted: "TAKE A PRACTICE SWING!"

With this, the golfer stepped backward and took a swing. Feeling more confident, he approached the tee when the voice again rang out: "USE THE OLD BALL!"

Simon Jensen, the pastor of St. Peter's Lutheran Church, awoke at dawn one Sunday morning. As he was having his first cup of coffee, he heard the radio weather forecast say that it would begin to rain that afternoon and continue through the rest of the week. Monday was his day off, and he loved golf!

Simon hated to think he would miss his game on his day off because of rain. Since it was quite early, he thought he would have time to go to the golf course, play nine holes, and still have time to get back for the 11:00 A.M. service. Since it was the middle of summer, there was no Sunday School class for him to worry about.

Soon, he was on the course alone. Satan noticed the minister there on Sunday morning and immediately reported it to the Lord, asking, "Isn't that one of your men?"

The Lord answered, "Yes, it is."

"Aren't you going to do anything about it?"

The Lord replied, "I'll take care of it."

The minister approached a par four hole where the green was easily visible from the tee. He addressed the ball and came through with a mighty stroke.

Then the Lord took charge. He blessed the ball and it kept going and kept going and kept going. To the minister's astonishment, the ball rolled across the green and into the cup. A hole in one on a par four hole! He was beside himself with ecstatic joy!

Satan protested, "I thought you were going to take care of him. Why did you let a thing like that happen?"

The Lord simply said, "I took care of it. Who's he going to tell about it?"

—*Costly Company*

First golfer: I have the greatest ball in the world. You can't lose it.

Second golfer: How so?

First golfer: If you hit it into the sand, it beeps. You hit it into the water, it floats. If you want to play golf at night, it glows.

Second golfer: Hey, sounds good. Where did you get it?

First golfer: Found it in the woods.

A basketball coach reportedly told some friends about a dream he had. "I was walking down the street," he said, "when this Rolls Royce pulled up beside me. Inside, there was a beautiful young woman—blonde, mid-twenties. She asked me to get in. She took me to a fantastic restaurant, where we ate and drank and she paid the bill. Then she asked me if I wanted to go home with her. And I said yes. And we did." The coach was silent for a minute.

"Then what happened?" the friends urged, sensing that the coach was getting to the hottest part of his story.

"The best part of all!" the coach drooled. "She introduced me to her two brothers—both of them over seven feet tall!"

Joe Garagiola writes:

While I was playing with the Pirates, I gave a speech to the Pittsburgh Junior Chamber of Commerce. Trying to make the best of a terrible season, I said, "We may not be high in the standings, and we don't win many ballgames, but you've got to admit we play some interesting baseball."

A voice from the back of the room yelled, "Why don't you play some dull games and win a few?"

 My dad and I once paused to watch some kids in a sandlot baseball game. "What's the score, son?" my father asked one of the players.

"We're behind 27 to 0 right now," said the kid.

"Wow," said my dad. "Aren't you a bit discouraged?"

"Nope," was the answer. "We ain't been to bat yet."

Question asked of Bob Uecker, actor, sportscaster, and former major leaguer:

"How did you handle pressure as a player?"

Answer: "It was easy. I'd strike out and put the pressure on the guy behind me."

Every decade or so, I attempt to play tennis, and it always consists of thirty-seven seconds of actually hitting the ball and two hours of yelling, "Where did the ball go?" "Over that condominium!" With bowling once you let go of the ball, it's no longer your legal responsibility. They have these wonderful machines that find it for you and send it right back.

—Dave Barry

Football player injured on field to teammate: "That was the Statue of Liberty play, all right. I got creamed by the huddled masses."

—Bob Thaves

Professional sports are getting so violent. Next season they're having Monday Night Drive-By Football.　　　—Bill Jones

Walking down the street, a man passes a house and notices a child trying to reach the doorbell. No matter how much the little guy stretches, he can't make it.

The man calls out, "Let me get that for you." He bounds onto the porch and rings the bell.

"Thanks, mister," says the kid. "Now let's run."

One Halloween night, a neighborhood practical joker decided to frighten the young "trick-or-treaters" who rang his doorbell. He put on a floor-length black cape, a black hat fitted with devil's horns, and a hideous mask that seemed to combine the most gruesome features of Dracula, Frankenstein's Monster, and the Wolf Man. Then he waited.

Finally, his doorbell rang. He turned off all the lights and, shining a flashlight on his mask, he opened the door and pierced the night air with an eerie scream. Then he looked down and saw standing before him a tiny, golden-haired five year old, dressed as a dainty fairy.

The little tyke stared wide-eyed for a moment. Then she raised her eyes up along the massive black cape, looked straight into the hideous mask, and asked, "Is your mommy home?"

I collect rare photographs. I have two. . . . One of Houdini locking his keys in his car. . . . The other is a rare picture of Norman Rockwell beating up a child.　　　—Steven Wright

Turning to the best player of the bridge foursome, the novice asked, "How would you have played that last hand of mine?"

The expert replied promptly, "Under an assumed name."

My friend Ralph, who is an accomplished marksman, was driving through a small town in Virginia. There he saw evidence of amazing shooting. On trees, walls, fences, and barns were numerous bullseyes with the bullet hole in the exact center.

In a field, he spotted a young man carrying a BB gun. Ralph waved him over and asked if he knew the identity of the remarkable shooter.

"Sure," said the boy. "I did all that shooting."

"How did you do it?" asked Ralph. "What's your secret?"

"There's nothing to it, really," the boy replied. "I shoot first and draw the circles afterwards."

A racetrack patron ran up to the window three times to place heavy bets on Major Dandy in the third race. When he appeared at the window for a fourth time, another patron tapped him on the shoulder.

"I reckon this ain't any of my business" he said, "but if I was you, I wouldn't be risking all that money on Major Dandy. He ain't gonna win the third race."

"Says you," sneered the better. "What makes you think that?"

"Well, if you must know," replied the other, "I happen to own Major Dandy and I just know he ain't goin' to win that race."

The other man thought for a minute. "Maybe so," he conceded, "but if that is a fact, all I can say is it's going to be a mighty slow race. I own the other four horses."

Frank was a man who believed in the deeper meaning of numbers. He was born on May 5, 1905, and was fifty-five years old. He had five children, and he lived at 555 East 55th Street. For the past five years, he had earned $55,000 as an executive at Sak's Fifth Avenue.

On his fifty-fifth birthday, Frank went to the track and was astonished to find that a horse named Numero Cinqo was running in the fifth race. Five minutes before the race began, he went to the fifth window and put down five thousand dollars in five-dollar bills on Number Five.

Sure enough, the horse finished fifth.

Karate is a form of martial arts in which people who have had years and years of training can, using only their hands and feet, make some of the worst movies in the history of the world.

—Dave Barry

When I was a young boy, I always protested vigorously when Mother asked me to take my little sister along fishing. "The last time she came," I objected, "I didn't catch a single fish."

"I'll talk to her," Mother said, "and I promise this time she won't make any noise."

"It wasn't the noise, Mom," I replied. "She ate all my bait."

Granddad and I went fishing one time up at the North Avenue Pier in Chicago. We fished all day, tried every kind of bait—worms, flies, minnows, doughballs, shad guts—but couldn't catch anything. Didn't get a nibble all day.

Just about sundown—sunburned, hot, thirsty, and tired—Granddad finally reached in his pocket, got a handful of change, just threw it all out into the lake, and said, "Here, go buy something you like."

When I was in Indiana a few years back, I ordered an iced tea and asked the waitress if she would like to hear a good Notre Dame joke.

A look of stern disapproval formed on her face. "Listen," she whispered. "See those two big guys on your left? They are both linemen on the Notre Dame football team. And that huge fellow on your right was a world-class wrestler at Notre Dame. That guy in the corner is Notre Dame's all-time champion weight lifter. And that fellow with him lettered in three sports at Notre Dame. Now, are you absolutely positive you want to go ahead and tell your joke here?"

"Nah, guess not," I replied. "I wouldn't want to explain it five times."

My Aunt Laura was in charge of last month's luncheon for her bridge club. She chose an expensive restaurant. However, after her group of elegantly dressed socialites was seated, Aunt Laura had no luck getting the waiter's attention.

Borrowing a cellular phone from a realtor who happened to be seated at the next table, she called the restaurant and asked to have menus sent to her table.

It worked!

Camping isn't what it used to be. "Honey, I'm gonna go get some firewood; do you have change for a twenty?"

—Nick Arnette

Whoever invented bungee jumping must have watched a lot of Road Runner cartoons.

—Nick Arnette

One mountaineer to another: "It almost cost us our lives climbing to the top of Mount Everest to plant the American flag. But it was worth it. Hand me the flag."

"Me? I thought you brought it."

—Paul B. Lowney, *The Best in Office Humor* (Peter Pauper Press)

8.
ON THE JOB
(BUT OUT TO LUNCH)

My brother is very superstitious—he won't work any week that
has a Friday in it.
—Milton Berle

Mark met his old friend Steve and told him that he was in desperate need of five thousand dollars. He begged Steve to loan it to him, but Steve refused.

"I have to remind you, then," said Mark, "of what happened twenty-five years ago when we were in Vietnam together. You were lying wounded in the jungle. I crawled out to you, dodging bullets, threw you over my shoulder, and dragged you back. For this, I got the Medal of Honor. But the important thing was, I saved your life. Now, will you let me borrow the five thousand dollars?"

"No," said Steve, unimpressed.

"Let's go back to fifteen years ago," said Mark. "I'd like to remind you who introduced you to your wife. Who set you up with her when you were afraid to ask her out? Who gave the money for your honeymoon, Steve? Me! Now will you let me have the five thousand dollars?"

The response was again, "No."

Still determined, Mark continued. "How about ten years ago," said Mark, "when your daughter was struck by that rare disease and your doctor was desperately trying to find the right blood to give her a transfusion? Whose was it that finally matched? Your pal Mark. I gave her seven blood transfusions, and it pulled her through. You'll let me have the money, won't you, Steve?"

"No, I won't," said Steve.

"Think back to five years ago," urged Mark. "Remember when your back was against the wall and you had to have twenty-seven thousand dollars or the bank would foreclose on your company. Who signed the note that guaranteed your loan? Good old Mark! I saved your business for you then, didn't I, Steve? Now you will find it in your heart to loan me the five thousand dollars!"

Steve still had no problem refusing.

"What kind of friend are you, anyway?" yelled Mark, exasperated. "Twenty-five years ago I saved your life, fifteen years ago I introduced you to your wife, ten years ago I saved your daughter's life, five years ago I saved your business. In light of that, I can't imagine why in the world you won't loan me the five thousand dollars!"

"What have you done for me lately?" asked Steve.

—Walter Schwimmer

They say there are six phases to any project:
- Enthusiasm
- Disillusionment
- Panic
- Search for the guilty
- Punishment of the innocent
- Praise and honors for the nonparticipants

Lance, a city man, bought a farm and was visited by his neighbor Fred, who owned the farm next to his. "Can you tell me," asked Lance, "where the property line runs between our farms?"

Farmer Fred looked him over and asked, "Are you talking owning or mowing?"

An economist was asked to talk to a group of business people about the recession. She tacked up a big sheet of white paper. Then she made a black spot on the paper with her pencil and asked a man in the front row what he saw. The man replied promptly, "A black spot."

The speaker asked every person the same question, and each replied, "A black spot."

With calm and deliberate emphasis the speaker said: "Yes, there is a little black spot, but none of you mentioned the big sheet of white paper. And that's my speech."

Billionaire J. P. Getty was once asked the secret of his success. Said Getty, "Some people find oil. Others don't."

There cannot be a crisis next week. My schedule is already full.
—Henry Kissinger

When small men begin to cast big shadows, it means that the sun is about to set.
—Lin Yutang

A salesman dropped in to see a business customer. Not a soul was in the office except a big dog emptying wastebaskets. The salesman stared at the animal, wondering if his imagination could be playing tricks. The dog looked up and said, "Don't be surprised, buddy; this is part of my job."

"Incredible!" muttered the man. "I can't believe it! I'm going to tell your boss what a prize he has in you—an animal that can talk!"

"No, no," pleaded the dog. "Please don't! If that bum finds out I can talk, he'll make me answer the phones!"

 "I think it's wrong," says comedian Steven Wright, "that only one company makes the game Monopoly."

Early one morning, a woman made a mad dash from her house when she heard the garbage truck pulling away. She was still in her bathrobe. Her hair was wrapped around big curlers. Her face was covered with sticky cream. She was wearing a chin-strap and a beat up old pair of slippers. In short, she was a frightful picture. When she reached the sidewalk, she called out, "Am I too late for the garbage?"

The reply came back: "No, hop right in."

A young man of thirty-two had been appointed president of the bank. He'd never dreamed he'd be president, much less at such a young age. So he approached the venerable Chairman of the Board and said, "You know, I've just been appointed President. I was wondering if you could give me some advice."

The old man uttered just two words: "Right decisions!"

The young man had hoped for a bit more than this, so he said, "That's really helpful, and I appreciate it, but can you be more specific? How do I make right decisions?"

The wise old man simply responded, "Experience."

The young man said, "Well, that's just the point of my being here. I don't have the kind of experience I need. How do I get it?"

Came the terse reply, "Wrong decisions!"

History credits Adam and Eve with being the first bookkeepers. After all, they invented the first loose-leaf system.

—Henny Youngman

John came home flushed with pride. "I've been promoted," he announced. "I have a new job! They've made me an expediter."

"What's an expediter?" asked his wife.

"Well, it's hard to explain, but if you did what I'm supposed to do, it would be called nagging."

Give a horse to him who tells the truth. He'll need it to escape on.

—Persian proverb

If you want your ship to come in, you must build a dock.

My son used to work in Texas. Now and then he would fly to the western part of the state on an airline called TTA. He called it "Treetop Airlines." That's about they way they flew.

One day, he was on this plane headed for San Angelo from Dallas. He was sitting up near the front, the door to the cockpit was open, and the pilot got on the horn. He called the tower and said, "I'd like a time check."

The tower came back and said, "Tell me what airline you are, and I'll tell you what time it is."

The pilot said, "What difference does it make what airline it is? I want to know what time it is."

The tower replied, "Well, it makes a lot of difference. If you're Delta, it's 1800 hours; if you're American, it's 6:00 P.M.; if you're USAir, it's Thursday; and if you're TTA, the big hand's on the twelve and the little hand's on the six."

I saw a subliminal advertising executive, but only for a second.

—Steven Wright

Every man is a fool for at least five minutes every day; wisdom consists of not exceeding the limit.   —Elbert Hubbard

"I'll make a new suit for you," agreed an overworked tailor, "but it won't be ready for six weeks."

"Six weeks!" protested the customer. "Why, the Lord created the entire world in six days."

"True," said the tailor. "And have you taken a good look at it lately?"

Cecil B. De Mille was well known for his spectacular motion pictures, especially those based on the Bible. Unfortunately, he had a tendency to allow his lavish special effects to drown the simple morals of the scriptural stories. He had filmed the life of Jesus, the story of Samson and Delilah, the Exodus of the children of Israel from Egypt. Shortly before his death, he undertook the most breathtaking of all his magnificent spectacles.

He was filming the six days of creation—the coming of light, the forming of the Earth, the separation of the sea from the land, the appearance of sun, moon, and stars, and the start of life itself.

This carefully planned sequence would cost more than fifty million dollars. For this purpose a huge valley in Spain was equipped with astonishing mechanical devices. The sequence could be performed only once. To try it twice would have meant undoing all the first attempt had brought about and running up costs greater than any studio could possibly afford.

To cover all eventualities, therefore, De Mille set up four separate camera crews on four separate peaks overlooking the valley, each under instructions to film everything.

At the appointed time, De Mille waved his hand at the special effects crew, and the magnificent display began.

Everything worked perfectly. The creation had been recreated. De Mille himself was reduced to speechless tears at its magnificence. When he recovered his composure, De Mille hastened to check on the camera crews.

He lifted his walkie-talkie and contacted Camera Crew One. "How did it go?" he asked.

"Gosh, C.B.," came back a shocked voice. "I don't know how to tell you this, but when the creation started, we were all so fascinated by it that we actually never thought to roll the cameras."

Under his breath, De Mille uttered a few choice curses. Then he silently praised himself for his careful preparations. After all, he had expected trouble. That was why he had four camera crews. He put in a call to Crew Two.

"Gosh, Mr. De Mille," came back a terrified voice. "I can't explain it. We were all set, but it turned out we just didn't have any film. Somehow no one had ever thought to bring any. I don't know what to say. I'm so upset I could just die."

"Do that," barked De Mille, and he rang up the third crew.

"Gosh, C.B., came back a hysterical voice, "we were ready, we were running, we were loaded, we took everything, but C.B. —I don't know how it happened, but we somehow never took the cap off the lens."

Now De Mille was dazed and stupefied. With a trembling hand, he called the final film crew.

For once a cheerful voice answered, "Hello, Mr. De Mille!"

De Mille said, "Is everything all right?"

"Couldn't be better," said the camera operator confidently.

Wild hope sprang up within De Mille's heart. "You have film?"

"Plenty."

"The right film?"

"Naturally."

"The cap is off the lens?"

"Of course."

"There is nothing wrong?"

"Not a thing."

"Thank goodness."

"Relax," said the fourth camera operator. "We're in perfect shape, so get started whenever you want, C.B."

Things were simpler years ago. Rip Van Winkle slept for twenty years and when he woke up nobody asked him to endorse a mattress.

I used to be an airline pilot. I got fired because I kept locking the keys in the plane. They caught me on an eighty-foot stepladder with a coat hanger.   —Steven Wright

Waiter to couple seated at a restaurant table: "If you need anything else, here's my beeper number."

—Dave Carpenter in *The Wall Street Journal*

A well-meaning customer of the famed Neiman-Marcus department store felt prompted to send Stanley Marcus this letter:

Dear Mr. Marcus:

I have been receiving beautiful and expensive brochures from you at regular intervals. It occurs to me that you might divert a little of the fortune you must be spending for this advertising matter to raise the salaries of your more faithful employees. For instance, there's an unassuming, plainly dressed little man on the second floor who always treats me with extreme courtesy when I visit your store and generally persuades me to buy something I don't really want. Why don't you pay him a little more? He looks as though he could use it.

Yours truly,
Mrs. W. S.

By return mail came Marcus' reply:

Dear Madam:

Your letter impressed us so deeply that we called a directors' meeting immediately, and thanks solely to your own solicitude, voted my father a twenty-dollar-a-week raise.

Yours truly,
Stanley Marcus

—Bennett Cerf in *Saturday Review*

The bank executive's secretary was having a bad day. Every time she started working on an assignment from the boss, he would change his mind and ask her to do it another way. After this happened several times, the boss heard her muttering, "I think I know what's wrong with this country!"

"Don't mumble, Miss Jackson," said the bank executive, "Speak up. Just what is wrong with this country?"

Staring at her fingernails, she laconically replied: "We're trying to run it with only one vice president."

Fred Watkins, the local barber, is the most negative person in our town. John Jordan, the president of the Rotary Club, was sitting in his chair one day, extremely excited. "Guess what, Fred," he said.

Fred muttered, "What?"

"My wife and I are going to Italy for a month."

"I've heard all about Italy," Fred replied. "The people are rude. The food is terrible. The countryside is ugly."

John paid no attention and continued, "And I'm going to spend a week in Rome."

"Big deal," said Fred. "Bunch of broken down old buildings."

Undeterred, John went on. "And I'm going to visit the Vatican. I'm even going to have an audience with the Pope."

"Oh, yeah," said Fred, "I know about those so-called papal audiences. You'll be packed into the square with a million other dopes and the Pope will wave from the balcony. Big deal."

A month went by and John was once again in the barber chair. "So how was your trip to Italy?" asked Fred. "As bad as I thought it would be, right?"

"Not at all," John responded. "The people were warm and friendly. The food was wonderful. The countryside was gorgeous."

"But Rome is a dump. Am I right?" the barber persisted.

"No," John answered, "Rome was delightful. We could have stayed a year and not run out of fascinating places to see."

"And how about your visit with the Pope?" asked the barber, expecting his prediction to be fulfilled.

John answered, "Well, I have to admit, you were half-right about that. The Pope was up there on the balcony and I was back in the crowd with thousands of people, but two uniformed Swiss guards came over and told me the Pope wanted to talk to me. They escorted me right up onto the balcony with him."

"What did he tell you?" asked the barber.

"He didn't tell me anything. In fact, he had a question for me."

"Well, what did he ask?" asked the incredulous barber.

John took a minute to allow the suspense to mount. "The Pope said to me, 'Tell me, my son, where did you get that terrible haircut?'"

There is a story about a monastery in Europe perched high on a cliff several hundred feet in the air. The only way to reach the monastery was to be suspended in a basket, which was pulled to the top by several monks who had to pull and tug with all their strength. Obviously the ride up the steep cliff in that basket was terrifying. On his way up, one tourist noticed that the rope by which he was suspended was old and frayed. With a trembling voice he asked the monk who was riding with him in the basket how often they changed the rope. The monk thought for a moment, shrugged, and answered, "Whenever it breaks."

Dear Santa,

I've been such a good girl this year, networking like crazy in kindergarten. My lemonade stand had the highest after-tax profit in town. My brother, Justin, has been super, too. He was the first kid on our block to restructure the debt of his Little League franchise. So we just know that you'll get us everything on this list. We've made it easy for you. All our requests come from the F.A.O. Schwartz catalog, as follows.

First, I want the cute little ranch mink coat (p. 5, $2,500). I'd also like the gold-plated carousel music box (p. 4, $12,000).

Justin wants the Ferrari Testarossa Junior (p. 1, $14,500) so he can zip through the playground at 28 miles per hour. Also, he'd like the "Birthday Party of a Lifetime" (p. 3, $18,000). His friends will love staying at the Plaza and taking the horse-drawn carriage ride through Central Park. I told him the party might be just one of those things that grown-up catalog writers promise, maybe for publicity, and never expect to deliver. But Santa, he says you're only three once!

Jennifer

P.S. This isn't like a bribe or anything, but there'll be Godiva chocolates waiting by the fireplace and some *crudités* for the reindeer.

When Connie was applying for a new job, she asked the interviewer if the company would pay for her medical insurance. The interviewer replied that the cost of medical insurance was deducted from the employee's paycheck.

"The last place I worked, the company paid for it," she said.

"Did they pay for your life insurance too?"

"Yes," she said.

"And for your dental insurance?"

"Yes, they did," she answered. "Not only that, but we got unlimited sick leave, a month's vacation, a Christmas bonus, two hour lunch breaks, and free child care."

"So why did you leave such a perfect place?" the incredulous interviewer asked.

"The company went bankrupt," she replied.

Many schools are in crisis. I like what comedian Joe Hickman said: "At first I wanted to be a cop, but you have to be 6'1", know karate, and carry a gun. Then I thought I'd be a schoolteacher, but you have to be 6'1", know karate, and carry a gun."

Q: What do you need to make a small fortune on Wall Street?
A: A large fortune.

A railroad agent in India had been reprimanded for making decisions without first getting direct orders from his superior in headquarters. One day his superior received the following startling telegram: "Tiger on platform eating conductor. Wire instructions."

"So you want another day off," snorted the office manager to his clerk. "I'm anxious to hear your excuse this time. You've been off for your grandfather's funeral four times already."

Replied the clerk, "Today my grandma is getting married again."

Two friends who hadn't seen each other in years met in a supermarket. One woman asked, "Tell me, Ruth, how is your son, George?"

"He's getting along fine," Ruth replied. "He's a poet. He just received his master's degree in Literature from the university."

"And what about Mary?"

"She's just as smart as George," Ruth replied. "She graduated from college with a degree in Modern Art."

"Wonderful! And how is little Freddy? What is he doing?"

"Well," Ruth said, "Freddy is still Freddy. He wouldn't go to college—he became a plumber, instead. If it weren't for him, we'd all be starving."

A market research interviewer was stopping people in the grocery store after they picked up their bread. One fellow picked up a loaf of Wonder Bread, and the interviewer asked him, "Sir, would you be willing to answer a couple of questions about your choice of bread?"

The man responded, "Yes, I'd be happy to."

"Fine," the interviewer said, "the question I'd like to ask you is this: Do you feel that your choice of Wonder Bread has been at all influenced by their advertising program?"

The fellow looked shocked and said, "Of course not. I'm not influenced by that sort of thing at all!"

"Well then," said the interviewer. "Could you tell me just why you did choose Wonder Bread?"

"Of course I can!" the man replied. "Because it builds strong bodies twelve ways!"

A fourth-grade teacher came into her room one Valentine's Day and found a handmade card bearing the message: "All the fourth grade loves you, Mrs. Jones."

This touched her deeply—until the next morning when she found a note with a corrected tally on her desk. It read: "All the fourth grade loves you, Mrs. Jones. All but two."

A HYMN FOR EVERY PROFESSION

- Dentists: Crown Him with Many Crowns
- Contractors: The Church's One Foundation
- Obstetricians: Come, Labor On
- Golfers: There Is a Green Hill Far Away
- Politicians: Standing on the Promises
- Gardeners: Lo, How a Rose E'er Blooming
- Librarians: Let All Mortal Flesh Keep Silent
- Lawyers: In the Hour of Trial
- Accountants: Ten Thousand by Ten Thousand
- Clothiers: Blest Be the Tie
- Students: Ask Ye What Great Things I Know
- Dry Cleaners: O for a Faith that Will Not Shrink
- Weather Forecasters: From Every Stormy Wind that Blows
- Orators: O Could I Speak the Matchless Word
- Choir Directors: Sing Them Over and Over Again to Me
- Traffic Engineers: Where Cross the Crowded Ways of Life
- IRS Agents: We Give Thee but Thine Own
- There's even a hymn for absent church members: Jesus, I am Resting.

Former President Ronald Reagan liked to tell a story about a newspaper photographer out in Los Angeles whose editor called him to say, "There's a fire raging out in Palos Verdes, a hilly area to the south. Your assignment is to rush down to the regional airport, board a small plane that'll be waiting for you, get some pictures of the fire, and be back in time for the afternoon edition.

Breathlessly, the photographer raced to the airport and drove his car to the end of the runway. Sure enough, there was a plane waiting with the engines all revved up, ready to go. He got aboard, and at about five thousand feet, he began getting his camera out of the bag. He told the fellow flying the plane to get him over the fire, so he could take his pictures and get back to the paper. From the other side of the cockpit there was a deafening silence. Then he heard these unsettling words: "Ah . . . aren't you the instructor?"

Facing failure after failure, Orville and Wilbur Wright persevered in their attempts to get their new flying machine off the ground. Finally, their efforts were crowned with success. On a December day at Kitty Hawk, North Carolina, Orville achieved the first recorded manned flight in a heavier-than-air vehicle. What a moment of triumph! The brothers ran to the nearest Western Union office and wired their sister Katherine, "We did it. We have actually flown in the air 120 feet. Will be home for Christmas."

Excited about her brothers' achievement, Katherine took the telegram to the local newspaper editor. He glanced at the message and seemed duly impressed. His story in the next edition of the local newspaper was headlined, "Orville and Wilbur Wright Will Be Home for Christmas."

A man stopped to chat with a farmer who was erecting a new building. He asked, "What are you putting up?"

The farmer replied, "Well, if I can rent it, it's a rustic cottage. If I can't, it's a cow shed."

Are you struggling with an impossible-looking task? Don't give up just because people tell you, "It can't be done." Almost every great idea or invention in history started the same way.

When trains were first invented, several "experts" agreed that if a train went at the frightful speed of fifteen miles an hour, the passengers would get nosebleeds. In addition, they would suffocate when going through tunnels . . .

In 1881, the New York YMCA announced typing lessons for women. Protests were made on the grounds that the female constitution would break down under the strain. . . .

When the telephone was first invented, Joshua Coppersmith was arrested in Boston for trying to sell stock in a company that would build them. The experts said that all well-informed people know it is impossible to transmit the human voice over a wire. . . .

— from *Net Results*, Net Results Resource Center, Lubbock, TX, February 1990

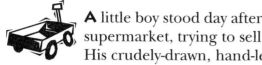 **A** little boy stood day after day in front of the local supermarket, trying to sell his mixed-breed puppy. His crudely-drawn, hand-lettered sign, attached to his small red wagon, read, "OK dog for sale. $3 or best offer." A salesman drove by each day, and after a week he began to pity the boy who was still trying to sell his dog.

The salesman stopped and said, "Son, do you really want to sell this dog?"

The boy replied, "I sure do."

"Well," said the salesman, "you're never going to sell him until you learn to See It Big. What I mean is, take this dog home, clean him up, doll him up, raise your price, make people think they're getting something big, and you'll sell him."

The next morning the salesman drove by and there was the boy with a puppy that was groomed, perfumed, and bedecked with multicolored ribbons alongside a big sign:

TREEMENNDOUS Puppy For Sale—$5,000

The salesman gulped and realized that although he had told the boy to See It Big, he had forgotten to explain the importance of Keep It Simple, Stupid. That evening he stopped by to tell the boy the other half of the formula. But this time, the boy and the puppy were gone, and the sign lay there with "SOLD" written across it in huge letters. The salesman was astounded. There was no way the boy could have sold that dog for five thousand dollars. His curiosity got the best of him, so after discovering the boy's address from the checker at the supermarket, he drove to the boy's house and rang the doorbell.

The boy came to the door and the salesman blurted, "Son you didn't really sell that dog for five thousand dollars, did you?"

The boy replied, "Yes, sir, I did, and I want to thank you for your help."

The salesman said, "How in the world did you do it?"

The boy replied, "It was easy! I traded the dog for two $2,500 cats!"

Before signing his name and title to important papers, a respected personnel manager always checked something in his desk drawer. When he retired, employees found in the drawer a scrap of paper that said: "2 *Ns*—1 *L*."

Two passengers seated next to one another on a jet plane headed for Hawaii struck up a conversation. It turned out they were both salesman. They began boasting to each other of their salesmanship.

"I'm from Seattle," said the first man, "and you may not believe it, but the other day I sold Boeing fifty thousand dollars' worth of cardboard boxes."

"Big deal," snorted the other guy. "I run a clothing store in Cedar Rapids. Yesterday, a woman came in to buy a suit to bury her husband in—and I sold her an extra pair of pants."

The chief executive officer of an electronics company called in his public-relations director. "Listen, Wilson. Someone is trying to buy us out. Get the price of our stock up so it'll be too expensive for them. I don't care how you do it, just do it!"

The P.R. man did so. When the CEO asked how, he replied, "I started a rumor Wall Street obviously liked."

"What was that?"

"I told them you were resigning."

A story is told about an engineer, a psychologist, and a theologian who were hunting in the wilds of northern Canada. Suddenly, the temperature dropped, and a snow storm descended, lashing them with its fury. As they trudged on, they came across an isolated cabin, far removed from any town. Because friendly hospitality is a virtue practiced by those who live in the wilderness, the hunters knocked on the door to ask permission to rest.

No one answered their knocks, but, discovering the cabin was unlocked, they entered. It was a simple place—two rooms with a minimum of furniture and household equipment. Nothing was surprising about the cabin except the stove. Not the stove itself—it was large, potbellied, and made of cast iron. What was unusual was its location: it was suspended in midair by wires attached to the ceiling beams.

"Fascinating," said the psychologist, stroking his beard. "It is obvious that this lonely trapper, isolated from humanity, has elevated his stove so he can curl up under it and vicariously experience a return to the womb."

"Nonsense!" replied the engineer as he scratched some calculations in the dust on the cabin floor. "The man is familiar with the laws of thermodynamics. By elevating his stove, he has a way to distribute heat more evenly throughout the cabin."

"With all due respect," interrupted the theologian, folding his hands in a gesture of piety, "I'm sure that hanging his stove from the ceiling has religious meaning. Fire 'lifted up' has been a religious symbol for centuries."

The three debated the point for several hours without resolving the issue. When the trapper finally returned, they immediately asked him why he had hung his heavy potbellied stove by wires from the ceiling.

His answer was succinct: "Had plenty of wire, not much stove pipe!"

Mary Lou Williams decided to apply for work in a church office. She heard that Church of the Savior was a bustling place and that they were looking for a secretary. She went over there one day and filled out a job application. A few days later she was interviewed by the pastor, Reverend Clarence Hewitt.

Pastor Hewitt noted that she had not filled in the year of her birth. "I see that your birthday is July tenth," said the pastor. "May I ask what year?"

"Every year," she replied.

I knew my partner was a workaholic. The sign over his desk read: "Thank God it's Monday."

Now I lay me down to sleep,
I pray my Cuisinart to keep,
I pray my stocks are on the rise,
And that my analyst is wise,
That all the wine I sip is white,
And that my hot tub's watertight.
That racquetball won't get too tough,
That all my sushi's fresh enough.
I pray my cordless phone still works,
That my career won't lose its perks.
My microwave won't radiate,
My condo won't depreciate.
I pray my health club doesn't close,
And that my money market grows.
If I go broke before I wake,
I pray my Volvo they won't take.

—*Washington Post*

Pastor Earl Rudnick told me that writing letters of recommendation for people with dubious qualifications was wearing him to the bone. I suggested he use the following letter:

> To Whom It May Concern:
>
> I most heartily recommend this candidate with no qualifications whatsoever. I am sure that no person would be better for the job. He'd like to work for you in the worst possible way. You will be very fortunate to get this person to work for you.
>
> Sincerely . . .

 Hal Hopkins, an itinerant house painter, offered his services at very low prices. Unfortunately, Hal had the nasty habit of thinning the paint with turpentine to insure some margin of profit.

One day, he was painting the steeple high atop a church. He thinned down the paint even more than usual for this job.

"After all," he said to himself, "nobody can really see the steeple from way down there on the ground." So he started painting with a solution that barely covered the wood. Just as he was finishing, the sky clouded over and a gale storm began to blow. The rain and wind beat against the painter and washed the paint off the steeple. Hopkins looked at the now-unpainted steeple, and cried out, "What will I do now?"

From the clouds, a deep voice replied, "Re-paint, and thin no more!"

Wilfred Benton was an active layperson at the Grace Presbyterian Church. He went to see his minister, Carl Wattling, for advice. Wilfred complained that he was severely depressed—business was bad, his wife had left him, the bill collectors were after him, and he was on the verge of a nervous breakdown.

The minister gave him what solace he could, then said "Go home, pick up the Bible and open it at random. Ask the Lord for guidance. Then read the first two words you see. They will provide the advice you need for your situation."

"Just the first two words I happen to see?" repeated Wilfred.

"That's right," said the pastor.

Pastor Wattling did not hear from Wilfred for several months. Then one day while in town, the minister saw Wilfred drive up in a Rolls Royce. He got out of the car with a beautiful young woman on his arm. The minister walked up to him and said "Well, I see your situation has changed. You look very prosperous."

"Yes," replied the man. "I took your advice, went home, opened the Bible at random and read the first two words."

"Well, what were the two words that served you so well?" asked the minister.

"Chapter Eleven," replied Wilfred.

A salesman should never be ashamed of his calling. He should be ashamed of his not calling.

—Albert Lasker

What is a committee? A group of the unwilling, picked from the unfit, to do the unnecessary.
—Richard Harkness

The graduate with a Science degree asks, "Why does it work?" The graduate with an Engineering degree asks, "How does it work?" The graduate with an Accounting degree asks, "How much will it cost?" The graduate with a Liberal Arts degree asks, "Do you want fries with that?"

A good listener is not only popular everywhere, but after a while he knows something.
—George Ade

When two people in a business always agree, one of them is unnecessary.
—William Wrigley, Jr.

Don't fret about finding your station in life. Someone's sure to tell you where to get off.
—Sinclair Lewis

Any critic can establish a wonderful batting average by just rejecting every new idea.
—J. D. Williams

A good leader takes a little more than his share of the blame, a little less than his share of the credit.
—Arnold Glassgow

Experience is what enables you to make the same mistake again without getting caught.
—Ralph Peterson

Only a mediocre person is always at his best.
—Somerset Maugham

My Uncle Irv is a self-educated man. Despite his busy career in business and in politics, he has found time to read thousands of books. I asked him one day, "Uncle Irv, how did you manage to do all that reading during those busy years?"

He replied, "Simple. I kept an open book on my desk, and read it whenever someone on the phone said, 'Just a moment, please.'"

At a Milwaukee post office, a woman complained to the clerk that a Pony Express rider could get a letter from Milwaukee to St. Louis in two days, and now, delivering the mail takes three days. "I'd like to know why," she scoffed.

The clerk thought a moment and then suggested, "The horses are a lot older now?"
—Bill Markert

Two business retailers were discussing the problems of their trade. "I can't remember business ever being this bad," Joe reflected. "My April and May sales were the worst I've seen in several years. Then June came in. What a disaster. And July was even worse."

"You haven't seen anything," mumbled the other. "My son dropped out of college and joined a commune. My teenage daughter said yesterday that she was pregnant and plans to drop out of high school. And now my wife for the last twenty-three years tells me there is no love left in our relationship. It doesn't get any worse that this."

"Oh yes, it does," countered Joe. "My August sales!"

Whenever anything bad happens to me, I write a joke about it. Then it isn't a bad experience, it's a tax deduction.
—Denise Munro

My Uncle Irv always contended: "The trouble with getting to work on time is that it makes the day so long."

Boss: "I can assure you that the value of the average employee will continue to increase."

Employee: "That's because there will be fewer of us doing more work, right?"

Boss: "Right. Except for the 'us' part."

—Scott Adams, United Features Syndicate

Dennis Miller's definition of body piercing: "A powerful, compelling visual statement that says, 'Gee, in today's competitive job market, what can I do to make myself less employable?'"

At a tiny diner in New Mexico, I asked for a cup of coffee with cream and sugar. I was rather annoyed that the waitress forgot to bring a spoon with my coffee. After trying unsuccessfully to get the waitress's attention, I announced in a voice loud enough to be heard from one end of the establishment to the other, "This coffee is going to be pretty hot to stir with my fingers."

Within seconds, the waitress appeared with another cup of coffee. "This one isn't so hot, sir," she beamed.

One always fears that in certain corporate environments Thomas Edison might not have had the freedom to invent the light bulb. Instead, Mr. Edison might have come up with—a bigger candle.   —Philip E. Rollhaus, 1986

When John Kennedy was campaigning for President in 1960, he visited a West Virginia Coal mine. One of the workers there confronted him and said, "I hear you're the son of one of the wealthiest men in the country. Is that right?"

Kennedy said it was.

The miner said, "I heard you got everything you ever wanted. Is that true?"

Kennedy said, "Pretty much so."

The miner asked, "Is it true you've never done a day's work with your hands in your entire life?"

Kennedy said it was true.

The miner said, "Let me tell you this, you haven't missed a thing."

Boss: I've decided to use humor in the workplace. Experts say humor eases tension, which is important in times when the work force is being trimmed. Knock knock.
Employee: Who's there?
Boss: Not you anymore.

—Scott Adams, *The Dilbert Principle* (Harper Business)

I just bought a new car. I asked for the passenger-side air bag. They gave me the salesman.
—Nick Arnette

The embarrassing thing is that the salad dressing is out-grossing my films.
—Paul Newman

Last week a friend of mine lost his job at the orange juice factory. He couldn't concentrate.

I love the way everybody is getting fancy job titles. Gas station attendants are now called "petroleum consultants." They saunter over, "I'd recommend the 89 octane unleaded. It's an unpretentious little fuel with a surprising kick. Would you care to sniff the nozzle?"
—Robert G. Lee

I used to sell life insurance. But life insurance is really strange. You really don't get anything for it. It works like this: You pay me money. And when you die, I'll pay you money.

—Bill Kirchenbauer

A noted astronomer found a bishop seated next to him on an airplane. In the course of conversation, the astronomer said, "I never had much interest in theology. My religion can be summed up in 'Do unto others as you would have them do unto you.'"

The bishop responded, "Well, I've had little time for astronomy. My views about it are summed up in 'Twinkle, twinkle, little star.'"

Interviewer: "Congratulations on winning the eighty million dollar lottery."
Farmer: "Thank you."
Interviewer: "Do you have any special plans for spending the money?"
Farmer: "I'm just gonna keep farming 'til it's gone."

My cousin Victor had just graduated from Yale but was unable to find a job. He went to work for his father, at the steel shelving factory my uncle owned.

Catching Victor napping in a supply closet, Hank commanded, "Go out and sweep the sidewalk."

"But Dad," Victor protested, "I'm a college graduate!"

"Oh, I forgot about that," Uncle Hank replied. "OK, I'll come out and show you how."

Three-year-old Stephen was having a terrific time on his first plane trip. He pushed every button in sight, ran through the aisles at top speed and finally crashed into the flight attendant as she was serving a tray of coffee.

Barely keeping her balance, she forced a smile and cooed, "Little boy, why don't you go outside and play?"

The worst job I ever had was working in a Fotomat booth. I was the only one at the Christmas party.
—Mark Dobrient

If lawyers are disbarred, and clergymen defrocked, then doesn't it follow that . . .
- electricians can be delighted,
- musicians denoted,
- cowboys deranged,
- models deposed,
- tree surgeons debarked, and
- dry cleaners depressed?

Hal Adams, a Kentucky farmer, had an ambitious son who graduated from Princeton University and upon his graduation (magna cum laude), he went to New York to make his fortune.

The breaks were against him, however, and he ended up as a bootblack in Grand Central Station.

Hal continued to work his farm, so now the father makes hay while the son shines.

One nephew of Deion Sanders' was a little short of cash, so he wrote to his rich and famous uncle and asked for a short-term loan. The usually generous Sanders was annoyed that the young man would ask him for money, considering that they had not seen one another for years. The multi-talented athlete wrote a chilly note to his nephew, suggesting in blunt, simple terms that he earn the money through his own diligence. The young man promptly sold the letter for a thousand dollars.

My Aunt Lucille was a schoolteacher in Chicago for many years. After her retirement, she was ticketed for speeding on the Eisenhower Expressway. Adamantly maintaining that she never exceeded the speed limit, she appeared in traffic court to protest the ticket.

When the judge recognized her as his former fifth-grade teacher, he smiled broadly and exclaimed, "Madam, I have been sitting here for years waiting for this moment. Now, you sit down at that table and write, 'I must not drive faster than the posted limit' five hundred times."

My father's cousin Josh was a fantastic salesman. He actually made a handsome living going door to door selling signs that read, "No salespeople allowed."

Wife: "You look tired, dear. Did you have a bad day at the office?"

Husband: "I'll say. I took an aptitude test, and believe me, it's a good thing I own the company!"

No matter how tired you may be, your exhaustion is justified, as can be proven by simple arithmetic. The U.S. has a population of 200 million. Of these, 72 million are over sixty-five years old, leaving 128 million to do the work. When you subtract the 75 million people under age twenty-one, you get 53 million. There are also 24 million employed by the Federal Government, which leaves 29 million to do the work. The 12 million in the Armed Forces leave only 17 million to do the work. When you subtract from this the 15,765,000 who are in state and city offices and 520,000 in hospitals, mental institutions and similar places, the work force is reduced to 715,000. Fine, but—462,000 are bums and vagrants, leaving only 253,000 to do the work. There are 252,998 people in jail, leaving —you guessed it—just two people. You and me. And I'm getting tired.

9

"PHYSICIAN, HEAL THYSELF"

Our doctor is an eye, ear, nose, throat, and wallet specialist.

—Bessie and Beulah

A pipe burst in a doctor's house. He called the plumber. The plumber arrived, unpacked his tools, repaired the pipe, and handed the doctor a bill for six hundred dollars.

The doctor exclaimed, "This is ridiculous! I don't even make that much as a doctor!"

The plumber quietly replied, "Neither did I when I was a doctor."

An expectant mother was being rushed to the hospital but didn't quite make it. She gave birth to her baby on the hospital lawn. Later, the father received a bill, listing "Delivery Room Fee: $50.00."

He wrote the hospital and reminded them that the baby was born on the front lawn. A week passed, and a corrected bill arrived: "Greens Fee: $200.00."

Four out of five doctors say that if they were stranded on a desert island with no lawyers, they wouldn't need any aspirin.

My wife works for an Health Maintenance Organization. In her circles, the following story is making the rounds:

The scene is heaven, just outside the Pearly Gates, and three distinguished looking men are waiting to request admittance. Finally, St. Peter arrives and asks each man to identify himself and state his greatest contribution to the human race.

The first man says, "I am Christian Barnard, and I performed the first successful heart transplant. Because of my work, thousands of lives have been saved."

St. Peter seems duly impressed and says, "You may enter into your eternal rest." The gates open, celestial music is heard, and Dr. Barnard disappears.

The second man states, "I am Jonas Salk, and I discovered the polio vaccine which has saved millions of lives."

Once again, St. Peters seems impressed and says, "You may enter into your eternal rest." The gates open, celestial music is heard, and Dr. Salk disappears.

The third man says, "I am John Nelson, and I invented the notion of managed health care. Because of me, millions of dollars have been saved."

St. Peter strokes his beard and says, "You, too, may enter into your eternal rest—but only for three days."

Samuel F. B. Morse, who was an eminent painter before he invented telegraphy, once asked a physician friend to look at his painting of a man in death agony. "Well," Morse inquired, after the doctor had scrutinized it carefully, "what is your opinion?"

"Malaria," said the doctor.

The surgeon and the internist were rushing to catch the hospital elevator, but just as they got to it, the doors started to close. That's when the surgeon, instead of holding the doors open with his hands, stuck his head between them.

"Don't you think," asked the internist, "that sticking your head between the doors is an odd way of getting them to stop?"

"Not at all," replied the surgeon. "I need my hands to operate."

A physician went to heaven and met God, who granted him one question. So the physician asked, "Will health care reform ever occur?"

"I have good news and bad news," God replied. "The answer is yes, but not in your lifetime."

—Stephen Huber, MD, in *Medical World News*

Rodney Dangerfield says that he was so ugly when he was born that the doctor slapped his mother. He was so unlucky when he was a child, that his rocking horse died. He went to see his psychiatrist, and the psychiatrist said he wanted to check to see if Rodney had an inferiority complex. So they put him through a series of tests. Studying the test results, the doctor said, "I have some good news and some bad news. The good news is, you do not have a complex. The bad news is, you really are inferior!"

While she was enjoying a transatlantic ocean trip, Billie Burke, the famous actress, noticed that a gentleman at the next table was suffering from a bad cold. She asked him sympathetically, "Are you uncomfortable?"

The man nodded.

She said, "I'll tell you just what to do for it. Go back to your stateroom and drink lots of orange juice. Take two aspirins. Cover yourself with all the blankets you can find. Sweat the cold out. I know just what I'm talking about. I'm Billie Burke from Hollywood."

The man smiled warmly and said, "Thanks. I'm Dr. Mayo of the Mayo Clinic."

Aunt Aggie went to see her physician. She complained, "Doctor, I don't know what to do. You've got to help me; I just can't remember a thing. I've no memory at all. I hear something one minute, and the next minute I forget it. Tell me, what should I do?"

Her doctor replied, "Pay in advance!"

Brad Oxnam woke up in a hospital bed and called for his doctor. He insisted, "Doc, give it to me straight. How long have I got?"

The physician replied that he doubted that his patient would survive the night. Oxnam said, "Call for my lawyer." When the lawyer arrived, Oxnam asked for his physician to stand on one side of the bed, while the lawyer stood on the other. Oxnam then lay back and closed his eyes. When he remained silent for several minutes, the physician asked what was going on. Oxnam replied, "Jesus died with a thief on either side, and I thought I'd check out the same way."

My father became a podiatrist. When he was going to medical school he couldn't afford to buy the whole skeleton.

My dad is a doctor. He really wanted to become a tree surgeon but discovered that he couldn't stand the sight of sap.

Sign on a medical building:
Mental Health Prevention Center

Sign in a veterinarian's office:
The doctor is in. Sit. Stay.

My car skidded on wet pavement and struck a light pole. I was stunned and momentarily unable to speak. Several bystanders ran over to help me. A tall, middle-aged woman was the first to reach my car. She started to speak when a burly truck driver rushed in and pushed her back. "Step aside, lady," he shouted. "I've taken a course in first aid."

The woman watched him for a few minutes, then tapped his shoulder. "Pardon me," she said. "But when you get to the part about calling a doctor, I'm right here."

WHAT THE DOCTOR SAYS (AND WHAT HE REALLY MEANS)

- *This should be taken care of right away.* "I'd planned a trip to Hawaii next month but this is so easy and profitable that I want to fix it before it cures itself."
- *Welllll, what have we here?* . . . Since he hasn't the foggiest notion of what it is, the Doctor is hoping you will give him a clue.
- *We'll see.* "First I have to check my malpractice insurance."
- *Let me check your medical history.* "I want to see if you've paid your last bill before spending any more time with you."
- *Why don't we make another appointment later in the week?* "I'm playing golf this afternoon, and this is wasting my time."
- *I really can't recommend seeing a chiropractor.* "I hate those guys mooching in on our fees."
- *Hmmmmmmmm.* Since he hasn't the faintest idea of what to do, he is trying to appear thoughtful while hoping the nurse will interrupt. (Proctologists also say this a lot.)
- *We have some good news and some bad news.* The good news is he's going to buy that new BMW, and the bad news is you're going to pay for it.
- *Let's see how it develops.* "Maybe in a few days it will grow into something that can be cured."
- *Let me schedule you for some tests.* "I have a forty percent interest in the lab."
- *I'd like to have my associate look at you.* "He's going through a messy divorce and owes me a small fortune."
- *How are we today?* "I feel great. You, on the other hand, look like death warmed over."
- *I'd like to prescribe a new drug.* "I'm writing a paper and would like to use you for a guinea pig."
- *If it doesn't clear up in a week, give me a call.* "I don't know what on earth it is. I sure hope it will go away by itself."
- *That's quite a nasty-looking wound.* "I'm trying not to throw up."
- *This may smart a little.* "Last week two patients bit through their tongues."
- *Well, we're not feeling so well today, are we?* "I can't remember your name, nor why you are here."
- *This should fix you up.* "The drug salesman guaranteed that it kills all symptoms."

- *Everything seems to be normal.* "I guess I can't buy that new beach condo after all."
- *I'd like to run some more tests.* "I can't figure out what's wrong. Maybe the kid in the lab can solve this one."
- *Do you suppose all of this stress could be affecting your nerves?* He thinks you are crazy and is hoping to find a psychiatrist who will split fees.
- *Why don't you slip out of your things?* "I don't enjoy this any more than you do, but I've got to warm my fingers up somehow." The doctor may also resort to this when she hasn't had a good laugh all day.
- *There's a lot of that going around.* "Wow, that's the third one this week. I'd better learn something about this."
- *If those symptoms persist, call for an appointment.* "I've never heard of anything so disgusting. Thank goodness I'm off next week."

Overheard at my doctor's office:
- Excuse me, but what medical journal am I going to be in?
- Do you by chance still have those pills I gave you last week? They were a string of beads my wife wanted restrung.
- Yours is a common enough personality problem—you're obnoxious.
- Imagine! Telling me I'm in perfect health. How does a quack like that stay in business?
- Pulse, 80; temperature, 103; income, $100,000 net.
- There's really nothing unusual about your condition, Mr. Hendricks, except for the fact that it is so seldom encountered in a person who is still living.
- Agnes, I wish you wouldn't refer to hypodermic injections as your needlework.
- Dear me, Doctor, I've been waiting so long I think I've recovered.
- Take one upon going to bed, and the other if you wake up in the morning.
- Would you mind going to the medical convention with me this week, all expenses paid?

Overheard at the hospital:

- How are the children and my good dishes?
- Bill, go downstairs to the phone booth, call this place, ask them how I'm doing, and come back and tell me, will ya?
- Let me put it this way . . . if you were a building, you'd be condemned.
- I hope I'll get to the root of your trouble, Reverend, because I've had the same thing myself for years.
- What you have is a common cold, and there is no known cure for it. But cheer up—it may run into pneumonia—and we know what to do for that!
- She's a practical nurse—she only nurses rich old men.
- Don't worry about the hospital bills, dear—they're less than you would spend if you were well!
- I'll have you out of here in a week—one way or the other.

After giving a woman a full medical examination, the doctor explained his prescription as he wrote it out. "Take the green pill with a glass of water when you get up. Take the blue pill with a glass of water after lunch. Then just before bed, take the red pill with another glass of water."

"Exactly what is my problem, Doctor?" the woman asked.

"You're not drinking enough water."   —*Quote*

Sheila had been in therapy with the woman psychiatrist for twelve years, but finally the doctor dismissed her, explaining, "You don't need me anymore."

Three mornings later, Sheila made a frantic call. "Doctor," she moaned, "I need you. You're like a mother to me. I depend on you for everything!"

"Don't be silly," soothed the psychiatrist. "I'm not your mother. Where are you now?"

"I'm home having breakfast."

"What are you having?" asked the doctor.

"Just a cup of coffee."

"You call that breakfast?"

A psychiatrist ushers a man into his office. The man is five feet tall and weighs over four hundred pounds. He's wearing rubber hip-boots with spurs, leather lederhosen with bright purple suspenders, a cummerbund, a denim jacket with one sleeve torn off, and a woman's pillbox hat with a veil. One side of his face is clean-shaven, the other is bearded. There's a roofing nail in his nose, the eraser end of a pencil sticking out of his right ear, and perched on his left shoulder is a bantam chicken which has been plucked naked. As he walks into the office, the man lets out blood-curdling shrieks followed by piteous sobs and raucous laughter.

"Good day, sir," the psychiatrist says, "What seems to be the problem?"

"Well, Doc," the man begins, "I'm worried about my brother."

Two psychiatrists, one old and one young, both show up each day for work immaculately dressed and alert. At the end of the day, the young doctor is frazzled and disheveled; the older man, fresh as ever. "How do you do it?" the young psychiatrist asked his colleague. "You always stay so fresh after hearing patients all day."

The older doctor replied, "I never listen."

My psychologist complimented me. She said, "You're really coming along fine. Already you've progressed from 'everybody's out to get me' to 'nobody cares about me.'"

I ran into my psychologist yesterday. She was pushing a sofa down the street.

"Why the couch?" I asked.

"House call," she replied.

My cousin Ed is a psychiatrist. He firmly believes in shock treatment. He gives his clients their bills in advance.

THE PSYCHIATRIC HOTLINE

Hello, welcome to the Psychiatric Hotline.

If you are obsessive-compulsive, please press one repeatedly.

If you are co-dependent, please ask someone else to press two.

If you have multiple personalities, please press three, four, five, and six.

If you are paranoid-delusional, we know who you are and what you want. Just stay on the line so we can trace the call.

If you are schizophrenic, listen carefully and a little voice will tell you which number to press.

If you are manic-depressive, it doesn't matter which number you press. No one will answer.

So many things went wrong in my life that I thought I was a loser. So I started seeing a psychologist, Barbara Wallace, Ph.D., to work on improving my self-image.

One morning I rushed into Dr. Wallace's, shouting, "I'm not a loser anymore, Doc. I just dropped my English muffin on the kitchen floor. Look, it landed butter side up!"

Dr. Wallace carefully examined the evidence and then with a sigh handed it back. "Lowell," she said gently, "you buttered the wrong side."

After twelve years of therapy, my psychiatrist said something that brought tears to my eyes: "No hablo ingles." —Ronnie Shakes

10.
LAWYERS

The trouble with lawyer jokes is that lawyers don't think they're funny, and nobody else thinks they're jokes.

The two oldest jokes I know are about lawyers. One is a Breton legend about St. Yves, and the other is this early American story of "The Pope and the Devil."

An attorney observed a boy about nine years of age, diverting himself at play, whose eccentric appearance attracted his attention.

"Come here, my lad," he said. The boy accordingly came, and after chatting a bit, asked the attorney what case was to be tried next. "A case between the Pope and the devil," answered the attorney, "and which do you suppose will gain the action?"

"I don't know," said the boy, "I guess 'twill be a pretty tight squeeze. The Pope has the most money, but the devil has the most lawyers." —*The New England Almanac,* 1801

Yves was a saintly lawyer from Nantes and is now the patron saint of all lawyers. A popular Breton legend has it that when he died, he accompanied a group of deceased nuns to St. Peter's Gate. When the nuns asked to enter, St. Peter told them that Heaven already had plenty of nuns, so they would have to wait in Purgatory. Then Yves asked to enter, and St. Peter was overjoyed. "You can enter immediately. We don't yet have a single lawyer." —*New York Times*, June 7, 1991.

A modern retelling of the story of St. Yves.

A physician, theologian and lawyer each had become world renowned for the brilliance and creativity of their thought and erudition. Each had contributed major treatises advancing the scholarship in their respective professions. Each had been called upon by the world's leaders to volunteer their invaluable time and intellectual talents toward the betterment of human kind and to help foster peace among the peoples of the world. As fortune would have it, all three were traveling toward a summit meeting of the world's scholars to once again contribute their great talents, when their plane crashed and all three were instantly killed.

As the first of these great minds, the physician approached the heavenly gates, St. Peter rushed out to greet him, grasped his hand and welcomed him warmly as a "good and faithful servant" to his eternal reward in heaven. Similarly, as the theologian approached Heaven's portal, St. Peter again rushed out and embraced the great savant with a warm embrace of welcome to his eternal reward.

At that moment, the lawyer, still a ways down the road, was seen approaching the gates of Heaven. Spontaneously the skies opened up with great songs and joyous hymns, the cherubim and seraphim were seen overhead singing angelic praises with Hosannas and Alleluias, and golden trumpets announced the pending arrival of the famous barrister. A great carpet was rolled out. From the skies, accompanied by flourishes from harps, rose petals fluttered down to mark her pathway as she approached nearer and nearer to the heavenly gate.

From just inside the portal, the physician and theologian were taken aback and approached St. Peter.

"We don't want to complain," they said. "We are happy to be here in heaven for all eternity, but we have a question.

"On earth, the two of us, like this attorney, were world famous for our scholarship and wisdom. Like her, we contributed our time and talents to the betterment of humankind. Yet, when we reached the heavenly gates, all we received was a warm handshake and a quiet welcome to our heavenly reward. She, on the other hand, is being greeted by all of the heavenly cherubim and seraphim, a great golden carpet has been rolled out to mark her way to heaven, the golden trumpets are announcing her arrival. . . . Why is she entitled to such a glorious entry?"

"Shhh!" responded St. Peter, "You must remember, this is the first lawyer to make it to heaven in three hundred years!"

"I object, Your Honor, I object to every word!" shouted Taylor, jumping to his feet. "The witness's entire testimony is a tissue of lies. It must be stricken from the record!"

"No need," said the judge calmly, motioning the attorney to be seated. "I wasn't listening."

Perturbed over the absenteeism of his parishioners at the worship services, a minister handed his secretary some church stationery and a list of ten members who were absent the most often. He asked her to write each of them a letter concerning their absence.

Within a few days the minister received a letter from a prominent physician who apologized profusely for having been absent so often. He enclosed a check for one thousand dollars to cover contributions he would have made had he been present, promised to be there the following Sunday at church service and, further, to be there every Sunday thereafter unless providentially hindered. The usual complimentary closing with his signature was given.

However, the following note was at the bottom of the page: "P.S. Please tell your secretary there is only one *t* in dirty and no *c* in skunk."

County Coroner Peter Jensen had a celebrated disdain for the legal profession. In a recent criminal trial, he was called on to testify. He was questioned by the attorney for the defense.

"Doctor Jensen, is it not the case that you do not know my client personally?"

"That is so," said the coroner.

"Is it not true that you never even met him?"

"True," answered the doctor.

"In fact, isn't it the case that you don't even know whether my client is living or dead?" thundered the lawyer, gathering steam.

"Quite true," replied the doctor calmly. "For all I know his brain could be in a jar on my desk in the morgue, but the rest of him might well be out practicing law somewhere."

A bumper sticker on a Porsche:
PLEASE HIT ME. I'M A LAWYER.

Mrs. Jamison came bursting into her lawyer's office and declared, "I want a divorce."

"But why?" asked the startled lawyer. "Do you have grounds?"

"Sure do! A house in Paramus and a cabin in the Poconos."

"No, what I mean is, do you have some kind of grudge?"

"Not exactly, but there's a carport in front of the house," Mrs. Jamison replied.

"That's not what I mean," said the lawyer, exasperated. "Your husband, does he beat you up or something?"

"Oh, no, I'm the first one up every morning."

"Mrs. Jamison!" yelled the lawyer. "Can you just tell me why you want a divorce?"

"Yes! It's because I just can't carry on a decent conversation with the man!"

Max Marlowe had a client who believed in reincarnation.

In his will he left everything to himself.

Phil Witzel, the trial lawyer, came dragging in after a hard day at work. "It was a terrible day in court," he told his wife. "I exhibited moral outrage when I meant to show righteous indignation."

The judge was disgusted to hear that the jury was deadlocked in what had appeared to be an open and shut case. Finally, he called them into the courtroom and, discovering they were still undecided, he announced, "I discharge this jury."

One juror bellowed back, "You can't discharge me!"

"And why not?" responded the judge.

"Because I don't work for you," said the juror. Pointing to the lawyer for the defense, he boasted, "I was hired by that man!"

The judge asked Marty Land, the prospective juror, "Is there any reason why you could not serve as a juror in this case?"

"I don't want to be away from my job that long," replied Land.

"Can't they get along without you at work?"

"I'm sure they can, but I don't want them to realize it."

The defendant lamented, "All I stole was a turkey. Any lawyer worth his salt ought to be able to get me off."

"I'd have a considerably easier job," the public defender relied, "if you hadn't told the court about preheating your oven before going out that day."

My Uncle Sid was notorious for his bad luck. After he returned from the Korean War, he was arrested while driving through a small town in Georgia and accused of burglary. Despite his protestations, he was found guilty.

Before the judge passed sentence, Sid's desperate lawyer said, "Your honor, I submit that my client did not break into the house. He found the living room window open, inserted his right arm, and removed a few trifling articles—a newspaper and a tangerine. Now, my client's arm is not himself, and I don't feel you should punish him for an offense committed by one of his limbs."

"Your argument is an interesting one," said the judge, "albeit not particularly convincing. I'll tell you what I'll do. I will follow your tenuous logic. Therefore, I sentence the prisoner's right arm to one year's imprisonment. He can accompany the arm or not, as he chooses."

The judge looked rather pleased with himself, but Uncle Sid had the last laugh. He calmly removed his artificial right arm, handed it to the dumbstruck judge, and walked out of court with his lawyer.

A judge in a Kentucky court asked, "Colonel Beaufort, according to my records you never served a day in the army. Can you tell me how you came to be called Colonel?"

The witness replied, "Well, suh, it's like the 'Honorable' in front of your name. It doesn't mean a thing."

A rich man in Springfield, Illinois, insisted that a certain poor man owed him $2.50. When the claim was denied, the rich man decided to sue him. He contacted a young lawyer named Abraham Lincoln, who at first hesitated to take the case. On second thought he agreed—if he'd be paid a fee of $10.00 cash in advance. The client readily produced the money, whereupon Lincoln went to the poor man and offered him $5.00 if he would immediately settle the alleged debt. Thus Lincoln received $5.00 for himself, the poor man got $2.50, and the claim was satisfied. The rich man foolishly paid four times the original debt, just to gain his rights.

A minister, a scientist, and a lawyer were adrift on a life raft in the tropics. At last they sighted land, but the wind died down while they were still a short way off the beach. The lawyer volunteered to go ashore with a line and pull the raft to land. The minister knelt and prayed for his safety.

Then the lawyer dived in. His companion saw the black fin of a shark making straight for him. The shark disappeared, then came upon the other side, having passed under the swimmer. Then they saw an even bigger shark darting toward him, but this one also swerved just in time.

After the lawyer had reached shallow water, the minister said to the scientist: "There, you Doubting Thomas, there is proof of the power of prayer."

"Power of prayer, my foot!" retorted the scientist. "That was just professional courtesy."

—Alex F. Osborn

When the King of Siam came to America for an eye operation some years ago, his American surgeon, accustomed to setting prices somewhat by ability to pay, couldn't decide exactly how much to charge His Royal Highness: one thousand dollars, to be a good neighbor? Or ten thousand, to prove the operation was worth the trip? After all, a king is a king.

Someone suggested that he check with the king's New York lawyer who might have some thought on the matter, and so he did. "No problem," said the lawyer. "The king is an honorable man. Like you, he understands value. Simply send him an invoice with no amount indicated, and then add a handwritten footnote: 'The king can do no wrong.'"

He did. Back came a check for seventy-five thousand dollars! The surgeon was overjoyed. He bought his wife a mink coat, ordered a new Cadillac, and blew the rest on a three-month trip around the world.

Upon his arrival home, the surgeon, now happier but no richer, opened his mail. In it was a bill from the king's lawyer—with no amount indicated, but with a handwritten footnote: "The honorable doctor can do no wrong."

A jury consists of twelve persons chosen to decide who has the better lawyer.

—Robert Frost

The bridge between heaven and hell is in desperate need of repair, and St. Peter calls over to the devil, "It's your turn to fix it."

"Sorry," says the devil. "We are too busy fixing our heating system to worry about a little thing like a bridge."

"If you don't fix it," says St. Peter, "I'll have to sue you for breach of contract."

"Is that so?" says the devil. "And just where do you think you're going to find a lawyer?"

Lloyd Paul Stryker, the trial lawyer, was famous for his courtroom techniques and legal arguments. His opponents feared him; his clients loved him.

He began writing articles for law journals describing his techniques and when to best employ them. Over the years, he developed a standardized lecture for speaking engagements. He traveled with his chauffeur, an intelligent middle-aged individual. The chauffeur was proud to be associated with this renowned lawyer. After years of listening to the same lecture, the bold chauffeur announced to Stryker that he had heard the same speech so often he could give it himself. This idea so intrigued Stryker that he arranged the switch. Stryker suggested that the next time they were out of town and no one would recognize them, they would exchange duties.

A month later, the opportunity presented itself. The lawyer stood at the back of the room while the chauffeur was introduced to a filled room of expectant lawyers. The chauffeur waxed eloquent, demonstrating techniques and addressing intricate details with precision. At the end of his speech, the audience gave the chauffeur a standing ovation. It was truly a splendid speech!

The moderator indicated that there were still a few minutes left on the program and asked the appreciative audience if they had any questions for their honored guest. One lawyer ventured to ask a question concerning the legal precedents for one of the techniques referred to early in the speech. Stryker, standing in the back of the room, felt his heart sink. He could easily field the question, but there was no way to let his chauffeur know the answer. They were about to be exposed!

The chauffeur began to laugh. With just a tinge of mockery he responded, "Why, that is such a simple and well-known precedent all of you should know the answer! The common lay person should know the answer to that question. In fact, to demonstrate my premise, I am going to let my chauffeur give you your answer."

The judge stared at a hardened criminal. "Because of the gravity of this case," he said, "I am going to give you three lawyers."

"Never mind three lawyers," replied the defendant. "Just give me one good witness."

Cecil Rhodes was an enormously wealthy man. One day a journalist said to him, "You must be very happy."

Rhodes replied, "Happy?! No! I spent my life amassing a fortune, only to find I have spent half of it on doctors to keep me out of the grave, and the other half on lawyers to keep me out of jail!"

"What possible excuse can you give for acquitting this defendant?" the judge shouted at the jury.

"Insanity, Your Honor," replied the foreman.

"All twelve of you?"

Old Cyrus Barker was the richest man in town. When he became terminally ill, there was much speculation among the villagers concerning the extent of his wealth. And when Cyrus died, one of the town busybodies made it his business to run to the deceased's lawyer and ask, "How much money did old Cyrus leave?"

The lawyer replied, "All of it, my friend, all of it."

People who love sausage and respect the law should never watch either one being made.

When my son was a law student in Missouri, he didn't know what to think when he saw this sign on the door of a classroom: INALIENABLE RIGHTS CANCELLED TODAY.

Ed Cell, the new lab technician, arrives at his first day of work to find a row of a dozen men seated passively in straight-backed chains lined against the wall. Each man is wearing a gray pin-striped suit and vest, an Ivy League school necktie, and wingtip shoes. Each man holds a briefcase in his lap.

"Who are they?" the technician asks the scientist in charge of the lab.

"They're lawyers," the scientist replies. "We use them instead of rats."

Ed is appalled. "What do you mean, 'we use them instead of rats'?"

"Why not? They're perfect for it," the scientist says. "There are a lot more unemployed lawyers than rats. You can catch all you want by just hanging a dollar bill out the window. And there are other advantages. For one thing, the lab technicians never get emotionally attached to them. For another, lawyers breed faster than rats. Also, there's not as much public outrage over the use of lawyers in lab experiments."

"Besides," the scientist added, "there are some things that a rat just won't do."

Willard was having a terrible day on the golf course. His tee-shot disappeared into the trees. Moments later, he found his ball next to a man who was lying on the ground and moaning.

"I'm a lawyer," the injured man yelped, pressing his hand against the growing knot on his head. "This will cost you five thousand dollars."

"I'm terribly sorry," Willard replied contritely, "but I distinctly remember yelling 'fore.'"

"Well, OK," said the attorney. "You've got a deal."

Quentin O'Connor, the noted lawyer, died and went to heaven. He had no sooner gotten inside the Pearly Gates when a tremendous chorus of angels began to sing gloriously in his honor. The air was filled with a golden aura, clouds of incense wafted everywhere, and approaching O'Connor was St. Peter himself.

"O'Connor," said the celestial gatekeeper, "we have long been awaiting you. You are the first human being ever to break Methuselah's mark for longevity. You have lived 1,037 years."

"What are you talking about?" said O'Connor, astonished. "I died at the age of sixty-five."

"At the age of sixty-five?" said St. Peter, astonished in his turn, "Aren't you Quentin O'Connor? The corporate lawyer?"

"Yes."

"From Philadelphia?"

"Yes."

"But the Record Book has you down for 1,037 years."

"There must be some mistake. I'm only sixty-five."

"Something must be wrong," said St. Peter. "Let me study the book."

He did so and suddenly clapped his hand to his forehead. "Ah, I see where we made our mistake. We added up the hours you billed to your clients."

There was a young couple, very much in love. The night before they were to be married, they were tragically killed in an automobile accident. They found themselves at the Pearly Gates of Heaven being escorted in by St. Peter.

After a couple of weeks in Heaven, the prospective groom took St. Peter aside and said, "St. Peter, my fiancee and I are very happy to be in Heaven but we miss very much the opportunity to have celebrated our wedding vows. Is it possible for people in Heaven to get married?"

St. Peter looked at him and said, "I'm sorry, I've never heard of anyone here wanting to get married. I'm afraid you'll have to talk to the Lord about that. I can get you an appointment for two weeks from Wednesday."

On the appointed day, the guardian angels escorted the couple into the august presence of the Lord God Almighty, where the young lovers repeated their request. The Lord looked at them solemnly and said, "Wait five years and if you still want to be married, come back and we will talk about it again."

Five years went by, and the couple still very much wanting to be married, came back. Again the Lord God Almighty, said, "Please, you must wait another five years and then I will consider your request."

Finally, they came before the Lord God Almighty the third time, ten years after their first request, and asked the Lord again. This time, the Lord answered, "Yes, you may marry. This Saturday at 2:00 P.M., we will have a beautiful ceremony in the main chapel. The reception will be on me!"

The wedding went beautifully. All the guests thought the bride was beautiful.

Alas, the couple was married but a few weeks when they realized they had made a horrible mistake. They just could not stay married to one another.

So they made another appointment to see the Lord God Almighty, this time to ask if they could get a divorce in Heaven. When the Lord heard their request, he looked at them and said, "Look, it took us ten years to find a minister here. Do you have any idea how long it will take to find a lawyer?"

Sign in the office of an estate attorney:
        Where there's a will, there's delay.

There was a young lawyer who showed up at a revival meeting and found himself called upon to offer a prayer. Unprepared, he gave a prayer straight from his lawyer's heart:

"Stir up much strife amongst thy people, Oh Lord," he prayed, "lest thy servant perish."   —Senator Sam Ervin

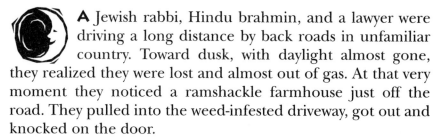 A Jewish rabbi, Hindu brahmin, and a lawyer were driving a long distance by back roads in unfamiliar country. Toward dusk, with daylight almost gone, they realized they were lost and almost out of gas. At that very moment they noticed a ramshackle farmhouse just off the road. They pulled into the weed-infested driveway, got out and knocked on the door.

The farmer welcomed them warmly, inviting them to stay the night. "There's only one problem," said the farmer, "I only have beds for two. One of you will have to sleep in the barn."

Being concerned for the comfort and well-being of his friends, the rabbi volunteered to go to the barn. Soon, they all retired for the night.

Twenty minutes later there was a knock at the door. There stood the rabbi, terribly embarrassed: "There are pigs in the barn," he explained, shaking his head sadly. "Pigs are forbidden in my religion. I find it impossible to stay the night in the barn."

Immediately the Hindu Brahmin volunteered to sleep in the barn, comforting the rabbi with understanding of the awkward situation.

Again they all retired, only to be aroused fifteen minutes later by another knock at the door. There stood a red-faced Brahmin, who with tears said: "To my terrible chagrin, I discover there are cows in the barn. Cows are sacred to my religion, and I cannot spend the night in their presence."

For a few embarrassing moments there was silence. Finally the lawyer realized he was the only choice left. "All right," he said reluctantly, "I'll sleep in the barn."

Once more they retired, but minutes later there was yet another knock at the door.

There stood the pigs and cows.

A mother and son were walking through a cemetery and passed by a headstone inscribed "Here lies a good lawyer and an honest man."

The little boy read the headstone, looked up at his mother, and asked, "Mommy, why did they bury two men there?"

Q: Why does California have the most lawyers and New Jersey
the most toxic waste dumps?
A: New Jersey got first pick.

The CEO of a large corporation was interviewing an engineer,
a physicist, and a lawyer for a major position. The CEO interviewed the engineer first, and asked him a long list of questions, ending with "How much is two plus two?"

The engineer excused himself, and made a series of measurements and calculations before returning to the board
room and announcing, "Four."

Next the CEO interviewed the physicist and asked the same
questions. Before answering the last question, the physicist
excused himself, went to the library, and did a great deal of
research. After consulting with the United States Bureau of
Standards and making many calculations, he also announced
that the answer was "Four."

Finally, the CEO interviewed the lawyer and asked the same
questions. At the end of his interview, after being asked the last
question, the lawyer drew all the shades in the room, looked
outside the door to see if anyone was there, checked the telephone for listening devices, and whispered, "How much do
you want it to be?"

Bill Kingsley walked into a curio shop and began to browse. A
brass rat on a shelf behind the counter attracted his attention.
He asked the shopkeeper for a price, and was told to make an
offer. Presently they agreed on a price, and the brass rat
changed hands.

The shopkeeper warned the customer as he took the
money, "This sale is final. If you leave the shop with the brass
rat, I won't take it back under any circumstances." The customer agreed and left with the rat.

As he walked home, he noticed that a live rat came scurry-
ing out of an alley and began to follow him. Soon there were
more, all following him and milling about his feet.

Kingsley began to run, but the rats kept up, and more joined the procession. After a few minutes, thousands of rats were chasing after him. Kingsley ran frantically for the river, and threw the brass rat into the water. The live rats followed the brass rat, and soon all had drowned.

Kingsley returned to the curio shop. As he entered, the shopkeeper shouted, "I told you, the sale was final! You cannot return the brass rat!"

Kingsley replied, "That's no problem. I just wondered if you had a brass lawyer."

An attorney passed on and found himself in Heaven. But he was not at all happy with his accommodations. He complained to St. Peter, who told him that his only recourse was to appeal his assignment. The attorney immediately advised that he intended to appeal, but was then told that he would be waiting at least three years before his appeal could be heard. The attorney protested that a three-year wait was unconscionable, but his words fell on deaf ears.

The lawyer was then approached by the devil. The devil told him that he would be able to arrange an appeal to be heard in a few days, if the attorney was willing to change venue to Hell. When the attorney asked why appeals could be heard so much sooner in Hell, he was told, "We have all the judges."

An attorney was sitting in his office late one night, when Satan appeared before him. The Devil told the lawyer, "I have a proposition for you. You can win every case you try, for the rest of your life. Your clients will adore you, your colleagues will stand in awe of you, and you will make embarrassing sums of money. All I want in exchange is your soul, your wife's soul, your children's souls, the souls of your parents, grandparents, and parents-in-law, and the souls of all your friends and law partners."

The lawyer thought about this for a moment, then asked, "What's the catch?"

About forty years ago, lawyer Lester Waterman was involved in a very difficult business case. He impatiently awaited the jury's verdict. When the jury came back with its decision, his client, "Nevada" Dipko, was out of town. As it turned out, Waterman and Dipko had won. Waterman immediately sent a telegram to his client, declaring, "Justice has triumphed!"

Dipko wired back, "Appeal at once!"

Hank Eisley, a pillar of the community, was the most popular businessman in a small town in Oregon. Hank's hardware store had been held up twice in one week by the same thief, which enraged this ordinarily humane and gentle store owner. When the crook returned a third time, Hank was waiting with a loaded shotgun. He shot and killed the robber.

Being a man of tender conscience, Hank was filled with remorse and pleaded guilty to first-degree murder. The punishment mandated by law was hanging. But the jury, all friends of Hank's, determined to save him in spite of himself. They brought in a verdict of not guilty.

"How in the world," said the judge, "can you bring in such a verdict when the defendant has pleaded guilty?"

"Well, your honor," said the foreman, "the defendant is such a liar that we can't believe him."

Lorenzo Dow, an evangelist of the last century, was on a preaching tour when he came to a small town one cold winter's night. He entered the local general store to get some warmth, and saw the town's lawyers gathered around the pot-bellied stove, discussing the town's business. Not one offered to allow Dow into the circle. Dow told the men who he was, and that he had recently had a vision in which he had gone on a tour of Hell, much like the traveler in Dante's Inferno. When one of the lawyers asked him what he had seen, he replied, "Very much what I see here: All of the lawyers are gathered in the hottest place."

Question: What's the difference between a lawyer and a boxing referee?

Answer: A boxing referee doesn't get paid more for a longer fight.

A lawyer was driving his big BMW down the highway, singing to himself, "I love my BMW, I love my BMW." Focusing on his car, not his driving, he smashed into a tree.

He miraculously survived, but the accident totaled his car. "My BMW! My BMW!" he sobbed.

A good Samaritan drove by and cried out, "Sir, sir, you're bleeding. And—your . . . your left arm is gone!"

Horrified, the lawyer screamed, "My Rolex! My Rolex!"

One day, a group of terrorists hijacked a Bar Association charter flight. The terrorists announced that, until their demands were met, they would release one lawyer per hour.

There is an interesting new novel about two ex-convicts. One of them studies to become a lawyer, the other decides to go straight.

A specially chartered plane was carrying the Pope, the Secretary General of the United Nations, the smartest lawyer in the world, and an Eagle Scout on an international goodwill tour, when it ran into a storm. When three of the engines and the hydraulic system started to fail, the pilot got on the plane's intercom.

"Gentlemen," he announced to his nervous passengers, "this aircraft is not going to reach its destination. Not only that, we have only four parachutes for the five of us on board. I hate to be selfish about this, but the early bird gets the worm." The passengers watched in horror as his parachute opened.

The Secretary General of the United Nations immediately pointed out that his survival was crucial to world peace and stability. "I must think of the peoples of the world . . . and save myself!" With that, he seized a parachute and jumped.

The lawyer immediately jumped up and pointed out that after all he was the smartest lawyer in the world. "At this very moment I have five cases before the U.S. Supreme Court on which hang the civil liberties of generations to come," he continued. "My career has been a beacon for thousands, and I cannot allow it to come to such an untimely end." Reaching into the pile, he too bailed out.

The Pope, a kindly man, turned to the Eagle Scout. "I've lived a long, full life and am quite prepared to meet my Lord and Savior. Son, you take that last parachute for yourself."

"Don't worry, your Holiness," said the Eagle Scout with a grin. "The world's smartest lawyer just jumped out of the plane wearing my knapsack."

Zorba Dukakis, a wealthy art dealer, discovers he has a terminal illness. He calls his three best friends, a doctor, a priest and a lawyer, and gives them five hundred thousand dollars apiece. He tells them, "I know I can't take it with me, but I want to try. I want your assurances that each of you will put this half million in cash into my casket at my funeral and have it buried with me."

A month later, Zorba died. Following the funeral, the three friends got together. The doctor said, "I've got to confess, I didn't put the money in the casket. I gave it to the hospital's foundation to build a new children's wing."

The priest said, "I've got to confess too. I didn't put that half million in the casket either. I gave it to the Little Sisters of the Poor to build a new treatment center at the nursing home."

The lawyer said, "Well, I'm aghast. I just want you to know that he was buried with my personal check for the full $500,000 in his casket!"

 If a lawyer and an IRS agent were both drowning, and you could only save one of them, would you go to lunch or read the newspaper?

A criminal with a long record of transgressions was on trial for his latest crime. The jury found him guilty on thirty-three counts and the judge sentenced him to 189 years. Realizing that even with time off for good behavior he would be over one hundred when he was released, the prisoner burst into tears. Noting this display of remorse, the judge reconsidered. He said, "I didn't mean to be so severe. Thinking it over, I can see that I've imposed an extremely harsh sentence. So you don't have to serve the whole time." The prisoner beamed with new-found hope, until the judge leaned toward him and said, "Just do as much as you can."

A young attorney was attending a funeral service, and stood near the back. Another mourner arrived late and asked the lawyer, "Where are they in the service?"

The attorney gestured at the minister and replied, "He's just opening for the defense."

As your attorney, it is my duty to inform you that it is not important that you understand what I'm doing or why you're paying me so much money. What's important is that you continue to do so.   —*Hunter S. Thompson's Samoan Attorney*

Question: While driving down a desert highway, you see the worst terrorist in the world on one side of the road, and a lawyer on the other. Which do you hit first?
Answer: The terrorist. Business before pleasure.

Some American academics, discussing the Six Day War with an Israeli general, were eager to know how it had ended so quickly. The general told them, "We had a crack regiment at the most sensitive front. It was made entirely of lawyers and accountants. When the time came to charge, boy, did they know how to charge!"

The two law partners were having lunch one day, when one of them suddenly jumped up and exclaimed, "Oh, no! I've got to get back to the office! I left the safe unlocked!"

The other lawyer looked at his partner calmly and replied, "What are you worried about? We're both here."

Two boys were walking in the woods when one boy spied a large walnut on the ground. When the other boy picked it up, they started to argue. One boy said, "The nut is mine, I saw it first."

The other boy said, "No, it's mine, I've already got it."

They were just about to fight when, luckily, along came a lawyer. The boys appealed to the lawyer to adjudicate their dispute.

The lawyer thanked the boys for the opportunity and, picking up the nut, said, "I will settle your dispute this way. Because you saw the nut first, I will give you this half. Because you had the nut in your possession, I will give you this half. And for my fee, I'll keep the nut's meat."

Rev. Winston Jackson, pastor of the First Assembly of God Church, reported for jury duty. The minister asked to be excused. "On what grounds?" asked the judge.

"Because I'm prejudiced," replied the preacher. "I hate to admit it," said the cleric, pointing to the man seated in front of the judge, "but I took one look at those shifty eyes, Your Honor, and I knew right away he was just as guilty as sin."

"Sit down," barked the judge. "The man you're pointing at happens to be the defendant's lawyer."

Question: What do you get when you cross a librarian with a lawyer?
Answer: All the information you need—but you can't understand a word of it.

A quote attributed to one of America's founders, John Adams, in the play *1776* goes like this: "I have come to the conclusion that one useless man is called a disgrace, two useless men are called a law firm, and three or more become a Congress."

The police accused Brick Carlson of stealing a Mercedes Benz. After a long trial, the jury acquitted him. Later that day Carlson came back to the judge who had presided at the hearing. "Your Honor," he said, "I wanna get out a warrant for that dirty lawyer of mine."

"Why?" asked the judge. "He won your acquittal. Why do you want to have him arrested?"

"Well, Your Honor," replied Carlson, "I didn't have the money to pay his fee, so he went and took the car I stole."

There is a finite number of physicians that a population of fixed size will support. The same theory holds for teachers and engineers. However, this principle does not seem to apply to lawyers. The more you have, the more you need.

These two guys, George and Harry, set out in a hot air balloon to cross the Atlantic Ocean. After thirty-seven hours in the air, George says, "Harry, we better lose some altitude so we can see where we are." Harry lets out some of the hot air in the balloon, and the balloon descends to below the cloud cover.

George says, "I still can't tell where we are. Let's ask that guy on the ground."

So, Harry yells down to the man, "Hey, could you tell us where we are?"

The man on the ground yells back "You're in a balloon, a hundred feet up in the air."

George turns to Harry and says, "That guy must be a lawyer."

Harry says, "How can you tell?"

George says, "Because the advice he gave us is one hundred percent accurate and totally useless."

The day after a verdict had been entered against his client, the attorney rushed to the judge's chambers. The lawyer demanded that the case be reopened. He said that he had new evidence that made a huge difference in his defense.

"What new evidence could you have?" said the judge.

The attorney replied, "My client has an extra ten thousand dollars, and I just found out about it!"

A lawyer's dog, running around unleashed, beelines for a butcher shop and steals a roast. The butcher goes to the lawyer's office and asks, "If a dog running unleashed steals a piece of meat from my store, do I have a right to demand payment for the meat from the dog's owner?"

The lawyer answers, "Absolutely."

The butcher says, "Then you owe me $12.50. Your dog was loose and stole a roast from me today." The lawyer, without a word, writes the butcher a check for $12.50.

Two days later, butcher opens the mail and finds an envelope from the lawyer. Inside is a note that reads: "$200 due for legal consultation."

There is no doubt that my lawyer is honest. For example, when he filed his income tax return last year, he declared half of his salary as "unearned income."

—Michael Lara

When an elementary school teacher heard children wailing , she rushed to the playground to see what was wrong. She found Marc and Chuck standing next to Laura, who was crying furiously.

Marc told her, "Chuck took Laura's orange. Then Laura hit him on the head and called him dirty names, and Marc kicked her in the stomach."

The teacher replied, "Then, we'll all have to go to the principal's office. Where is the orange now?"

Marc smiled and produced the orange from his pocket. "I have the orange. I'm Laura's lawyer."

One day in Contract Law class, Professor Diamond asked one of his better students, "Now if you were to give someone an orange, how would you go about it?"

The student replied, "I'd say, 'Here's an orange.'"

The professor was livid. "No! No! Think like a lawyer!"

The student pondered for a moment, then said, "OK, I'd tell him, 'I hereby give and convey to you all and singular, my estate and interests, rights, claim, title, claim and advantages of and in, said orange, together with all its rind, juice, pulp, and seeds, and all rights and advantages with full power to bite, cut, freeze, and otherwise eat the same, or give the same away with or without the pulp, juice, rind and seeds, anything herein before or hereinafter or in any deed, or deeds, instruments of whatever nature or kind whatsoever to the contrary in anywise notwithstanding.'"

The professor beamed.

My parents sent my brother through law school. He graduated. Now he's suing them for wasting seven years of his life.

—Mike Binder

Osgood Thistlebank called his lawyer, Sydney Fellows, one day to ask a routine question about an ongoing matter with which both parties were familiar. Fellows gave a quick routine answer, and the entire phone conversation took less than a minute. Osgood was understandably a little dismayed to find a bill from the lawyer in his mail a few days later. The bill charged for one quarter hour of consultation time, the minimum billing increment, at the lawyer's rate of two hundred dollars per hour. Osgood grumbled considerably as he wrote out the check for fifty dollars.

Two weeks later, while out for a walk, Osgood happened to walk past the lawyer's house. Fellows was outside, watering his lawn, and waved to his client. Osgood walked over and said, "Nice day, isn't it?—Wait a minute. *Don't answer that!*"

Excerpts from letters written by lawyers at firms in Southern California:

- Please find enclosed copies of the plaintiff.
- Plaintiff weighs 125 pounds with a driver's license.
- The bus operator claims he ran over the plaintiff because he was behind schedule.
- The court, in its discretion, is permitted to strike irrelevant, redundant and redundant matters.
- Have you suffered a loss of smell in either ear?
- He suffered a fracture to his left foreman.
- Please notify us immediately if you do not receive this letter.
- It appears that we will have a difficult time obtaining a defense verdict if this case is tried before a live jury.
- We are refraining from providing you with copies of the medical records, which are enclosed.
- Enclosed is our status report on this matter. Please be advised that this case is a mess.
- Plaintiff states it is her belief that her neck injuries were caused by a jerk.

—reported by Steve Kluger in *Say the Darndest Things*

Victor Sterling, a very rich contractor, was shaken by the doctor's diagnosis. The physician said that unless Victor had a heart transplant, he had only weeks, perhaps days, to live. Fortunately, advised the doctor, there were several hearts available, although each was quite expensive.

"How much?" Victor asked.

"Well, I've got one heart of an individual who was thirty-five years old," said the surgeon. "He exercised moderately and never ate fatty foods. It's in pretty good shape and goes for only one hundred thousand dollars."

"What else do you have?" Victor asked, "Anything better?"

"There is the heart of a twenty-year-old Olympic decathlon winner. He never smoked or drank. He was in perfect physical condition. That one will cost $250,000."

"Look Doc, this is my life," said the patient. "What's the best you got?"

"Well there is one heart, very rare but the very best. It belonged to a sixty-five-year-old man. He drank and smoked to excess, he was thirty pounds overweight and he never exercised. His cholesterol count was over three hundred. This heart goes for one million dollars."

"Why is it so expensive?" asked the patient.

"It's the heart of an attorney," explained the surgeon. "It's never been used."

Franklin Walters was shocked to learn that he had lost his case. He was even more upset when his lawyer handed him the bill. "It says here that I have to pay you five thousand dollars now and five hundred a month for the next five years! It's as if I were buying a top-of-the-line Mercedes!"

The lawyer smiled and replied, "You are."

I broke a mirror in my house. I'm supposed to get seven years of bad luck, but my lawyer thinks he can get me five.

—Steven Wright

All during the dinner party, whenever he was engaged in conversation with other guests, people kept interrupting Dr. Sinclair, the young cardiologist who had recently moved into the community, to ask him medical questions about themselves or members of their families. It happened once again while he was chatting with Phillips, a local attorney.

Turning back to the lawyer after responding to the interrupting question, he inquired: "What can I do to stop people from asking me medical questions outside of my office? Do people ask you legal questions?"

"Oh, indeed they do," replied Phillips, "But most of them stopped after I started sending them legal bills."

That seemed a bit harsh to the young physician, and upon reaching his office the next morning, he was still ambivalent about whether to give it a try—until he opened his mail and found a bill from Phillips.

Maynard Begley, the wealthy patent attorney, had a lovely summer house in rural Maine. Each summer, the lawyer would invite a different friend to spend a week or two up at this place.

One year, he invited a Czech friend to stay with him. The two friends had a splendid time in the country, rising early and hiking in the great outdoors.

Early one morning, the lawyer and his Czech companion went out to pick berries for their morning breakfast. As they went around the berry patch, along came two huge bears, a male and a female.

Well, the lawyer, seeing the two bears, immediately dashed for cover. His friend, though, wasn't as fleet afoot, and the male bear reached him and swallowed him whole.

The lawyer ran back to his Mercedes, tore into town as fast has he could, and got the local sheriff. The sheriff grabbed his shotgun and dashed back to the berry patch with the lawyer.

Sure enough, the two bears were still there.

"He's in that one!" cried the lawyer, pointing to the male, while visions of lawsuits from his friend's family danced in his head. He just had to save his friend.

The sheriff looked at the bears, and without batting an eye, leveled his gun, took careful aim, and shot the female.

"What'd ya do that for?" exclaimed the lawyer. "I told you my friend was in the other bear!"

"Exactly," replied the sheriff, "and would you believe a lawyer who told you the Czech was in the male?"

 NASA was interviewing professionals to be sent to Mars. Only one could go—and couldn't return to Earth.

The first applicant, a physician, was asked how much he wanted to be paid for going, "A million dollars," he replied, "I want to leave it for the advancement of medical research."

The next applicant, an engineer was asked the same question. He asked for two million dollars. "I want to give a million to my family," he explained, "and I'll donate the other million to MIT."

The last applicant was a lawyer. When asked how much money he wanted, he whispered in the interviewer's ear, "Three million dollars."

"Why so much more than the others?" asked the interviewer.

The lawyer replied, "If you give me three million, I'll give you a million, I'll keep a million, and we'll send the doctor to Mars."

Joe Hanover was resting in his usual chair at the barbershop, as young Dr. Armstrong was completing his weekly sartorial visit. The conversation among the barbershop habitués had turned to the condition of a lawyer they both knew, Benson by name, who had suffered a massive heart attack only a few days earlier.

"He's not doing too well," the young doctor noted solemnly, "In fact, Benson is lying at death's door."

"Now that's something," commented Hanover. "At death's door and still lying!"

Will Rogers never met a lawyer!

Two attorneys, Cary Babcock and Gordon Lee, took a safari vacation in the African backcountry. One day, they took a rest, removed their packs, and leaned their rifles against a tree. They were startled when a large, hungry-looking lion emerged from the jungle and began eyeing them with anticipation.

It was clear that the attorneys' rifles were too far away to do them any good. Babcock began to remove his shoes, and Lee asked him why he was doing that.

Babcock replied, "Because I can run faster without them."

Lee declared, "I don't care how fast you can run. You'll never outrace that lion."

The now barefoot Babcock told him, "I don't have to out-run the lion. I just have to outrun you."

A farmer noticed that his prize cow was missing from the field through which the railroad passed. He filed suit against the railroad company for the value of the cow. The railroad company sent a big city lawyer to the town nearest the farmer to defend the case.

The trial was to be conducted before the justice of the peace in the back room of the general store. The attorney immediately cornered the farmer and tried to get him to settle out of court. The farmer finally agreed to take half of his original claiming.

After the farmer signed the release and took the check, the young lawyer couldn't help but gloat a little over his success. He said, "I hate to tell you this, but I put one over on you. The engineer was asleep and the fireman was in the caboose when the train went through your farm that morning. I didn't have one witness to put on the stand, and I couldn't have won the case."

The old farmer replied, "Well, I'll tell you, young feller, I was a little worried about winning that case myself. That durned cow wandered home this morning!"

After graduating from law school and passing the bar exam, Earl Schein went to work for his father. Several years later, the elder Schein retired and Earl took over his father's practice. One evening, in a mood of obvious elation, he rushed to his father's home. "Dad, I've got great news," he shouted. "I settled that old Anderson suit at last."

"Settled it!" cried the astonished father. "Why, I gave you that case as an annuity for life."

A lawyer named Reginald Strange had just purchased a new cemetery plot for himself and was shopping for a tombstone. After he had made his selection, the stone cutter asked him what inscription he would like on it.

"Here lies an honest man and a lawyer," responded the lawyer.

"Sorry, but I can't do that," replied the stone cutter. "In this state, it's against the law to bury two people in the same grave. However, I could carve in foot-high letters, 'Here lies an honest lawyer.'"

"But that won't leave room for my name. How will people know who it is?" protested the lawyer.

"No problem," retorted the stone cutter. "People will read the inscription and say, 'That's Strange!'"

From an actual courtroom transcript:
Question: Do you know how far pregnant you are right now?
Answer: I will be three months on the eighth of November.
Question: Apparently then, the date of conception was August eighth?
Answer: Yes.
Question: What were you and your husband doing at that time?

Called for jury duty, Harriet Trenneman asked to be excused on the grounds that she was opposed to capital punishment.

"But this is a civil suit," explained the judge. "A woman is suing her ex-husband. It seems she put money aside for six years to buy herself a mink coat, but he took it and blew it all on another woman."

"In that case," she replied, "I guess I could change my views on capital punishment."

A lawyer is someone who writes a sixty-page document and calls it a brief.

11.
COPS & ROBBERS

The measure of a man's character is what he would do if he knew he would never be found out. —Thomas Macaulay

Not long ago, a young immigrant disembarked in New York Harbor from Ireland. Newly arrived, he started across one of those busy city streets—against the light.

One of New York's finest, a big police officer, grabbed him and asked, "And where d'you think you're going?"

He said, "I'm only trying t' get to the other side of the street there!"

When that New York police officer, Irish himself, heard that brogue, he said, "Now, lad, wait. You stay here until the light turns green, and then you go to the other side of the street."

"Ah," the young fellow said, "the light turns green."

The opposing light turned orange for just a few seconds, as it does, and then the light in question turned green, and he started out across the street. He got about fifteen feet out, then turned around and shouted, "They don't give them Protestants much time, do they?"

I grew up in a neighborhood that was so tough that when the men were drafted into the Army, every time they fired a weapon on the firing range they wiped off their fingerprints.

I grew up in a neighborhood so rough, I learned to read by the light of a police helicopter. That neighborhood is so dangerous, America On Line can't even deliver e-mail there.

—Bill Jones

Bill Watson, a longtime sales representative became dissatisfied with his career and decided to become a police officer. Several months later, a friend asked him how he liked his new job. "Well," he replied, "the pay isn't great and the hours are long, but one thing I really like is that the customer is always wrong."

When the Police League of Indiana sponsored a Best Speeding Alibi contest, one honorable mention award went to an exasperated father who was stopped with a load of fighting, squalling children in his back seat. He had told the officer, "I was trying to get away from all the noise behind me."

An ad in our community's weekly newspaper offered "a thoroughbred police dog" for only forty dollars. This seemed like a reasonable price, so I called the number in the ad and made an appointment to see the dog. Imagine my dismay when the dog in question looked like a cross between a poodle and a schnauzer. A bit outraged, I asked, "What do you mean, calling that mutt a thoroughbred police dog?"

"Don't be deceived by his looks," was the solemn reply. "He's under cover."

Pastor Jenkins found a dead mule in front of his home and phoned the police about it. The officer on the desk knew the minister. Thinking to have some fun, the officer said, "I thought you members of the clergy took care of the dead."

The minister was not amused. "We do," he replied testily, "but it is always proper to first get in touch with the relatives."

An officer in a police helicopter spotted a car speeding down the Interstate. He radioed his partner on the ground and the patrol officer in the car stopped the speeder and began writing a citation.

"How in the world did you know I was speeding?" the man asked.

The patrol officer didn't say anything but pointed skyward.

"Aww," the man moaned. "You mean, He's turned against me, too?"

"That's quite a slice you had on that golf ball," said the angry police officer to the sheepish duffer. "It curved clear off the course and broke the windshield of my squad car. Just what do you intend to do about it?"

"Well," said the golfer, "I was thinking that probably the best thing to do would be to try moving my thumb a little farther up on the club."

Stopped by a police officer for driving without a taillight, the driver was visibly distressed.

"Don't take it so hard," said the officer, "it's only a minor offense."

"That's not the point," replied the troubled driver. "What worries me is, what's happened to my trailer and my wife?"

A sheriff's deputy pulled alongside a speeding car on the freeway. Glancing at the car, he was astounded to see that the woman at the wheel was knitting!

The deputy cranked down his window and yelled, "PULL OVER!"

"NO," the woman yelled back, "IT'S A SCARF!"

My grandfather invented the burglar alarm, but someone stole it from him.

—Victor Borge

RULES FOR BANK ROBBERS

According to the FBI, most modern-day bank robberies are "unsophisticated and unprofessional crimes," committed by young male repeat offenders who apparently don't know the first thing about their business. This information was included in an amusing article titled "How Not to Rob a Bank," by Tim Clark, which appeared in the 1987 edition of *The Old Farmers Almanac.*

Clark reported that in spite of the widespread use of surveillance cameras, seventy-six percent of bank robbers use no disguise, eighty-six percent never study the bank before robbing it, and ninety-five percent make no long-range plans for concealing the loot. Thus, he offered this advice to would-be bank robbers, along with examples of what can happen if the rules aren't followed:

- *Pick the right bank.* Clark advises that you don't follow the lead of the fellow in Anaheim, California, who tried to hold up a bank that was no longer in business and had no money. On the other hand, you don't want to be too familiar with the bank. A California robber ran into his mother while making his getaway. She turned him in.

- *Approach the right teller.* Granted, Clark says, this is harder to plan. One teller in Springfield, Massachusetts, followed the holdup man out of the bank and down the street until she saw him go into a restaurant. She hailed a passing police car, and the police picked him up. Another teller was given a holdup note by a robber, and her father, who was next in line, wrestled the man to the ground and sat on him until authorities arrived.

- *Don't sign your demand note.* Demand notes have been written on the back of a subpoena issued in the name of a bank robber in Pittsburgh, on an envelope bearing the name and address of another in Detroit, and in East Hartford, Connecticut, on the back of a withdrawal slip giving the robber's signature and account number.

- *Beware of dangerous vegetables.* A man in White Plains, New York, tried to hold up a bank with a zucchini. The police captured him at his house, where he showed them his "weapon."

- *Avoid being fussy.* A robber in Panorama City, California, gave a teller a note saying, "I have a gun. Give me all your twenties in this envelope." The teller said, "All I've got is two twenties." The robber took them and left.
- *Don't advertise.* A holdup man thought that if he smeared mercury ointment on his face, it would make him invisible to the cameras. Actually, it accentuated his features, giving authorities a much clearer picture. Bank robbers in Minnesota and California tried to create a diversion by throwing stolen money out of the windows of their cars. They succeeded only in drawing attention to themselves.
- *Take right turns only.* Avoid the sad fate of the thieves in Florida who took a wrong turn and ended up on the Homestead Air Force Base. They drove up to a military police guardhouse and, thinking it was a tollbooth, offered the security men money.
- *Provide your own transportation.* It is not clever to borrow the teller's car, which she carefully described to police. This resulted in the most quickly solved bank robbery in the history of Pittsfield, Massachusetts.
- *Don't be too sensitive.* In these days of exploding dye packs, stuffing the cash into your pants can lead to embarrassing stains, Clark points out, not to mention severe burns in sensitive places—as bandits in San Diego and Boston painfully discovered.
- *Consider another line of work.* One nervous Newport, Rhode Island, robber, while trying to stuff his ill-gotten gains into his shirt pocket, shot himself in the head and died instantly. Then there was the case of the hopeful criminal in Swansea, Massachusetts, who, when the teller told him she had no money, fainted. He was still unconscious when the police arrived.

In view of such ineptitude, it is not surprising that in 1978 and 1979, for example, federal and state officers made arrests in sixty-nine percent of the bank holdups reported.

—Kevin Hickman

In Harrieta, Michigan, a thirty-year-old man entered a Methodist Church on Sunday morning and held the congregation hostage with a rifle.

While police were en route, one parishioner asked how much the gun cost; he said five hundred dollars. Another offered him five hundred dollars for it, and he accepted. The hostages took up a collection for the five hundred dollars, he handed the rifle over . . . and the police arrested him.

Your sins will find you out:
- The Ohio thief was sure that the church was a safe hideout. Just inside he spied a rope hanging. Up he climbed, only to hear the church bell ringing his whereabouts.
- A Mexico City man snatched a woman's purse and dashed into a doorway to hide. It turned out to be the door of a police station, where he was questioned and later identified by his victim.
- In New York, a man picked up an alarm clock and headed for the nearest exit. The clock, concealed under his coat, went off before he could get out of the store.

From the *Pittsburgh Press*:
George Shamblin insisted to police that he was trying to save his wife from drowning when he threw rocks at her as she struggled in the Kanawha River. "I was trying to drive her back to shore," he said.

A cement mixer collided with a prison van on the Kingston Bypass. Motorists are asked to be on the lookout for sixteen hardened criminals. —Ronnie Corbett

The lady across the hall tried to rob a department store . . . with a pricing gun. . . . She said, "Give me all of the money in the vault, or I'm marking down everything in the store . . ."
—Steven Wright

Years ago, the people of Arizona were being plagued by José Ortega, a Mexican bandit who again and again snuck across the border and robbed their banks. With each successful robbery, he became bolder and bolder. And yet the Arizona lawmen could never catch him before he skedaddled back across the border to his hide-out in the mountains of Mexico. Finally, in frustration the Bankers Association hired a famous Pinkerton detective and sent him down into Mexico to get back their money.

The detective set off for the small mountain town reputed to be the hideout of Ortega. The detective found the town, strode into the saloon, and there standing at the bar he found the man he was after, José Ortega.

The detective pulled his pistol and exclaimed, "Aha! Now I've got you!"

Thrusting his gun into the bandit's face, he shouted, "Where have you hidden the millions you have stolen from our banks in Arizona? Tell me, or I'll blow your head off!"

At this point another man, Juan Garcia, who was also in the saloon, stepped up to the detective and said. "Sir, you are wasting your time talking to José like this. He doesn't understand a word of English. He has no idea what you just said. Would you like me to translate for you?"

The detective said, "Yes, of course. Say this to him, 'Tell me where the money is or I'll shoot you dead.'"

So Juan Garcia turned to José and jabbered away at him for a few moments in Spanish. There was much arm waving and chattering as a terrified José told Juan in Spanish that if he would lead the man to the corral a mile out of town, climb down into the well and remove the red brick, there he would find over three million dollars in gold.

When José was finished speaking, Juan turned to the detective and said, "I'm sorry, Señor, but he says he has absolutely no idea where the gold is."

When a Jackson, California, lumber yard owner found that his office safe had jammed, he called the nearby state prison where my son Matt was once a guard and asked whether any of the inmates might know how to open it. Soon, a convict and a prison guard showed up at the office. The inmate spun the dials, listened intently, and calmly opened the safe door.

"I can't thank you enough," said the lumberman. "How much do you figure I owe you?"

"Well," said the prisoner, "the last time I opened a safe, I got twenty-five thousand dollars."

It's a quiet Saturday afternoon in Goose Bend, Wyoming in 1876, and the boys are having a leisurely drink when Ol' Jeb comes racing into the saloon hollering, "Big John is coming to town! Big John is coming to town!"

The frenzied crowd rushes for the door. Drinks are abandoned on the bar. Hand-rolled cigarettes lie smoldering where they were dropped. Dancing girls shriek in panic and flee out the back way. The bartender locks up the liquor and is barring the front door.

Before the bartender can secure the saloon, however, a man comes galloping down Main Street on a huge bull buffalo and reins up out front. He dismounts, grabs the buffalo by the horns, bites down on its upper lip, kicks it in the ribs, and orders "Stay!" The buffalo cowers submissively at the hitching post.

The man rips the saloon's bat-wing doors from their hinges, stomps in, and catches the bartender heading for the back door. "Hold up!" the stranger orders. "I crave red-eye."

Momentarily paralyzed with fear, the bartender eyeballs the stranger. He is six and a half feet tall, and outweighs a full-grown grizzly. He wears rattlesnake chaps, a greasy rawhide shirt, a filthy torn Stetson, and steel-tipped fighting boots, and he smells like he hasn't as much as looked at a bathtub in years. On one hip he's carrying a sawed-off 12-gauge shotgun and on the other is a 32-inch Arkansas toothpick. On his scarred, stubbled face is a look of cruel, insane meanness.

"Right away, sir." The trembling bartender fetches a bottle.

The stranger seizes the bottle, smashes off the neck on the edge of the bar, tilts it back, and drains the contents in one gulp.

"W-would you like another, sir?" the bartender stammers.

The stranger wipes his mouth with the back of his hand. "Not on your life! I'm getting the heck out of here." The stranger glances around anxiously. "Haven't ya heard? Big John is coming to town!"

12.
GOVERNMENT & MILITARY

Most problems don't exist until a government agency is created to solve them.

—Kirk Kirkpatrick

POLITICAL SYSTEMS DEFINED
- *Feudalism.* You have two cows. Your lord takes some of the milk.
- *Pure Democracy.* You have two cows. Your neighbors decide who gets your milk.
- *Representative Democracy.* You have two cows. Your neighbors pick someone to decide who gets your milk.
- *Pure Communism.* You have two cows. Your neighbors help take care of them, and you all share the milk.
- *Pure Socialism.* You have two cows. The government takes them and puts them in a barn with everybody else's cows. You have to take care of all the cows. The government gives you as much milk as you need.
- *Bureaucratic Socialism.* You have two cows. The government takes them and puts them in a barn with everybody else's cows. They are cared for by ex-chicken farmers. You have to take care of the chickens the government took from the chicken farmers. The government gives you as much milk as the regulations say you should need.
- *Fascism.* You have two cows. The government takes both, hires you to care for them, and sells you the milk.

- *Dictatorship.* You have two cows. The government takes both and drafts you.
- *Bureaucracy.* You have two cows. At first, the government regulates what you can feed them and when you can milk them. Then it pays you not to milk them. Then it takes both, shoots one, milks the other and pours the milk down the drain. Then it requires you to fill out forms accounting for the missing cows.
- *Pure Anarchy.* You have two cows. Either you sell the milk at a fair price, or your neighbors try to take the cows and kill you.
- *Anarcho-Capitalism.* You have two cows. You sell one and buy a bull.
- *Surrealism.* You have two giraffes. The government requires you to take harmonica lessons.

You may not agree with every department in the government, but you really have to hand it to the IRS.

We are finding it increasingly difficult to support both the government and family on a single salary.

Taxpayers: A special class of people who don't have to pass civil service examinations in order to work for the government.

Someone has noted that besides being Income Tax Day, April 15 is also the day the Titanic sank and the day that Lincoln was assassinated.

Congressman Santos began his speech like this. "Ladies and gentlemen, please let me tax your memories for a moment—"

Someone in the crowd interrupted, "Well, you've tried to tax everything else!"

If you think you're getting too much government, just be thankful you're not getting as much as you're paying for.

—Will Rogers

What gets me is that estimated tax return. You have to guess how much you are gonna make. You have to fill it out, fix it up, sign it, send it in. I sent mine in last week. I didn't sign it. If I have to guess how much I'm gonna make, let them guess who sent it.

—Jimmy Edmondson (Professor Backwards)

Have you gotten your income tax papers yet? They've done away with all those silly questions now. There are only three questions on the form:

1. How much did you earn?
2. How much do you have left?
3. Send it in.

—Sandy Powell

The politician's promises of yesterday are the taxes of today.

—Mackenzie King

Dateline, Sacramento: Today, the California governor signed into law a billion-dollar tax break that will cut $60.00 off the tax bill of a family earning $40,000 per year, and $300.00 off the taxes of a family earning $100,000 a year. Which proves once again, it pays to be rich.

—Will Durst

A presidential aide said, "Mr. President, I was wondering, sir, if it might be possible for my son to work somewhere in the White House."

"Of course," answered the president. "What does he do?"

The aide threw up his hands and said, "Nothing."

"Excellent," noted the president. "We won't even have to train him."

A surgeon, an engineer, and a politician were debating which of their professions was the oldest.

"Eve was made from Adam's rib," said the surgeon, "and that, of course, was a surgical procedure."

"Yes," countered the engineer, "but before that, order was created out of all chaos—and that most certainly was an engineering job."

"Aha!" exclaimed the politician triumphantly. "And just who do you think created the chaos?"

Political orator: All that I am or will be, I owe to my dear mother.
Heckler: Why don't you give your mom ten cents and square the account?

My father's mother learned several years after her husband's death that he had never become a U.S. citizen. For more than forty years, she had lived under the assumption that by marrying him she had herself become a citizen. So at age sixty-five she began studying for her citizenship exam. My Aunt Harriet and I helped her cram for the test. It was a treat to hear her spew out the names of the Supreme Court justices in her Russian-Yiddish accent!

At the ceremony to obtain her citizenship, she was asked, "Would you ever advocate the overthrow of the constitutional government by either coercion or violence?"

Grandma thought for a few seconds and blurted out, "By violence."

During the presidential primaries, there's always good news and bad news. The good news is, the field of candidates narrows as the season progresses. The bad news is, so do their minds.

I think that the undecideds could go one way or the other.
—George Bush in 1988

Mr. and Mrs. Smith were leaving the White House after a tour when they bumped into the president. "Mr. President," said Mr. Smith, "I know this is a great imposition, but—would you mind?"

"Of course not," said the Commander-in-Chief.

So they gave him their camera and posed in front of the White House.

A man walked into a hotel. "I'd like a room for tonight," he told the clerk.

"I'm sorry, sir, but we have no vacant rooms," the clerk answered.

"Not even one room?" the man asked.

"No, sir, we're full tonight," said the clerk.

The man thought for a moment. "Please tell me, if the President of the United States came in and asked for a room, would you give him one?"

"If the President of the United States asked for a room, I would find one for him!" the clerk replied.

"Well, the President is not coming here tonight. So give me the room you'd give him!"

First Woman: "On my vacation, I toured Abraham Lincoln's boyhood home. It's exactly like it was over a hundred years ago."
Second Woman: "We must have the same landlord."

Father: "Son, do you realize when Lincoln was your age he was already studying hard to be a lawyer?"
Son: "Right, Pop, and when he was your age, he was already President of the United States."

Father: "I'm ashamed of you. When I was your age, I could name all the Presidents in order.
Son: "But, Dad, there were only two of them then!"

A congressman involved with agriculture issues received this hilarious letter and passed it on to the *Washington Times* column "Inside the Beltway," by John McCaslin.

Rural Route #2
Fremont, NE 68025

September 8, 1987

Honorable Secretary of Agriculture
Washington, DC

Dear Sir:

I need your advice with an agricultural situation, please. My friend Ed Peterson, who lives in Wells, Iowa, received a check for one thousand dollars from the government for NOT raising hogs. So, I want to go into the business of "not raising hogs" next year.

What I want to know is, in your opinion, what is the best kind of farm not to raise hogs on, and what is the best breed of hogs not to raise?

I want to be sure that I approach this endeavor in keeping with all governmental policies. I would prefer not to raise razorbacks, but if that is not a good breed not to raise, then I will just as gladly not raise Yorkshires or Durocs.

As I see it, the hardest part of this program will be in keeping an accurate inventory of how many hogs I haven't raised.

My friend Peterson is very joyful about the future of the business. He has been raising hogs for thirty years or so and the best he ever made on them was $422 in 1968, until this year when he got your check for not raising hogs.

If I get one thousand dollars for not raising fifty hogs, will I get two thousand for not raising a hundred? I plan to operate on a small scale at first, holding myself down to about four thousand hogs not raised, which will mean about $80,000 the first year. Then I can afford an airplane.

Now another thing, these hogs I will not raise will not eat one hundred thousand bushels of corn. I understand that you also pay farmers for not raising wheat and corn. Will I qualify for payments for not raising corn and wheat not to feed the four thousand hogs I am not going to raise?

Also, I am considering the "not milking cows" business, so send me any information you have on that, too. In view of these circumstances, you understand that I will be totally unemployed and plan to file for unemployment and food stamps.

Be assured you will have my vote in the coming election.

Patriotically yours,

Harry Callahan

P.S. Would you please notify me when you plan to distribute more free cheese?

Our presidents seem to have enjoyed a more than average wittiness. John F. Kennedy, one of my favorite leaders, was queried about his first days in the White House and replied, "The thing that surprised us most was to find that things were just as bad as we'd been saying they were!"

A small boy asked President Kennedy how he became a war hero. Kennedy replied: "It was easy. The Japanese sank my boat."

President Grover Cleveland and the Senate were constantly bickering with one another. However, the House of Representatives and Cleveland got along great.

After a hectic day with the Senate, Cleveland, exhausted, retired early at home. In the middle of the night, the butler heard some noises and rushed to Cleveland's bedroom, shook him and whispered: "Mister President, I think there are burglars in the house!"

The President woke up just enough to say: "In the Senate, maybe, but not in the House!"

The President of the United States, the Prime Minister of England, and the Communist leader met and started discussing the dreams they had. The President of the U.S. said: "I dreamed that I was made President of the World."

The Prime Minister of England announced: "I dreamed I was made Prime Minister of the World."

The Communist leader cried: "That's funny. I have no recollection of appointing either of you!"

Do you think that when they asked George Washington for ID that he just whipped out a quarter?   —Steven Wright

One morning Thomas Jefferson woke up in a modest Washington rooming house, dressed, and then left the house in order to attend his inauguration as the third president. When he got back, duly sworn in, he found no space left for him at the dinner table. Quietly accepting the democratic principle of first come, first served, the President of the United States went up to his room without dinner.

Bill Moyers, Johnson's press secretary, said grace at lunch one day. "Speak up, Bill," cried Johnson. "I can't hear a thing."

"I wasn't addressing you, Mr. President," say Moyers quietly.

Leaving the White House after a dinner gathering, drama critic George S. Kaufman gave this parting quip to First Lady Eleanor Roosevelt: "You have a good location, good food, and I'm sure the place should be a great success when it's noised around a bit."

According to a wholly unsubstantiated rumor repeated in White House circles shortly after former President Nixon retired to his San Clemente estate, it seems that only hours after his arrival in California, Mr. Nixon telephoned Gerald

Ford. When the new president got on the line, Mr. Nixon is unreliably reported to have sung this memorable line: "Pardon me, boy, this is the chap who knew to choose you."

During his stint as governor of Georgia, Lester Maddox explained why his state should not create a consumer protection agency as follows: "Honest businessmen should be protected from the unscrupulous consumer."

Uncle Irv ran for alderman in Chicago. He came home late on election night and gave his wife the glorious news, "Darling, I've been elected!"

"Honestly?" she replied, too delighted to believe the news.

"Hey," he said, "why bring that up?"

My friend Ed was a sheep rancher in Idaho. One day a stranger walked up to him and asked, "If I can guess how many sheep you've got, may I have one?" Thinking this impossible, Ed agreed. The stranger declared, "You have 1,795 sheep."

"Now how did he figure that out?" Ed wondered as the man selected an animal, slung it over his shoulder and turned to leave.

"Wait," called the Ed. "If I can guess your occupation, can I have that animal back?"

"Sure," said the man.

"You're a government bureaucrat."

"How did you figure that out?" asked the stunned man.

"Well," grinned Ed, "put my dog down and I'll tell you."

There was a fellow who applied for a job as a press aide for a Congressman. Not long after he submitted his application, he received word from the official's office: "Your resume is full of exaggerations, distortions, half-truths, and lies. Can you start work Monday?"

In 1787 Washington led the convention that wrote the U.S. Constitution. He spoke little during this historic event. Then someone suggested that the Constitution set a limit of five thousand men in the army.

Washington could be quiet no longer. "If that is so," he said, "let the Constitution also say that no foreign militia should ever invade our country with more than three thousand troops."

Former Undersecretary of the Interior John C. Whitaker is reminded how easy it is to lose perspective about one's importance in government. He tells a story of an eighty-five-year-old woman who has lived her whole life in one spot in Nova Scotia. The population there swells to nine in summer and stays steady at two during the winter.

Whitaker, who has been fishing there every year since he was twelve, flew in one day. Miss Mildred welcomed him into her kitchen and said, "Johnny, I hate to admit I don't know, but where is Washington?"

When Whitaker realized that she wasn't kidding, he explained: "That's where the President is. That's like where you have the Prime Minister in Ottawa."

When she asked how many people lived there, Whitaker replied that there were about two million. She said, "Think of that! Two million people living so far away from everything."

Will Rogers said that all he needed for his humor was the Congressional Record. He said, "There's no trick to being humorous when you have the whole United States government working for you."

A Jefferson City, MO, paper reports:
Columbia, Tenn., which calls itself the largest outdoor mule market in the world, held a mule parade yesterday, headed by the governor.

Einstein dies and goes to heaven. In the first few hours he meets four men. "Hello," he says to the first one. "I'm Albert Einstein."

"Glad to meet you," says the man. "By the way, my I.Q. is 180."

"Is that right?" say Einstein. "Then we'll be able to discuss quantum physics."

"And I," says the second man, "have an I.Q. of 155."

"Splendid," says Einstein. "We can discuss the latest mathematical theories."

"As for me," says the third man, "my I.Q. is 125."

"Delighted to meet you," says Einstein. "We can discuss the current state of the arts. And you, sir," says the scientist, offering his hand to the fourth man, "I'm glad to meet you too."

"I'm honored," says the fourth man, "but my I.Q. is only eighty-five."

"Oh, that's all right," says Einstein. "How are things in Washington?"

It is inexcusable for scientists to torture animals; let them make their experiments on journalists and politicians.   —Henrik Ibsen

A canny politician campaigning for re-election to congress went from farm to farm, drumming up votes. In one back yard he found a young woman milking a cow. He had just started talking to her when the mother stuck her head out of the back door and called, "Mary, who's that feller you're talkin' to?"

Mary explained that the visitor was a famous politician.

"You come right into this house," commanded the mother. Then she added, "If that feller says he's a politician, you'd better bring the cow with you."

When the governor of the Virgin Islands was visiting Washington, DC, the toastmaster became flustered during his introduction and announced, "It's a great pleasure to present the Virgin of Governor's Island."

In the 1950 senatorial primary campaign in Florida, veteran Congressman Claude Pepper was opposed by George Smathers. Pepper was especially strong in the "Bible Belt," which includes the northern section of Florida.

To shake the hold Pepper had on these voters, Smathers is said to have developed a special speech, making use of the facts that Pepper, a Harvard Law School graduate, had a niece who was a staff member of a Senate Subcommittee, and a sister who acted in New York. For these county courthouse rallies, Smathers would say: "Are you aware, my friends, that in his youth Claude Pepper was found matriculating in Harvard? That before marriage he habitually indulged in celibacy? Not only that, he was practicing nepotism in Washington with his own niece; and he has a sister who is a thespian in wicked Greenwich Village! Worst of all, my friends, Claude Pepper is known all over Washington for his latent tendency toward overt extroversion. And are you aware that Claude Pepper vacillated one night right on the Senate floor?"

Pepper lost the election.

(. . . and went on to many years of distinguished service in the House of Representatives. Smathers retired from the Senate in 1971, vigorously denying the story till the end, nonetheless acknowledging that the tale has by now "gone into the history books.")

In one of the smaller towns in Texas, a completely new school board was voted into office in the 1988 election. After taking over, they dutifully issued a budget for fiscal year 1990, carefully balanced to projected revenues. When the state's Board of Education in Austin asked why they planned to spend absolutely no money on foreign language education that year, the answer was: "We don't hold with new-fangled ways. If English was good enough for Jesus Christ, it should be good enough for the children of our town."

Ad in the paper: "Young man, Democrat, would like to meet young lady, Republican. Object: third party."

Political ads are so scandalous, I always switch to a daytime talk show when they come on. —Bill Jones

I finally hired a new church secretary, a former Pentagon employee. She immediately reorganized my filing system, labeling one file cabinet SACRED and the other TOP SACRED.

 While on a business trip, a man came to a small Southern town. He decided to look up an old college chum who held the office of Mayor.

It being Saturday afternoon, the traveler asked a gas station attendant if he knew where he might find the mayor. The attendant replied, "That no good so-and-so? He's probably off fishing, just like every other day."

Then the man went to the local drugstore and asked the clerk if she knew where he might find the mayor on a Saturday. "That bonehead?" she replied. "I wouldn't tell you even if I knew."

After several more attempts produced similar hostile answers, the man decided to go to City Hall, on the chance that there might be someone there to direct him to his friend's house.

The building was almost empty, except for the mayor's office. There the man found his old friend, hard at work. "I'm here at my desk seven days a week," the mayor said.

"But," the out-of-towner asked, "why would you want a job that keeps you working that hard? Is it the salary?"

"Oh, no," the mayor said, "there's no pay at all."

Was it possibly the graft from paving contracts and the like?

"No," said the mayor, "all city contracts are awarded through competitive bidding."

Was it the patronage that he controlled?

"No," said the mayor, "All jobs are under civil service jurisdiction."

"Then why in the world do you take a job like this?"

The mayor replied, "For the prestige, of course."

While he was Soviet General Secretary, Mikhail Gorbachev was late for a meeting and told his chauffeur to step on it. The chauffeur refused, on the grounds that it would be breaking the speeding laws. Gorbachev ordered him into the back seat and got behind the wheel.

After a few miles, a police patrol stopped the car. The senior officer sent his subordinate to arrest the offender.

A moment later, the officer returned, saying that the person was much too important to prosecute.

"Who is it?" demanded the police chief.

"I am not sure, sir," replied the officer, "but Comrade Gorbachev is his chauffeur."

When Dan Quayle was elected Vice President, he tried to keep the pomp and glitter in perspective. And, boy, did he get help!

Once he and his family and the Secret Service dined at Red, Hot & Blue—an "in" ribs place in Washington, DC. When Quayle stood to leave, applause broke out. Quayle said he was pleased, until the headwaiter told him people in line were clapping because his party had just vacated three tables.

—*USA Today*

Air Force One comes in for a landing at the airport. A ramp is wheeled up and President Clinton appears, carrying a pig under each arm. As he comes down the ramp, the Marine at the bottom snaps to a salute. Clinton says, "You'll have to excuse me. I can't return your salute. My hands are full."

"Yes, sir. I see the pigs, sir!" responds the Marine.

"Now hold on," says Clinton. "These aren't just pigs. These are genuine Arkansas Razorbacks."

"Yes, sir! Razorbacks, sir!" says the Marine.

"I got this one for Chelsea and this one for Hillary," Clinton explains.

The Marine answers, "Yes, sir! An excellent trade if I may say so myself, sir!"

Psychiatrist Karl Menninger in his famous book *Whatever Became of Sin?* noted that American Presidents used to mention sin once in awhile, but that none has done so since 1953. The Republicans refer to the twin problems of "pride" and "self-righteousness." The Democrats refer to "shortcomings." But none use the grand old sweeping concept of sin anymore. Thus, it seems, we as a nation stopped sinning decades ago!

—Dr. Donald Strobe

A candidate running for Congress hired two assistants: one to dig up the facts, and the other to bury them.

A politician is a guy who shakes your hand before an election and your confidence afterwards.

The more you read about politics, you got to admit that each party is worse than the other.

—Will Rogers

In America you can go on the air and kid the politicians, and the politicians can go on the air and kid the people.

—Groucho Marx

Two brothers were born to a family in Kentucky. When they grew up one ran off to sea, and the other became Vice President of the United States. Neither one was ever heard from again.

—Alben Barkley

Martha Washington to husband, as he ponders their overnight accommodations: "Oh, for heaven's sake, George. Two hundred years from now, what difference will it make where we slept?"

Now and then an innocent man is sent to the legislature.
—F. McKinney Hubbard

The politician is trained in the art of inexactitude. His words tend to be blunt or rounded, because if they have a cutting edge they may later return to wound him. —Edward R. Murrow

Congressmen and fellows like me are alike in some ways, I guess. But when I make a joke, it's a joke. When they make a joke, it's a law. —Will Rogers

Many a politician starts to behave, not because he saw the light, but because he was starting to feel the heat.

When the polls are in your favor, flaunt them.
When the polls are overwhelmingly unfavorable, ridicule and dismiss them, or stress the volatility of public opinion.
When the polls are slightly unfavorable, play for sympathy as a struggling underdog.
When too close to call, be surprised at your own strength.
—Paul Dickson

We have a presidential election coming up. And I think the big problem, of course, is someone will win. —Barry Crimmins

As one story goes, when Soviet leader Mikhail Gorbachev called the White House to speak with President Ronald Reagan, a White House official rushed to the President and said, "The good news, Mr. President, is that General Secretary Gorbachev is calling to say he is in favor of free speech. The bad news is, he's calling collect."

Think of what would happen to us in America if there were no humorists. Life would be one long Congressional Record.

—Tom Masson

Guidelines for bureaucrats:
When in charge, ponder.
When in trouble, delegate.
When in doubt, mumble.

—James H. Boren

A little girl asked her father, "Daddy, do all fairy tales begin with 'Once upon a time'?"

He replied, "No, there is a whole series of fairy tales that begin with 'If elected I promise . . . '"

In 1960 John F. Kennedy was campaigning for the presidency. He gave a stunning speech in San Antonio, Texas, to a large enthusiastic crowd assembled at the Alamo, where a handful of Texans once held off a large Mexican army.

After he finished, Kennedy wanted to make a quick exit. Turning to Maury Mathers, a local politician, he said, "Maury, let's get out of here. Where's the back door?"

Maury replied, "Senator, if there had been a back door to the Alamo, there wouldn't have been any heroes."

Lyndon Johnson tried to get his fellow Democrats to put away their regional differences. But then he added, "Of course, I do not want to go as far as the Georgia politician who shouted from the stump in the heat of debate, 'My fellow citizens, I know no North, I know no South, I know no East, I know no West.'

"To which a barefooted, freckle-faced boy shouted from the audience, 'Well, you better go back and study some geography!'"

Robert Orben says that the essence of America can be summed up in this exchange. A father told his son that all Americans belong to a privileged class.

The son said, "I disagree."

And the father said, "That's the privilege."

According to ancient tradition, the Gospel of Matthew was written by a tax-collector, and if this is true, the clarity and the simplicity of this Gospel comes as a surprise to anyone who reads it. Imagine, a Gospel written by a tax collector! What do you suppose a gospel written by the IRS might sound like today?

"Once there was an adult male named Joseph, a self-employed carpenter with two dependents: Mary, who was an unemployed housekeeper, and a minor son named Jesus. Jesus was born six days before December ended, and this provided Joseph with a full deduction for the entire year. Jesus was born in Bethlehem while Joseph and Mary were on a business-related trip, which could not be deducted. The family received considerable assets of gold, frankincense, and myrrh while in Bethlehem. A ruling has not yet been made on whether this increase in net worth should be reported as income on line twelve, page two."

—Dr. Eugene W. Brice

A fellow in Vermont said to his mother one day, "Mother, I don't believe you'd vote for God Himself if He ran on the Democratic ticket!"

To which she replied: "Of course not. If He switched parties at this late date, he wouldn't be very reliable, now, would He?"

I once read a speech by a president of the United States (he's dead, so don't start guessing) in which he declared on page one that his religion was the Sermon on the Mount, and then on page three, when dealing with foreign affairs, said: "Let's have no nonsense about turning the other cheek."

—Dr. Donald Strobe

Benjamin Franklin once said, "In this world nothing is certain but death and taxes."

A cynic has said, "Death and taxes may always be with us, but at least death doesn't get any worse."

Is there no escape from bureaucrat-speak?

If Ben Franklin were alive today, would he say, "In this world nothing is certain but negative patient-care outcome and revenue enhancement"?

If Tolstoy were writing now, would he write a novel entitled *Violence Processing and a State of Permanent Pre-Hostility*?

When John F. Kennedy was president, a prominent citizen of Washington, DC invited him to play golf. On the first hole Kennedy floated a nice shot about three feet from the pin. He walked up to the ball and glanced over at the man who had invited him. Kennedy was looking for the man to concede him the putt. The man ignored him, and stared up at the sky.

"You're certainly going to give me this putt, aren't you?" Kennedy asked.

"Make a pass at it," the man replied. "I want to see your stroke. A putt like that builds character. Besides, it will give you a little feel for the greens."

With an anguished look, Kennedy said, "I work in the Oval Office all day for citizens like you," he said. "And now you're not going to give me this putt?" The man said nothing.

"OK," Kennedy sighed. "But let's keep moving. I've got an appointment after we finish with the Director of Internal Revenue."

"The putt's good," the man said hastily. "Pick it up."

One wag called Christopher Columbus the Father of Modern Government. He didn't know where he was going when he started, he didn't know where he was when he got there, and he did it all on borrowed money.

President Lyndon Johnson insisted that Lawrence F. O'Brien take his oath of office as Postmaster General in a little post office in Hye, Texas. At the ceremony, Johnson recalled mailing his first letter at that very post office when he was four. "It was about fifty-three years ago," said LBJ. "And Larry O'Brien told me a few moments ago that he is going out to find that letter and deliver it."

A father took his small son to visit the US Capitol. From the gallery they watched as the House of Representatives came to order and the Chaplain led in prayer. "Why did the minister pray for all those men, Dad?" asked the lad.

"He didn't, son," the father exclaimed. "First, he looked them over, then he prayed for our country!"

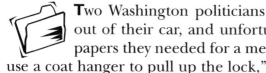 Two Washington politicians had locked themselves out of their car, and unfortunately some important papers they needed for a meeting were inside. "Let's use a coat hanger to pull up the lock," suggested the first.

"Oh, no," argued the second. "Someone might see us and think we were trying to break in."

"Then we could use my pocketknife to cut away the rubber around the window and stick our fingers through to pull up the lock."

"No, no! People would think we're too stupid to know how to use a coat hanger to open cars."

"Well, we'd better do something fast. The top's down and it's starting to rain."

Woody Allen has said, "The government is unresponsive to the needs of the little man. Under five-seven, it's impossible to get your congressman on the phone."

After reading his prepared statement at a press conference, the feisty senator threw the meeting open for questions.

"Is it true," asked one sarcastic reporter, "that you were born in a log cabin?"

"You're thinking of Abraham Lincoln," replied the senator nonchalantly. "I was born in a manger."

Nothing can mess up your lifestyle like dying. Just ask a guy who died last month in Greenville, South Carolina.

Some of you might be asking how you can ask a dead guy anything. Well, his being dead didn't stop the Greenville County Department of Social Services from sending him a letter.

"Your food stamps will be stopped effective March 1992 because we received notice that you passed away," the letter to the dead guy said. It ended, "May God bless you."

Despite the nice touch at the end, the letter made it sound as if the decision to stop food stamps was final.

But this is not to say that the public agency was cold. The department offered the dead guy hope for the future. "You may reapply if there is a change in your circumstances," the letter said.

At first, Al Palanza Jr., brother of the dead guy, read the letter and said he was disgusted. Later he found it funny. He called it "living proof of how screwed up the system is."

Robin Kubler, the county's social services director, said it's not her system that's screwed up. She said the form letter was generated by a computer system.

And the "May God bless you"? That was added by a caseworker, she said, to soften the statement. —*Philadelphia Inquirer*

"Did you know that George Washington's inaugural speech lasted all of one and a half minutes?" asks Jay Leno. "I guess there's just not much to say if you're a politician who can't tell a lie."

In Washington DC, a visitor asked a passerby on C Street, "Which side is the State Department on?"

The reply: "Ours, I think."

When I was a speechwriter for a US Senator, I overheard the following conversation.

Newspaper reporter: "Why don't you cut spending if revenues are down?"

Congressman: "Don't be silly, sport. This is the government, not real life."

At a Washington cocktail party, two strangers struck up a conversation. After a few minutes of small talk, one said, "Have you heard the latest White House joke?"

The second fellow held up his hand. "Wait, before you begin, I should tell you that I work in the White House."

"Oh, don't worry," the first man replied. "I'll tell it very slowly."

Christmas is when kids tell Santa Claus what they want, and their parents end up paying for it.

A deficit is when adults tell the government what they want, and their kids end up paying for it.

—Ilana Stern

Former Secretary of Labor Raymond J. Donovan tells the story of a flight on Air Force One. He was in the back compartment of the jet while President Reagan was in the front. The phone rang in the back compartment and the voice said, "Mr. Donovan, the President would like you to join him for lunch." Secretary Donovan straightened his tie and thought to himself how important he was to have the President ask him to join him for lunch.

Just as Secretary Donovan walked through the doorway into the President's compartment, the Red Phone, the Presidential

Hotline, rang next to the President. "Wow," thought Donovan, "what a moment to be present."

The President picked up the phone and said, "Yes . . . uh huh . . . yes . . . What are my options?"

Donovan's heart almost stopped. His mind raced. Surely history was in the making, he supposed.

Then the President continued, "OK. I'll have the iced tea," and hung up.

Ronald Reagan used to tell of a shoemaker who was making a pair of shoes for him when he was a lad. The cobbler asked Ronald if he wanted a round or square toe. Ronald was unsure, so the cobbler told him to return in a day or two and let him know. A few days later the cobbler saw young Ronald on the street and asked what he had decided. Ronald was still undecided. The cobbler said the shoes would be ready the next day. When Ronald picked up the shoes, one had a round toe and one had a square toe. As an adult Reagan commented, "Looking at those shoes taught me a lesson. If you don't make your own decisions, somebody else makes them for you."

One night, President Clinton tossed and turned, finding it impossible to sleep. So he decided to go for a walk. He sauntered by the Jefferson Monument. He reflected for a minute and said: "Thomas Jefferson, what a great American. Boy, if I could just talk to you, I know you could give me some guidance."

Then a deep voice came from above: "Go to the People, Go to the People."

To which Clinton responded: "Are you *crazy*? 'Go to the people'? The people hate me. No, no, I can't go to the people."

Then Clinton strolled toward the Washington Monument, and said: "Now I know if I could speak with the Father of our Country with his wisdom, he could surely help me."

Then a deep voice came from above and said, "Go to Congress. Go to Congress."

And Clinton responded: "Are you crazy? 'Go to Congress'? Congress hates me. No, no. I can't go to Congress."

Now thoroughly disheartened, Clinton traipsed by the Lincoln Monument and looked at the grand figure of Lincoln. Clinton said: "I just know if you could speak, Mr. Lincoln, with your honesty, it would help my Presidency."

Then a deep voice came from above: "Go to the Theater. Go to the Theater."

A story is told that President Clinton was swimming off the beach at Martha's Vineyard one day when he got caught in an undertow and was pulled underwater out of reach of his bodyguards. Three boys diving in the area saw him and pulled him out of the water to safety.

"Thank you all so much for rescuing me," the president said. "What can I ever do to repay you for saving my life?"

The first boy said, "I would like to go to West Point."

"I will see that you do," Clinton replied.

The second boy said, "I would like to go to Annapolis."

"I will get on it right away," the president promised.

Then turning to the third boy, he asked, "And how can I repay you?"

"I would like to be buried in Arlington Cemetery," the boy replied.

"Arlington Cemetery!" said the amazed Chief Executive. "Why do you want that?"

Replied the boy, "Well, when my father finds out I saved your life, he's gonna kill me!"

Dateline, Sacramento: This year the California Governor signed 709 bills protecting us from such ravages as feral pigs, which now can be killed with the proper permit. Although beating a feral pig to death with a permit does not sound like a fantasy gig to me. Well, you can't say we don't get our money's worth from our elected representatives. OK, I guess you can say it, but you'd be wrong . . . as far as quantity goes.   —Will Durst

THE CALL OF THE POLITICALLY CORRECT
SHEPHERD TO HIS NYMPH
(WITH APOLOGIES TO CHRISTOPHER MARLOWE, WHO IS A DEAD WHITE EUROPEAN MALE AND THEREFORE UNWORTHY OF STUDY)

Come live with me and we shall be politically correct
We'll walk among the spotted owls and every rare insect
We'll not cheer for sporting teams whose names
    mock our ancestors
Or consort with other than the original fur-wearers
No toxic fission
No fossil fuels
No polyester
No grades in schools
Come live with me within the old-growth forest near the seas
Where the dolphins all are safe
    and swim through nets with ease
Where the union label grows
    in our greenhouse-gas-free dome
And the rain forest stretches out
    beyond our race-normed home
No fatty oils
No silicone
No ever-present
Cellular phones
We'll be perfectly tolerant of all (as if we cared!)
And we'll hope that we won't be procreationally impaired
And when we have politically correct young girls and boys
They'll play in their cloth diapers with our recycled toys
They'll get their truths from
Old bitter men
And never think nor learn
Lest they offend.

—Kevin M. Loney

Reagan won because he ran against Jimmy Carter. Had he run unopposed, he would have lost.

—Mort Sahl

Moses was leading the children of Israel as they fled from the Egyptians. When they came to the Red Sea, he begged God to rescue his people. Suddenly he heard a voice from on high saying, "There is some good news and some bad news."

"I hear you, Lord," said Moses, "Tell your servant everything."

"The good news," said the voice from on high, "is that I will part the sea, so that you and your people can escape."

"And the bad news?" asked Moses.

"You'll have to file the environmental impact statement."

MILITARY MOMENTS

During World War II, a general and his subordinate lieutenant were traveling from their base to a base in another state. They shared a booth on a passenger train with two civilians, an attractive young lady and her grandmother.

For most of the trip, they conversed freely. Then the train entered a long, dark tunnel. Once inside the tunnel, all four passengers in this particular booth heard two distinct sounds— the first was the smooch of a kiss; the second was a loud slap.

Now, here are these four people in this booth aboard the passenger train. They possess four differing perspectives.

The young lady is thinking to herself how glad she is that the young lieutenant got up the courage to kiss her, but she is somewhat disappointed at her grandmother for slapping him for doing it.

The general is thinking to himself how proud he is of his young lieutenant for being enterprising enough to find this opportunity to kiss the attractive young lady, but he is flabbergasted that she slapped him instead of the lieutenant.

The grandmother is flabbergasted to think that the young Lieutenant would have the gall to kiss her granddaughter, but she is proud of her granddaughter for slapping him.

And the young lieutenant is trying to hold back his laughter, for he found the perfect opportunity to kiss an attractive young lady and slap his superior officer all at the same time!

An Army sergeant sought to lead an Episcopal worship service in the absence of the base chaplain. He read the Call to Worship, the invocation, led the men through the Prayer of Confession, then started to read the Absolution of Sins. Right then he noticed in small print in the prayer book that only an ordained minister could give the Absolution. He knew that he was not ordained.

He was stumped for a minute. Then he remembered that he was a sergeant. He faced them squarely with chest out and chin in and sounded off, "As you were, men. As you were."

Captain Burnell approached the platoon sergeant with a somber look on his face and informed him of the of bad news. "Sergeant," he said, "we just got notice that Private Smith's grandmother died. You'd better go break the news to him."

The sergeant walked into the barracks, paused at the doorway and shouted, "Hey, Smith, your grandmother died."

The captain was horrified. "Sergeant, that's no way to tell a man that his grandmother has died. Look how you've shocked him. You have to use tact in a situation like this. I think we'd better send you to Diplomacy School."

So the sergeant spent a year studying at Diplomacy School. On the day he returned, the captain approached him.

"Well, sergeant, how did you do in school?"

"Fine," replied the sergeant. "I've really learned how to be tactful."

"That's good, because we've just gotten notice that Corporal Johnson's grandmother died. Go in and tell him."

The sergeant entered the barracks, paused at the doorway and called his men to attention. When they were lined up, he stepped before them and ordered, "All those with living grandmothers step forward. Hey, hey, not so fast, Johnson."

When I was crossing the border into Canada, they asked if I had any firearms with me. I said, "Well, what do you need?"

—Steven Wright

The disappointed young recruit in his second week of basic training was writing an irate letter to his congressman, complaining of the many indignities and outrages to which he was being subjected. He wrote, "And the food, I can describe it only as slop. Back home, I wouldn't feed it to pigs for fear that it would poison them. No decent garbage man would have anything to do with it. And to make matters worse, they serve such small portions."

At an afternoon tea for officers and their wives, the commanding general of the base delivered a seemingly endless oration. A young second lieutenant, listening with obvious disfavor, grumbled to the woman at his side, "What a pompous and unbearable old windbag that slob is."

The woman turned to him, her face red with rage and said, "Lieutenant, do you know who I am?"

"No, ma'am."

"I am the wife of the man you just called 'an unbearable old windbag.'"

"Indeed," said the young lieutenant, looking steadfast and unruffled, "and do you know who I am?"

"No, I don't," said the general's wife.

"Thank goodness," said the lieutenant, as he disappeared into the crowd.

Eleanor Roosevelt was visiting a hospital ward when she came upon a sorry looking soldier, every part of whose body was encased in plaster casts.

"My goodness, what happened to you?" asked the concerned First Lady.

The GI responded, "I was on patrol in the jungle, when I heard this Japanese soldier yell, 'President Roosevelt eats rats!' So I yelled back, 'The Emperor eats skunks!'"

"And then you were wounded? By a mortar round perhaps?" asked Mrs. Roosevelt.

"No, not yet," the GI answered. "Then the Japanese soldier shouted, 'Gary Cooper can't act!' So I shouted back, 'The Emperor's wife can't cook!'"

"And then you were wounded? By a hand grenade perhaps?" asked a somewhat impatient Mrs. Roosevelt.

"No, not yet," said the GI.

"Well, what happened?" asked the First Lady.

Said the GI, "Then the Japanese soldier yelled, 'All of your generals are idiots.' And I yelled back, 'All of your generals are morons.' And while we were standing in the road shaking hands, I was run over by a tank!"

Sometimes I think war is God's way of teaching us geography.
—Paul Rodriquez

A slipping gear could let your M203 grenade launcher fire when you least expect it. That would make you quite unpopular in what's left of your unit.
—*PS Magazine*, the Army's magazine of preventive maintenance, August 1993

13.
TOO MANY LIGHT BULB JOKES

BY PROFESSION . . .

Question: How many conservative economists does it take to change a light bulb?

Answer: None. If the government leaves it alone, the darkness will improve all by itself.

Q: How many liberal economists does it take to change a light bulb?

A: One, plus forty billion dollars, a huge tax increase on the rich, more deficit spending, and the recognition that it's all the Republicans' fault the bulb burned out.

Q: How many bureaucrats does it take to change a light bulb?

A: Let's see. One to spot the burned-out bulb, one to authorize a requisition, twelve to file requisition copies, one to deliver the requisition order to the purchasing department, one to order the bulb, one to forward the purchasing order, one to fill the order, one to receive the bulb . . .

Q: How many politicians does it take to change a light bulb?

A: Two. One to assure everyone that everything possible is being done while the other screws the bulb into the water faucet.

Q: How many Hollywood actors does it take to change a light bulb?
A: Just one. He holds the bulb and the universe revolves around him.

Q: How many unemployed actors does it take to change a light bulb?
A: One hundred. One to change it, and ninety-nine to stand around and say, "Hey, I could've done that!"

Q: How many folk singers does it take to change a light bulb?
A: Ten. One to change it and nine to write songs about how great it was before electricity.

Question: How many lawyers does it take to change a light bulb?
Answer 1: How many can you afford?
Answer 2: It only takes one to change your bulb—into his.
Answer 3: Such number as may be deemed necessary to perform the stated task in a timely and efficient manner within the strictures of the following agreement: Whereas the party of the first part, also known as "The Lawyer," and the party of the second part, also known as "The Light Bulb," do hereby and forthwith agree to a transaction wherein the party of the second part (Light Bulb) shall be removed from the current position as a result of failure to perform previously agreed upon duties, i.e., the lighting, elucidation, and otherwise illumination of the area ranging from the front (north) door, through the entry way, terminating at an area just inside the primary living area, demarcated by the beginning of the carpet, any spill-over illumination being at the option of the party of the second part (Light Bulb) and not required by the aforementioned agreement between the parties. The aforementioned removal transaction shall include, but not be limited to, the following steps:

The party of the first part (Lawyer) shall, with or without elevation at his option, by means of a chair, step stool, ladder or any other means of elevation, grasp the party of the second part (Light Bulb) and rotate the party of the second part (Light Bulb) in a counter-clockwise direction, said direction being non-negotiable. Said grasping and rotation of the party of the second part (Light Bulb) shall be undertaken by the party of the first part (Lawyer) with every possible caution by the party of the first part (Lawyer) to maintain the structural integrity of the party of the second part (Light Bulb), notwithstanding the aforementioned failure of the party of the second part (Light Bulb) to perform the aforementioned customary and agreed upon duties. The foregoing notwithstanding, however, both parties stipulate that structural failure of the party of the second part (Light Bulb) may be incidental to the aforementioned failure to perform and in such case the party of the first part (Lawyer) shall be held blameless for such structural failure insofar as this agreement is concerned so long as the non-negotiable directional codicil (counter-clockwise) is observed by the party of the first part (Lawyer) throughout.

Upon reaching a point where the party of the second part (Light Bulb) becomes separated from the party of the third part ("Receptacle"), the party of the first part (Lawyer) shall have the option of disposing of the party of the second part (Light Bulb) in a manner consistent with all applicable state, local and federal statutes.

Once separation and disposal have been achieved, the party of the first part (Lawyer) shall have the option of beginning installation of the party of the fourth part ("New Light Bulb"). This installation shall occur in a manner consistent with the reverse of the procedures described in step one of this self-same document, being careful to note that the rotation should occur in a clockwise direction, said direction also being non-negotiable.

NOTE: The above described steps may be performed, at the option of the party of the first part (Lawyer), by said party of the first part (Lawyer), by his heirs and assigns, or by any and all persons authorized by him to do so, the objective being to produce a level of illumination in the immediate vicinity of the aforementioned front (north) door consistent with maximization of ingress and revenue for the party of the fifth part.

Question: How many psychiatrists does it take to change a light bulb?
Answer 1: Only one, but the light bulb must want to change.
Answer 2: None; the bulb will change itself when it is ready.
Answer 3: How long have you been having this fantasy?
Answer 4: How many do *you* think it takes?

Q: How many cops did it take to screw in a light bulb?
A: None. It turned itself in.

Q: How many journalists does it take to screw in a light bulb?
A: Three. One to report it as an inspired government program to bring light to the people, one to report it as diabolic government plot to deprive the poor of darkness, and one to win the Pulitzer Prize for reporting that the electric company hired a light bulb assassin to break the bulb in the first place.

Question: How many computer programmers does it take to change a light bulb?
Answer 1: Three. One to change it, one to write a manual, and one to work on the upgrade.
Answer 2: None. That's a hardware problem.
Answer 3: None. "It's not a bug, it's a feature."
Answer 4: Two. One always leaves in the middle of the project.

Q: How many high-technology reporters does it take to screw in a light bulb?

A: Four. One to write a review of all the existing light bulbs so you can decide which one to buy, another to write a remarkably similar article in another magazine the next month, a third to have a big report come out on glossy paper two months later that is by then completely out of date, and the fourth to hint in a column that a new and updated bulb is coming out that will make this one completely worthless.

Q: How many gorillas does it take to screw in a light bulb?

A: Only one, but it sure takes a lot of light bulbs!

BY STATE . . .

Q: How many Californians does it take to change a light bulb?

A: Four. One to screw in the bulb, and three more to share the experience.

Q: How many Virginians does it take to change a light bulb?

A: Three. One to hold the ladder, one to screw in the bulb, and one highly refined lady to remark how much lovelier the old bulb was.

Q: How many Oregonians does it take to change a light bulb?

A: Forty-two. One to hold the ladder, one to screw in the bulb, and forty to draft the environmental impact statement.

Q: How many New Yorkers does it take to change a light bulb?

A: One hundred and two. One to hold the ladder, one to change the bulb, one hundred cops to make sure the first two aren't mugged.

BY HOBBY . . .

Q: How many anglers does it take to change a light bulb?
A: Five, and you should've seen the light bulb! It must have been THIS big!

Q: How many jugglers does it take to change a light bulb?
A: One, but it takes at least three light bulbs.

Q: How many bluegrass musicians does it take to screw in a light bulb?
A: One to do it and two to argue about whether that was the way Bill Monroe would have done it.

Q: How many poets does it take to change a light bulb?
A: Three. One to curse the darkness, one to light a candle and one to change the bulb.

Q: How many Dadaists does it take to change a light bulb?
A: To get to the other side.

BY DENOMINATION . . .

Q: How many Baptists does it take to change a light bulb?
A: CHANGE??

Question: How many Calvinists does it take to change a light bulb?
Answer 1: None. God has predestined when the lights will be on.
Answer 2: Calvinists do not change light bulbs. They simply read out the instructions and pray the light bulb will decide to change itself.

Q: How many charismatics does it take to change a light bulb?
A: Five. One to change the bulb and four to bind the spirit of darkness in the room.

Q: How many neo-evangelicals does it take to change a light bulb?
A: No one knows. They can't tell the difference between light and darkness.

Q: How many TV evangelists does it take to change a light bulb?
A: One. But for the message of light to continue, send in your donation today.

Q: How many fundamentalists does it take to change a light bulb?
A: Only one, because any more would be compromise, and ecumenical standards of light would slip.

Q: How many liberal theologians does it take to change a light bulb?
A: At least ten, as they need to hold a debate on whether or not the light bulb exists. Even if they can agree upon the existence of the light bulb, they still may not change it to keep from alienating those who might use other forms of light.

Q: How many Anglicans or Catholics does it take to change a light bulb?
A: None. They always use candles.

Q: How many campfire worship leaders does it take to change light bulb?
A: One. But soon all those around can warm up to its glowing.

Q: How many Episcopalians does it take to change a light bulb?

A: Ten. One to actually change the bulb, and nine to say how much they liked the old one.

Q: How many Southern Baptists does it take to change a light bulb?

A: About sixteen million. However, they are badly divided over whether changing the bulb is a fundamental need or not.

Q: How many Nazarenes does it take to change a light bulb?

A: Two. One to change the bulb. Another to replace the new with the old after shaking it and finding it can be revived with a second blessing.

Q: How many United Church of Christ members does it take to change a light bulb?

A: Eleven. One to change the light bulb. And ten more to organize a covered dish supper that will follow the Changing of the Bulb Service.

Question: How many Lutherans does it take to change a light bulb?

Answer 1: There is some question here. But we have it on good authority that they have appointed a committee to study the issue and report back at their next meeting.

Answer 2: We read that we are to so fear and love God, that we cannot by our own effort or understanding comprehend the replacement of an electromagnetic photon source. It is, rather by faith, NOT by our efforts (effected toward the failed worldly incandescence), that we truly see, and that our own works cannot fully justify us in the presence of our Lord and Savior, Jesus Christ. Of course, it is still dark.

Q: How many Methodists does it take to change a light bulb?

A: Three hundred. Twelve to sit on the Board which appoints the Nominating and Personnel Committee. Five to sit on the Nominating and Personnel Committee, which appoints the House Committee. Eight to sit on the House Committee, which appoints the Light Bulb changing committee. Four to sit on the Light Bulb Changing Committee, which chooses who will screw in the Light Bulb. Those four then give their own opinion of "screwing in methods" while the one actually does the installation. After completion it takes one hundred individuals to complain about the method of installation and another 177 to debate the ecological impact of using the light bulb at all.

Q: How many Unitarians does it take to change a light bulb?

A: We choose not to make a statement either in favor of or against the need for a light bulb. However, if in your own journey, you have found that a light bulb works for you, that is fine. You are invited to write a poem or compose a modern dance about your personal relationship to your light bulb and present it next month at our annual light bulb Sunday service, in which we will explore a number of light bulb traditions, including incandescent, fluorescent, three-way, long-lived, and tinted; all of which are equally valid paths to luminescence through Jesus Christ.

BY THE WAY . . .

Q: How many board meetings does it take to get a light bulb changed?

A: This topic was resumed from last week's discussion, but is incomplete pending resolution of some action items. It will be continued next week. Do we have any new business? . . .

Q: How many Vulcans does it take to change a light bulb?

A: Approximately 1.0000000.

Q: How many evolutionists does it take to change a light bulb?
A: Only one, but it takes eight million years.

Q: How many Amish does it take to change a light bulb?
Q: What's a light bulb?

14.
AGING & HEALTH

In spite of the cost of living, it's still popular. —Kathy Norris

Ronald Reagan was beyond the age at which most Americans retire when he ran for the presidency in 1980. At age sixty-nine, he conducted a vigorous campaign, never passing up the chance to defuse the issue of his age with humor.

Probably his best such moment came during his second presidential election campaign, during his televised debate with Walter Mondale in 1984. A reporter asked Reagan if he was too old to serve another term. Reagan was more than ready for the question. "I'm not going to inject the issue of age into this campaign," he began. "I am not going to exploit for political gain my opponent's youth and inexperience."

YOU KNOW YOU'RE GETTING OLD WHEN:
- you feel like the morning after, and you haven't been any-where the night before.
- everything hurts and what doesn't hurt, doesn't work.
- you look forward to a dull evening.
- you find yourself giving good advice instead of setting a bad example.
- the candles cost more than the cake.

YOU KNOW YOU'RE GETTING OLD WHEN:

- the little gray-haired lady you help across the street is your wife.
- you go duck hunting just to please the dog.
- your doctor is just old enough to be your grand daughter.
- in the morning you hear snap, crackle, pop, and it isn't your breakfast cereal.
- your mind makes contracts your body can't fulfill.
- you know all the answers, but nobody asks you the questions.
- you call in sick and mean it.
- you give your grandkids thirty-five cents for an ice cream cone, and they look at you funny.
- the gleam in your eyes is from the sun hitting your bifocals.
- a dripping faucet causes an uncontrollable bladder urge.
- your grandchildren study things in history that you studied in current events.
- by the time you've lit the last candle on your cake, the first one has burned out.
- your idea of obscenity is jogging.
- you have too much room in the house and not enough room in the medicine cabinet.
- you get your full share of exercise acting as a pallbearer for those who took their exercise.
- you stop buying natural foods, because you need all the preservatives you can get.
- you feel like it's the morning after, but you haven't been anywhere the night before.
- you finally reach the top of the ladder and find it is leaning against the wrong wall.
- you get out of the shower and are glad the mirror is all fogged up.
- your little black book contains lots of names, all of which end in M.D.
- you get winded playing chess.
- your children begin to look middle aged.
- your favorite feature in the newspaper is "Twenty-five Years Ago Today."
- your knees buckle, but your belt won't.

- After painting the town red, you have to take a long rest before you apply the second coat.
- you remember today that yesterday was your anniversary.
- you just can't stand people who are intolerant.
- The best part of your day is over when the alarm clock goes off.
- you walk around with your head held high, trying to get used to the trifocals.
- you sit in a rocking chair and can't make it go.
- your idea of a long trip is to the back of the Wal-Mart.
- dialing long distance wears you out.
- your pharmacist offers to carry the bag of medicines to the car for you.
- you go to the barber shop and the barber asks why.
- you burn the midnight oil after 9:00 P.M.
- your pacemaker makes the garage door go up and down as you watch a pretty young girl walk by.
- your back goes out more often than you do.
- you really don't look forward to celebrating your next birthday.
- you not only get a senior citizen discount, but the clerk comments you should!
- your idea of a sports event is a wheelchair race.
- you get tired watching the fish swim around in the aquarium.
- most of your day is spent making appointments with various doctors.
- a funeral director calls and makes idle conversation, asking how you feel.
- pushing the buttons on the remote control for television is confusing.
- you sit and envy your parakeet for the energy it has to move around so much.
- you find TV ads for new laxatives interesting.
- you lose an argument with a phone answering device.
- your idea of a complete day is to be able to finish the crossword puzzle.
- you argue with your best friend about which denture adhesive is better.
- your idea of strenuous exercise is a bridge tournament.

YOU KNOW YOU'RE GETTING OLD WHEN:

- you take real interest in hospital admissions listed in the paper, to keep track of your friends.
- you go to visit a friend in the hospital, and the emergency room staff comes toward you with a wheelchair.
- while trying to figure out your last hospital bill, you have to take additional medication for your blood pressure.
- that last visit to the specialist cost you more than you earned in the first four years at work.
- you receive six pieces of mail in the same day, and five of them are from retirement villages, asking you to come and visit them.
- taking out a three-year subscription to a magazine is an act of positive thinking and real optimism.
- you decide to put off one more day what you had decided to put off one more day yesterday.
- you get excited simply watching the Weather Channel on television.
- you go to the mall not to shop but get a free blood pressure examination.
- you look forward to the next sale on support hose.
- licking stamps for your letters is a hard day's work.
- the doctor tells you that you are as sound as a dollar, and you get very upset.
- your idea of a wild drinking party is a king-size Coca Cola.
- you notice that your high school classmate looks older than sin.
- you can remember when going to a movie didn't cost you as much as the initial down-payment on a refrigerator.
- you can recall when service stations actually were.
- you call the ambulance dispatcher and he tells you your address.
- you begin to lose hope of ever finishing your Green Stamp book.
- you can remember when it wasn't necessary to call the bank before the plumber.
- you don't think "getting older" jokes are funny.

ANDERSEN'S TOP 20 LIST

How do you know when you're getting old? I truly believe that age is a state of mind, that you're only as old as you think you are. I know an octogenarian who has more energy, enthusiasm and drive than others half his age. I am also familiar with people in their thirties and forties who look like they already have one foot in the grave.

What are the warning signs, the tell-tale indicators that the years may be catching up with you? Here's a humorous checklist for you to enjoy. You know you're getting older when:

20. The telephone rings on a Saturday night and you hope it's not for you.
19. Your kids try to count the candles on your birthday cake, but are driven back by the heat.
18. You don't have to worry about avoiding temptation anymore, temptation avoids you.
17. Your Social Security number is two digits.
16. The only "vice" you can still handle is the one on your workshop bench.
15. You're 44 around the chest, 38 around the hips, 100 around the golf course and a pain around the house.
14. As you are picking up items off the floor, you ask if there is anything else you can do while you're down there.
13. You've finally got it all together, and then you forget where you left it.
12. You realize that whatever Mother Nature gave you, Father Time is starting to take away.
11. You're at that difficult age where you're too old to work and too poor to retire.
10. When they turn down your bed when staying overnight at a hotel, they leave a chocolate Ex-Lax on your pillow,
9. You read the obituary section of the newspaper first.
8. "Getting a little action" means your prune juice is working.
7. You're working your way through the three ages of hair: parted, unparted, departed.
6. You stop buying green bananas.
5. You take up jogging so you can hear heavy breathing again.

4. You decide to procrastinate but never get around to it.
3. Every new person you meet reminds you of someone you already know.
2. People keep telling you how great you look.
1. You finally know your way around but no longer want to go.

—Roger Andersen in *Laughing Matters*

Forget about jets, racing cars and speed boats. Nothing goes as fast as middle age.

I was sitting outdoors at a cafe in Miami Beach. The place was kind of a joke itself. It was a Chinese-Jewish-Cuban-Mexican-American restaurant. A tiny place with a huge multi-lingual menu.

As I perused the menu, two men sauntered toward me. One was an old man, probably well into his eighties yet erect and buoyant in his stride. He was attired in Florida rest home chic—black-and-white checked polyester slacks, a bright yellow golf shirt, white vinyl slip-on shoes with matching belt.

The other man was in his forties. He wore gray flannel slacks, a white shirt with rolled up sleeves, a conservative maroon tie, and cordovan wingtips. In his left hand, he carried an expensive snake skin briefcase. As he spoke, his right hand traced grand, sweeping gestures in the air.

When they strode past me, I noticed the emotional contrast between them. The older man appeared cheerful and relaxed, while the younger man seemed dramatically over-earnest. He was perspiring profusely in the south Florida humidity.

I could hear the younger man say in a rather pompous yet pleading tone, "Sam, we really should discuss your long term investment goals."

"Goals, shmoals," replied the elderly man, a broad smile illuminating his face. "At my age I don't even buy bananas by the bunch!"

Middle-age is when work is a lot less fun, and fun is a lot more work.

—Milton Berle

It's not your age that matters, it's how your matter ages.

—Martin A. Ragaway

An eighty-year-old man's golf game was hampered by poor eyesight. He could hit the ball well but he couldn't see where it went. So his doctor teamed him up with a ninety-year-old man who had perfect eyesight and was willing to go along to serve as a spotter.

The eighty-year-old man hit the first ball and asked his companion if he saw where it landed.

"Yep," said the ninety-year-old.

"Where did it go?" the eighty-year-old demanded.

The ninety-year old replied, "I don't remember."

"I used to eat a lot better when Ronald Reagan was president."

"Ah . . . so you think times were better back them?"

"No. I had my own teeth!"

Remember: fifty isn't old—if you're a tree!

"What are you so happy about?" a women asked the ninety-eight-year-old man.

"I broke a mirror," he replied.

"But that means seven years of bad luck."

"I know," he said, beaming. "Isn't it wonderful?"

Since I had my forty-first birthday, my wife has been kind enough to remind me of my age with the following: "Age is mind over matter. If you don't mind, it doesn't matter."

—Dan Ingman

An elderly Irish woman goes to confession. She says to the priest, "Father, forgive me for I have sinned. I've had sexual relations with a handsome young man."

"But, Mrs. O'Reilly," blurts out the startled priest, "You're over eighty years old! When did this happen?"

The woman replies, "Sixty-two years ago this week, but I love to talk about it!"

Sarah Adler, the noted actress, was never willing to admit to her true age. One day a nosy journalist asked her, "Madame Adler, I don't mean to embarrass you, but would you mind telling me your age?"

Without hesitating for an instant, she replied, "Sixty-eight."

The reporter objected, "But, Madam Adler, how can that be? I just asked your son Jack his age, and he told me he is sixty."

Still undaunted, Sarah replied, "Well, he lives his life and I live mine."

My wife says I am not "with it." She asked me if I liked the Stones. I replied, "The Stones? I love the Stones. I watch them whenever I can. My favorites are Fred and Barney."

—Steven Wright

"New TV shows are basically old shows reworked slightly," says comedy writer Bill Jones. "For example, Bob Vila will soon be in a show about middle-aged folks having plastic surgery. It's called 'This Old Spouse.'"

At twenty, we don't care what the world thinks of us. At thirty, we start to worry about what it thinks of us. At forty we realize that it isn't thinking of us at all.

The trouble with growing old is having to listen to your children's advice.

Remember when:
- a marriage was likely to outlast all three wedding present toasters?
- a drug problem was trying to get a prescription filled on Sunday?
- jokes that couldn't be told in mixed company weren't?
- paperbacks had more passion on the cover than in the contents?
- the only person you'd find in a store at three o'clock in the morning was a burglar?
- a whole family could go to the movies for what it now costs for a box of popcorn?   —Doug Larson, United Features Syndicate

A group of senior citizens at a retirement home was having a high old time discussing their various aches, pains and ills. Arthritis, indigestion, ulcers, insomnia, on and on it went. Finally an eighty-five-year-old man said, "Think of it this way, my friends. It just proves that old age isn't for sissies!"

You know you are middle-aged when your children tell you that you're driving too slow and your parents tell you that you're driving too fast.

Five-year-old Stephanie asked her seven-year-old brother Paul, "Why does grandmother read the Bible so much?"

Replied Paul, with all the wisdom of his additional two years, "I guess she must be cramming for her finals."

MEMORIES AND "FORGETORIES"

I don't let old age bother me. There are three signs of old age.
Loss of memory, and . . . I forget the other two.   —Red Skelton

My wife's Aunt Aggie told me once that that there are four
advantages to getting old and forgetful.

"One, you meet new friends every day; two, every joke you
hear is new; three, you can hide your own Easter eggs; and four
. . . I forget the fourth thing."

Nothing is more responsible for the good old days than a bad
memory.
                                                    —Franklin P. Adams

It's easy enough to have a clear conscience. All it takes is a
fuzzy memory.

 As Arnot L. Sheppard, Jr. once remarked, "Just when
you think you see the whole picture of life clearly, the
channel changes."

Years ago, a retrospective showing of Pablo Picasso's works was
held at the Museum of Modern Art in New York City. Nearly a
thousand of Picasso's works were displayed in chronological
order, beginning when he was a very young boy. The early works
were traditional landscapes and still-lifes. Then, as the artist
advanced in age, brilliant colors began to emerge, and the still-
lifes were no longer very still. Finally, of course, the works
turned into the kind of bold, zesty abstractions for which
Picasso is best known. One art critic who saw the show recalled
that once, when Picasso was eighty-five, he was asked the reason
his earlier works were so solemn and his later works so ecstatic
and exciting. "How do you explain it?" asked the interviewer.

"Easily," Picasso responded, his eyes sparkling. "It takes a
long time to become young!"

Aunt Aggie says, "My memory is starting to go. I locked the keys in my car the other day. Fortunately, I had forgotten to get out first."

Aunt Aggie was on an Amtrak train a few months ago. She searched through her purse and pockets for her ticket while the conductor waited patiently. Finally she said, "This is terrible. I know I had a ticket, but for the life of me I can't remember what I did with it."

The conductor said, "All is not lost, ma'am. You can pay me directly. Then when you find the ticket you can return it and get your money back."

"But that's not the point," said Aunt Aggie in bewilderment. "I don't remember where it is I'm going."

My brother Scott's memory is just as bad as mine. We're both convinced we're an only child.

My grandfather's a little forgetful, but he likes to give me advice. One day, he took me aside and left me there.

—Ron Richards

Years ago, my grandfather was talking to an old friend, our honorary Uncle Marty, who at the age of eighty-nine was still a bachelor. Grandfather jokingly asked, "Marty, you old codger, can you remember the first girl you ever kissed?"

Marty gave a hollow laugh. "Mike," he said dryly, "I can't even remember the last one."

You're getting older when it takes you more time to recover than it did to tire you out.

—Milton Berle

My dad says, "Every morning when I get up, I read the obituary page. If my name's not there, I shave and dress."

My parents live in Cape Coral, Florida, a haven for the elderly. My folks are a mere eighty-two years old each. Once my dad went to a local service club meeting. I asked him the age of the members.

"They were pretty old," he said. "In fact," he added after a moment's thought, "I would say that their average age was deceased."

Don't worry about temptation—as you grow older, it starts avoiding you.
—*Old Farmer's Almanac*

Middle age is when broadness of the mind and narrowness of the waist change places.

You get a little perspective when you pass thirty. I'm beginning to appreciate the value of naps. Naps are wonderful. It's like, what was I fighting all those years?
—Marsha Warfield

At a drugstore, a wife wanted to buy shaving lotion for her mate.
"What kind?" asked the clerk.
"Well," explained the wife, "he's seventy years old. Have you got any of that Old Spouse?"
—James Dent in Charleston, West Virginia *Gazette*

We just had a surprise party for my mom's ninetieth birthday. She was completely surprised . . . because she's eighty-one!

Uncle Irv, who is eighty-six, just returned from a trip to Paris. "I wish I'd done it forty years ago," he confided to me.

"You mean, when Paris was really Paris?"

"No, when Irv was really Irv!"

Eighty is a wonderful age—especially if you're ninety.

—Abel Green

You know you're getting older when you like to see cops go by.

—Jason Chase

Middle age occurs when you are too young to take up golf and too old to rush up to the net. —Franklin Pierce Adams

There are three ages of man: youth, middle age, and "Gee, you look good." —Red Skelton

To me, old age is always fifteen years older than I am.

—Bernard Baruch

Jay Trachman observes that the major differences among the generations are that "people over thirty-five generally know their Social Security numbers by heart; people under thirty-five memorize their credit-card numbers; and people under fifteen know all the cable channels."

You know you're getting old; there are certain signs. I walked past a cemetery and two guys ran after me with shovels.

—Rodney Dangerfield

After a family meal one night, three generations are sitting around chatting. Four-year-old Hillary is sitting on her grandfather's knee. She asks sweetly, "Grandpa, can you make a noise like a frog?"

Granddad replied, "What?"

Hillary again asked, "Can you make a noise like a frog?"

Granddad said, "Why do you want me to make a noise like a frog?"

Hillary replied, "Well, last night Daddy said that when you croak we can all go to Disneyland."

Luckily, Granddad took the comment in good humor.

GOOD HEALTH, AND HOW TO AVOID IT

Joined a health club last year, spent four hundred bucks. Haven't lost a pound. Apparently, you have to show up.

—Rich Ceisler

I joined a health spa recently. They had a sign for "Free Weights." So I took a couple.

—Scott Wood

I'm not working out. My philosophy: No pain, no pain.

—Carol Leifer

Thanks to jogging, more people are collapsing in perfect health then ever before.

—Jack Leonard

Everywhere is walking distance if you have the time.

—Steven Wright

If carrots are so good for my eyes, how come I see so many dead rabbits on the highways?

—Richard Jeni

I went to the eye doctor and found out I needed glasses for reading. So, I got some flip-up contact lenses.　　—Steven Wright

I hate it when my foot falls asleep during the day, 'cause that means it's going to be up all night.　　—Steven Wright

My friend Irv was troubled with frequent dizzy spells. He went from doctor to doctor and none could discover what his problem was. He tried everything. He jogged. He meditated. He prayed. He even went to a faith healer. Finally, his dizzy spells disturbed him so much he started to lose weight and couldn't sleep at night. He became a nervous wreck and his health began to deteriorate. He lost hope that he would ever recover. So he decided to prepare for the worst.

He made out his will, bought a cemetery plot and made arrangements with the local funeral home for his imminent demise. He even decided to buy a new suit of clothes to be buried in. He went to the men's clothing store, where he was carefully measured by a tailor before he picked out underwear, shoes, socks, suit jacket, trousers, and a beautiful silk tie. He turned to the tailor who had jotted down his measurements and asked for a shirt with a fifteen-inch collar to complete his wardrobe.

The tailor said, "But sir, you need a size 16 $1/2$ collar, not size 15."

Irv insisted he wore a size 15.

Finally, in frustration the clerk said: "But if you wear a size 15, you'll get dizzy spells!"

I walked into the phone company office to pay my bill. The line wasn't clearly formed, and there was an old man with a cane nearby me. It was unclear as to who was next.

The man gestured to me and said, "After you."

I smiled at him and said, "No, please, after you. I have all day."

Then he said, "No, you go ahead. My doctor says I have at least six months."

Mark Twain warned, "Be careful about reading health books. You may die of a misprint."

Robert Orben describes a friend who "always looks as if he's just finished seeing two hundred slides of his neighbor's three-week vacation in Cleveland."

Laughter is therapeutic. It can mend anything from a broken heart to the crack of dawn. From Alison Crane, executive director of the American Association for Therapeutic Humor, comes a story originally told to her by a middle-aged pastor:

"I had a very serious accident a few years ago; it was amazing I survived. And, of course, I was in the hospital for a long time recuperating.

Because I was there for so long, I became nonchalant with the nurses about the procedures they subjected me to—you can't keep decorum up for very long with no clothes on. I was also having trouble finding a relatively painless spot for them to put yet another injection of pain medication. . . .

One time I rang for the nurse, and when she answered on the intercom, I told her I needed another pain shot. I knew it would take just about as long for her to draw up the medication as it would for me to gather the strength to roll over and find a spot for her to inject it. I had succeeded in rolling over, facing away from the door, when I heard her come in. "I think this area here isn't too bad," I said, pointing to an exposed area of my rear.

But there was an awful silence after I said that. My face paled as I rolled over slowly to see who had actually come in—one of my twenty-two-year old female parishioners! I apologized and tried to chat with her, but she left shortly thereafter, horribly embarrassed.

Well, about thirty seconds after she left, the impact of the situation hit me and I started to laugh. It hurt like you can't imagine, but I laughed and laughed. Tears were rolling down my face, and I was gasping when my nurse finally came in. She asked what had happened. I tried to tell her, but couldn't say more than a word or two before convulsing into laughing fits again. Amused, she told me she would give me a few minutes to calm down and she'd be back to give me my shot.

I had just started to regain my composure when my nurse reappeared and asked again what had happened. I started to tell her, but got to laughing again, and she started to laugh just from watching me, which made it worse. Finally, she left again, promising to try back in fifteen more minutes. This scenario repeated itself a couple of more times, and by the time I could tell her what had happened, I felt absolutely no pain. None. I didn't need medication for three more hours. And I know it was an emotional turning point in my recovery."

The cost of living is going up and the chance of living is going down.
—Flip Wilson

MENTAL HEALTH WILL DRIVE YOU MAD

Wally Sneeringer, pastor at St. Luke's Presbyterian Church, was experiencing serious trouble. He claimed he slept like a baby. He explained, "I sleep for an hour. Then I wake up and cry for an hour. Then I sleep a while, and then wake up and cry a while. And I do this all night long!"

I suffer from two phobias: (1) Phobia-phobia—the fear you're unable to get scared, and (2) Xylophataquieopiaphobia—the fear of not pronouncing words correctly.
—Brad Stine

My cousin Ed says, "I know a lot of people with inferiority complexes, but theirs are all better than mine."

Vanna White's in a rehab center. She's hooked on phonics.

—Scott Wood

Lotta self-help tapes out there. Got one called "How to Handle Disappointment." I got it home and the box was empty.

—Jonathan Droll

He's turned his life around. He used to be depressed and miserable. Now he's miserable and depressed.   —David Frost

LIFE IS EASY, THEN YOU DIET

Diet tips:

- If no one sees you eat it, it has no calories.
- If you drink a diet soda with a candy bar, they cancel each other out.
- When eating with someone else, calories don't count if you both eat the same thing.
- Food used for medicinal purposes never counts, such as hot chocolate, brandy, toast, and Sara Lee cheesecake.
- If you fatten up everyone else around you, you look thinner.
- Movie-related foods such as Milk Duds, popcorn with butter, and Junior Mints don't count because they are simply part of the entertainment experience and not a part of one's personal fuel,.
 Enjoy your diet!

—Malcolm Kushner, *How to Use Humor for Business Success*

Auntie Kay: So, Annie, what are you going to do when you get to be as big as your mother?
Annie: Go on a diet.

While Wendell waited at the airport to board his plane, he noticed a computer scale that could display weight and fortune. He stepped on the scale platform, dropped a quarter in the slot, and the computer screen read: "You weigh 189 pounds, you're married and you're on your way to Chicago." Wendell stood there dumbfounded.

Another man put in a quarter and the computer read: "You weigh 155 pounds, you're divorced and you're on your way to Fresno."

Wendell was amazed. Then he rushed to the men's room, changed his clothes and put on dark glasses. He went to the machine again. The computer screen read: "You still weigh 189 pounds, you're still married, and you just missed your plane to Chicago!"

"**D**o you say a prayer before you eat?"

"No, we don't have to. My mother is a good cook."

Chubby girls are more fun than skinny girls. You go to a skinny girl's house, you're lucky to get mineral water and sprouts. You go to a chubby girl's house, you know there's food there.

And chubby girls give the best directions. If you want to know how to get somewhere, ask a chubby girl. "OK. You go up the street till you see the big Wendy's. Turn right and go past the McDonalds. There's a Burger King. Make a left. . . ."

—Jason Chase

It's time to go on a diet when the man from Prudential offers you group insurance. Or when you take a shower and you have to let out the shower curtain. Or when you're standing next to your car and get a ticket for double parking. I've been on a diet for two weeks and all I've lost is two weeks. —Totie Fields

Many of us don't know what poor losers we are until we start dieting.
—Tom La Mance

The second day of a diet is always easier than the first. By the second day you're off it.
—Jackie Gleason

My mother is on a diet. She's tried Slimfast, the Pritikin Diet, the Scarsdale Diet, the grapefruit diet. Now she's living off just garlic and limburger cheese. Nobody can get near her, so from a distance she looks thin.

Did you ever see the customers in health-food stores? They are pale, skinny people who look half-dead. In a steak house, you see robust, ruddy people. They're dying, of course, but they look terrific.
—Bill Cosby

When I was a child, I was so fat that in the school Nativity play I was the one chosen to play Bethlehem.

If you are thinking about buying a pair of skin tight designer jeans, let your contents be your guide.

The two women were on their coffee break and the conversation drifted to efforts to try to lose a few pounds. But then one of them produced a humongous sweet roll and began to devour it. "Is that allowed on your diet?" the other asked.

"It's only OK on my second diet," the first explained.

"You mean you're on two diets?"

"Uh huh."

"I don't get it."

"The first diet didn't give me enough to eat."

The tailor had just measured the naturalist's waistline. "Marco, dear," the customer's wife said, "it's amazing when you think about it. A Douglas fir with the same circumference would be seventy-five feet tall."

I wanted a light meal before an afternoon speaking engagement, so I ordered soup and salad. After I was served, I called the waiter over and complained, "There's a fly in my soup."

The waiter, looking rather bored, replied: "Quiet! Everybody will want one! Besides, what do you expect for a dollar, elephants?"

Joe Cannon (West Lane News) suggests it's time to consider losing weight when:

- you rent a canoe and they put large weights at the opposite end of the thing to balance it.
- you take a trip to the zoo and the children start throwing peanuts your way.
- five people trying to get a tan ask you to move because you're blocking out the sun.
- a child asks if he can use the life preserver around your waist, but you're not wearing one.

The two biggest sellers in any bookstore are the cookbooks and the diet books. The cookbooks tell you how to prepare the food, and the diet books tell you how not to eat any of it.

—Andy Rooney

Little Eric knelt, bowed his head and prayed, "Dear God, if You can discover ways to put the vitamins in chocolates and ice cream instead of in spinach and cod liver oil, I would sure appreciate it."

FOOD: ASK FOR IT BY NAME

A traveler's eye was caught by the sign in front of a small diner: "We have everything. Just ask." He entered and took a seat at the counter. When the owner appeared, the cynical traveler asked if it was true that they had everything. "Just ask," replied the owner.

"What if you don't have what I want?" the traveler persisted.

"Then I'll give you my new pickup truck," said the owner.

"OK," said the traveler, "I'll have buffalo head stuffed with pheasant eggs served in octopus gravy."

The owner turned around and shouted to the cook, "One number seventeen!"

I love our new juicer. It can make juice from anything. This morning I had a glass of toast.

I was on a twelve-city promotional tour for one of my books and was getting homesick. I went to a small diner for breakfast. The waitress came over to take my order and I said, "I'd like to have scrambled eggs, rye toast, decaf coffee, and some kind words."

She was back in a few minutes with the eggs, the toast, and the coffee. As she started to leave I touched her arm and said, "Miss, I appreciate what you brought, but I've been traveling for six weeks and I need those kind words more than I need anything else."

She leaned toward me and whispered, "Don't eat them eggs."

I'm older than most comedians. I take audiences back. Way back. Back to the fifties. Back when girls wore earrings and guys wore jockey shorts. So far back, sushi was called bait.

—Jason Chase

Nothing takes the taste out of peanut butter like unrequited love.
—Charlie Brown

Last night my father ordered a whole meal in French, and even the waiter was surprised. It was a Chinese restaurant.

Going out to eat is expensive. I was out at one restaurant and they didn't have prices on the menu. Just faces with different expressions of horror.
—Rita Rudner

Buffet: A French word that means "Get up and get it yourself."
—Ron Dentinger

There's a pizza place near where I live that sells only slices. In the back you can see a guy tossing a triangle in the air. . . .
  I went to a restaurant that serves "breakfast at any time." . . . So I ordered French Toast during the Renaissance.—Steven Wright

My father found glass in his pizza. When he complained to the manager, he was charged for an extra topping!

Bachelor cooking is a matter of attitude. If you think of it as setting fire to things and making a mess, it's fun. It's not so much fun if you think of it as dinner. . . . Nomenclature is an important part of bachelor cooking. If you call it "Italian cheese toast," it's not disgusting to have warmed-over pizza for breakfast.
—P. J. O'Rourke

The coffee business is getting ridiculous. There's a new coffee company that delivers overnight. It's called Federal Expresso.
—Bill Jones

I guess the Big Gulp at 7-Eleven wasn't big enough. Now they have the "Super Double" Gulp—72 ounces of soda. It comes with its own lifeguard. I looked inside the cup; they were filming an episode of *Baywatch* in there.

—Scott Wood

A hamburger by any other name costs twice as much.

—*The Humor Gazette*

Once I had achieved success as an entertainer, I wanted to impress my mom. I brought her to Las Vegas for dinner at Caesar's Palace. The first night there, we went to dinner at Caesar's Palace. Among other items, the menu listed "Twin Lobsters—$45.00"

"Why don't you order that, Mom?" I asked. "I know how much you like lobster."

She looked at me with the eyes of a skeptic and shook her head. "How do I know they're really twins?"

—Jay Leno

We have a new recipe for an exotic gourmet dinner: "First take two credit cards . . ."

—Bessie and Beulah

I can't cook. I use a smoke alarm as a timer.

—Carol Siskind

Today's housewife enjoys cooking . . . especially when it's done by the chef at one of the better restaurants.

I'll give you an idea how bad my cooking is—last Christmas the family chipped in together and bought me an oven that flushes.

—Phyllis Diller

Robert Orben muses: "Did you ever think you'd see the day when two grown people would sit down to a bottle of fizzy water, low-calorie quiche and decaffeinated coffee—and call it a power lunch?"

Waitress to diner: "I'm required by law to tell you that everything you ordered today may be harmful to your health."

If you actually look like your passport photo, you aren't well enough to travel. —Explorer Sir Vivian Fuchs

For three days after death, hair and fingernails continue to grow, but phone calls taper off. —Johnny Carson

15.
YOU'RE ALL
NOTHING BUT ANIMALS!

My dog is so obedient
He does what he is bid.
The park bench said "Wet Paint"
And that's exactly what he did!

—Agnes White Thomas in National Enquirer

I took my dog to obedience school, and the dog got a higher grade than I did.

Tommy, one of my grandsons, walked into the convenience store and asked the clerk for a box of laundry soap so that he could wash his dog, Petey. The clerk was appalled and told the boy, "Son, you can't use laundry soap on a dog. It might hurt him. Are you sure you want laundry soap?"

"Oh, yes," Tommy insisted. So the clerk sold the boy a box of laundry soap.

The next day, Tommy skulked into the store with a very sad look on his face. "What's the matter, Tommy?" the clerk asks.

"Petey died," the boy blurted out, tears wetting his cheeks.

"That's terrible," sympathized the clerk. "But remember, I told you that laundry soap might hurt your dog."

Tommy responded, "I don't think it was the laundry soap. I think it was the spin cycle."

One day a letter carrier was greeted by a boy and a huge dog. The mailman said to the boy, "does your dog bite?"

"No," replied the boy.

Just then the huge dog bit the mailman in the ankle. The letter carrier yelped, "I thought your dog doesn't bite!"

"He doesn't," replied the boy, "but this is not my dog!"

An agent arranged an audition with a TV producer for his client, a talking dog who told jokes and sang songs. The amazed producer was about to sign a contract when suddenly a much larger dog burst into the room, grabbed the talking pooch by the neck and bounded back out.

"What happened?" demanded the producer.

"That's his mother," said the agent. "She wants him to be a doctor."

A police dog responded to the ad for work with the FBI. "Well," says the personnel director, "you'll have to meet some strict requirements. First you must type at least sixty words per minute."

Sitting down at the typewriter, the dog types at eighty words per minute.

"Also," says the director, "you must pass a physical and complete the obstacle course."

This perfect canine specimen finished the course in record time. "There is one last requirement," the director continues, "you must be bilingual."

With confidence, the dog looks up at him and says, "Meow!"

I put this question to my dog,
A pet who has an air;
"What, may I ask, makes Man's Best Friend
Think he owns Man's Best Chair?"

—Dick Emmons in *The Wall Street Journal*

There's a guy with a Doberman pinscher and a guy with a Chihuahua. The guy with the Doberman says to the guy with the Chihuahua, "Let's go over to that restaurant and get something to eat."

The guy with the Chihuahua says, "We can't go in there. We've got dogs with us."

The guy with the Doberman says, "Just follow my lead."

They walk over to the restaurant, the guy with the Doberman puts on a pair of dark glasses, and he starts to walk in. A guy at the door says, "Sorry, Mac, no pets allowed."

The guy with the Doberman says, "You don't understand. This is my seeing-eye dog."

The guy at the door says, "A Doberman pinscher?"

He says, "Yes, they're using them now; they're very good."

The guy at the door says, "Come on in."

The guy with the Chihuahua figures, "What the heck," so he puts on a pair of dark glasses and starts to walk in.

The guy at the door says, "Sorry, pal, no pets allowed."

The guy with the Chihuahua says, "You don't understand. This is my seeing-eye dog."

The guy at the door says, "A Chihuahua?"

He says, "You mean they gave me a Chihuahua?"

A rancher in Idaho had a sheep dog named Max who met him at the door every day when he came home for dinner. The rancher came home one day, but the dog didn't meet him. He looked for the dog and found him curled up just inside the front door.

The rancher nudged the dog, and urged, "Let's go," but the dog didn't move. So the rancher picked up the dog, carefully placed him in his pickup truck, and drove to the office of Doc Hyde, the local vet. He told Doc Hyde, "Max is sick, can you help him?"

The vet checked the dog, and said, "Sorry, your dog is dead."

The rancher said, "He can't be. Check him again."

Doc Hyde examined the dog again and said, "I'm sorry, but your dog is definitely dead."

The rancher said "Are you sure?"

The vet walked into the other room. When he came back he had a cat. He put the cat on the table. The cat jumped onto the dog's back and dug in his nails. From there, the cat jumped on the dog's head. He scratched the dog's nose. He bit the dogs ear. Then the cat jumped down and walked away.

The rancher said, "You're right. Max is gone. So how much do I owe you?"

The vet said, "That'll be $545. Forty-five dollars for the office visit, and five hundred for the cat scan."

CAT BATHING: A MARTIAL ART

Some people say cats never have to be bathed. They say cats lick themselves clean. They say cats have a special enzyme of some sort in their saliva that works like new, improved Wisk—dislodging the dirt where it hides and whisking it away.

I've spent most of my life believing this folklore. Like most blind believers, I've been able to discount all the facts to the contrary, the kitty odors that lurk in the corners of the garage and dirt smudges that cling to the throw rug by the fireplace.

The time comes, however, when a man must face reality, when he must look squarely in the face of massive public sentiment to the contrary and announce: "This cat smells like a port-a-potty on a hot day in Juarez."

When that day arrives at your house, as it has at mine, I have some advice you might consider as you place your feline friend under your arm and head for the bathtub:

- Know that although the cat has the advantage of quickness and lack of concern for human life, you have the advantage of strength. Capitalize on that advantage by selecting the battlefield. Don't try to bathe him in an open area where he can force you to chase him. Pick a very small bathroom. If your bathroom is more than four feet square, I recommend that you get in the tub with the cat and close the sliding-glass doors as if you were about to take a shower. (A simple shower curtain will not do. A berserk cat can shred a three-ply rubber shower curtain quicker than a politician can shift positions.)

- Know that a cat has claws and will not hesitate to remove all the skin from your body. Your advantage here is that you are smart and know how to dress to protect yourself. I recommend canvas overalls tucked into high-top construction boots, a pair of steel-mesh gloves, an army helmet, a hockey face mask, and a long-sleeved flak jacket.

- Prepare everything in advance. There is no time to go out for a towel when you have a cat digging a hole in your flak jacket. Draw the water. Make sure the bottle of kitty shampoo is inside the glass enclosure. Make sure the towel can be reached, even if you are lying on your back in the water.

- Use the element of surprise. Pick up your cat nonchalantly, as if to simply carry him to his supper dish. Cats will not usually notice your strange attire. They have little or no interest in fashion as a rule.

- Once you are inside the bathroom, speed is essential to survival. In a single liquid motion, shut the bathroom door, step into the tub enclosure, slide the glass door shut, dip the cat in the water and squirt him with shampoo. You have begun one of the wildest minutes of your life.

- Cats have no handles. Add the fact that he now has soapy fur, and the problem is radically compounded. Do not expect to hold on to him for more than two or three seconds at a time. When you have him, however, you must remember to give him another squirt of shampoo and rub like crazy. He'll then spring free and fall back into the water, thereby rinsing himself off. (The national record for cats is three latherings, so don't expect too much.)

- Next, the cat must be dried. Novice cat bathers assume this part will be the most difficult, for humans generally are worn out at this point and the cat is just getting determined. In fact, the drying is simple, compared to what you have just been through. That's because now the cat is semipermanently affixed to your right leg. Simply pop the drain plug with your foot, reach for your towel and wait. (Occasionally, however, the cat will cling to the top of your army helmet. If this happens, the best thing to do is shake him loose and encourage him toward your leg.) After the water is drained from the tub, simply reach down and dry the cat.

In a few days the cat will relax enough to be removed from your leg. He will usually have nothing to say for about three weeks and will spend a lot of time sitting with his back to you. He might even become psychoceramic and develop the fixed stare of a plaster figurine.

You will be tempted to assume he is angry. This isn't usually the case. As a rule he is simply plotting ways to get through your defenses and injure you for life the next time you decide to give him a bath.

But at least now he smells a lot better.

 "**D**octor, Doctor," called Mr. Schultz frantically, "come quick. You know my wife always sleeps with her mouth wide open, and just now a mouse ran down her throat."

"I'll be over in a few minutes," said the doctor. "Meanwhile, try waving a piece of cheese in front of her mouth, and maybe the mouse will come out."

When the doctor reached the Schultz apartment, he found Mr. Schultz in his shirt sleeves waving a six-pound flounder frantically in front of the prostrate Mrs. Schultz's face.

"What's the idea?" said the exasperated doctor. "I told you to wave a piece of cheese. Mice don't like flounder."

"I know, I know," gasped Mr. Schultz. "But we've got to get the cat out first."

The rambunctious lion was stomping around the jungle, roaring his loudest roar, and looking for trouble. He grabbed a passing panther and asked, "Who is the king of the jungle?"

"You are, O mighty lion," answered the panther.

He grabbed a zebra and demanded, "Who is the king of the jungle?"

"You are, O mighty lion," answered the zebra.

He grabbed a chimpanzee and asked, "Who is the king of the jungle?"

"You are, O mighty lion," answered the chimp.

Next the lion met an elephant and asked, "Who is the king of the jungle?"

The elephant grabbed him with his trunk, whirled him around and around and threw him violently to the ground.

The bruised and dazed lion pulled himself to his feet and said, "Just because you don't know the answer is no reason to get so rough."

An antelope and a lion entered a diner and took a booth near the window. When the waiter approached, the antelope said, "I'll have a bowl of hay and a side order of radishes."

"And what will your friend have?"

"Nothing," replied the lion.

The waiter persisted. "Isn't he hungry?"

"Hey, if he were hungry," said the antelope, "would I be sitting here?"

A cowboy fell off his horse and broke his leg 'way out on the prairie. The steed grabbed his master's belt in his teeth, carried him to shelter and then went to fetch the doctor.

Talking it over a few weeks later, a friend of the cowboy's praised the horse's intelligence. "Quite a horse ya got there," he said. "Smart as a whip."

"Heck, he's not so smart," replied the cowboy. "He came back with the veterinarian."

A father took his son deer hunting. After they were deep in the forests, the father said, "We'll do better if we split up. You stay here by the tree. If you see a deer, shoot it."

The son, who had never hunted deer before, asked, "What does a deer look like?"

The father answered, "It has four legs, is brown and has long ears." Before leaving, the father added, "Just one more thing. There are poachers in these woods. If of one tries to get your deer, just hold him at gunpoint until I return."

A short time later, the father heard a gun shot. He ran toward the spot where he had left his son. As his son came into view, he saw the boy pointing a gun at a man, who had his hands in the air. As he got closer, he heard the man say, "All right, son, it's your deer. Just let me get the saddle off of it."

A city man took a winter vacation in an isolated rural area. After a few days of pure peace and quiet, though, he started to get restless.

"What do you do for fun and excitement here?" he asked one of the locals.

"We go down to the lake and watch the moose dance on the ice," was the reply. "It's delightful."

The city fellow didn't think too much of that idea, but after another night of watching the wallpaper, he decided it was better than nothing. So that evening he went down to the lake. The next day he saw the local man who had recommended the trip. "I went down to the lake last night to watch the moose dance on the ice," the city man said. "It was the worst thing I ever saw. Those animals were so clumsy and uncoordinated, they were falling all over themselves."

"Well of course they were," snorted the local. "Nobody goes to the lake on Wednesday. That's amateur night."

The wolves were decimating the farmers' sheep. So the farmers' association raised the bounty on them to a hundred dollars a pelt. Two hunters, Sam and Ed, decided they could use the money. So they got their gear together and headed out to the wide open spaces to shoot some wolves and make themselves rich.

They had just fallen asleep out under the stars when a noise woke Ed. By the light of the campfire he saw the eyes of a hundred wolves—teeth gleaming. He shook his friend and whispered hoarsely, "Sam! Sam! Wake up! We're rich!"

Years ago the Denver Zoo had a difficult decision to make. They were offered the gift of a large, beautiful polar bear, but the problem was that there was no existing room for the bear. At the time of the gift the Board of Directors was in the middle of a fund-raising campaign to renovate the zoo. They changed the strategy to include a magnificent habitat for the polar bear in their renovation plans.

In the meantime the bear was put in a small, temporary cage. The space was so small that it could only take three steps, turn around and walk three steps back.

Because of unforeseen delays the construction took three years, but its new home was indeed grand: waterfalls, spaciousness, caves. The bear entered its new home, looked around, took three steps, turned around, took three steps back, turned around . . .

Ralph and Norris went bear hunting in Montana. While Ralph stayed in the cabin, Norris went out looking for a bear. He soon found a huge bear, shot at it but only wounded it. The enraged bear charged toward him. His rifle jammed, so he dropped it and started running for the cabin as fast as he could.

Now Norris was pretty fleet of foot, but the bear was just a little faster and gained on him with every step. Just as Norris reached the open cabin door, he tripped and fell flat. Too close behind to stop, the bear tripped over him and went rolling into the cabin.

Norris man jumped up, closed the cabin door and yelled to his friend inside, "You skin this one while I go and get another!"

A minister's son was taken out camping one day. His companion warned him not to stray too far from the campfire because the woods were full of wild beasts of all kinds. The young boy had every intention, really, of following that advice but inevitably he was drawn by curiosity and wandered farther and farther from the fire.

Suddenly, he found himself face to face with a large and powerful looking bear. He saw no means of escape, and seeing the bear advance rather menacingly towards him, the minister's son did what he had been taught to do—he knelt down to pray for deliverance. He closed his eyes tightly, but opened them a few moments later and was delighted to see that the bear was also kneeling in prayer right in front of him. He said, "Oh, bear, isn't this wonderful! Here we are with such different viewpoints and such different lives and such different perceptions of life, and yet we're both praying to the same Lord!"

"Son," the bear said evenly, "I don't know about you, but I'm saying grace."

"I simply gotta divorce this woman," the disconsolate man explained to the court. "She insisted upon keeping a pet goat in our bedroom. The smell got so terrible I just couldn't stand it any longer."

The judge shook his head. "That sounds bad," he admitted, "but couldn't you open a window?"

"What?" cried the husband. "And let all my pigeons out?"

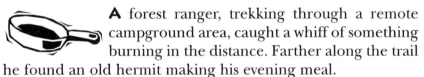 A forest ranger, trekking through a remote campground area, caught a whiff of something burning in the distance. Farther along the trail he found an old hermit making his evening meal.

"What are you cooking?" the ranger asked.

"Peregrine falcon," answered the hermit.

"Peregrine falcon!" the conservationist shouted. "You can't cook that! It's on the endangered-species list."

"How was I to know?" the hermit shrugged. "I haven't had contact with the outside world in ages."

The ranger told the recluse he wouldn't report him this time, but he wasn't to cook peregrine falcon ever again. "By the way," he asked, "what does it taste like?"

"Well," replied the hermit, "I'd say it's somewhere between a dodo bird and a spotted owl."

—Richard Schuldt

Felix Johnson, pastor of the Free Methodist Church in Union City, Michigan, stopped in a pet shop to buy a parrot. "But I don't want one that swears," he explained to the shopkeeper.

"I've got just the bird for you!" said the shopkeeper, Mel Lundy.

Lundy took Pastor Johnson into a back room where the parrot was perched, with a string on each foot.

Lundy pulled the string on the right foot and the bird recited the Lord's Prayer.

Then Lundy pulled the string on the left foot and the parrot burst into "Nearer My God to Thee."

"This is wonderful," said Pastor Johnson. "What would happen if I pulled both strings at the same time?"

"You idiot," squawked the parrot, "I'd fall on my keister."

Max Cohen comes home from the pet shop with a parrot and places it on its perch.

"*Shalom alaichem,*" Cohen says.

"*Alaichem shalom,*" the parrot replies.

Cohen is flabbergasted. "You're Jewish? You speak Hebrew?"

"Of course," the parrot replies, "I'm Orthodox."

"You pray?"

"Of course," the parrot says. He reaches under one wing, takes out a tiny skullcap and prayer shawl and puts them on. "In fact," the parrot insists, "since next week is Rosh Hashanah, I'd like you to take me to the synagogue with you."

Immediately Cohen sees a profit in the situation. The next day he tells his friends at the synagogue about his amazing pet. Just as he expects, they accuse him of having lost his mind. So he bets various parishioners a total of two thousand dollars that he has a parrot who prays.

Rosh Hashanah arrives, Cohen takes the parrot to the synagogue—and the parrot doesn't pray a single word. Cohen is two thousand in the hole.

When he gets the parrot back home, Cohen grabs the bird to wring its neck.

"Hold it, you idiot," the parrot says.

"Why should I?" Cohen demands. "I bet my friends you would pray, and when you didn't, I lost two thousand dollars."

"But Yom Kippur, the Day of Atonement, is in ten days," the parrot points out.

"So?" Cohen says.

"On Yom Kippur we Orthodox Jews sing the Kol Nidre."

"So?"

"So, bet everyone I can sing the Kol Nidre," the parrot says.

"But you didn't pray a word on Rosh Hashanah," Cohen says.

"And you should thank me for it," the parrot says. "Think of the odds you'll get on Yom Kippur."

A clergyman owned a parrot with an acquired vocabulary of cuss words from a previous owner. It was embarrassing. A woman in his congregation suggested a remedy. She would put him with her well-behaved parrot, since her female parrot said nothing except, "Let us pray."

The birds were put together. The pastor's bird took one look at the lady parrot and chirped, "Hi, Toots, how about a little kiss?"

The lady parrot responded gleefully, "My prayers have been answered!"

—Kit Hoag

The emperor was a gentle man and loved all wild animals. Instead of hunting them he allowed them to run loose throughout his domain. The people finally became annoyed, then revolted and overthrew their ruler.

It was the first time in history that the reign was called on account of game.

Mrs. Hildrick, the third grade teacher was quizzing her pupils on natural history. "Now, Jason, tell me where the elephant is found."

Jason struggled for the answer. Finally a look of pride lit up his face: "The elephant is so big that he's never lost."

"I tell you what I'm going to do," said Wayne to his friend Frank. "For a hundred dollars, I'm going to sell you an elephant. What do you think about that?"

"I think it sounds crazy," Frank replied. "I don't want an elephant. I don't even like elephants."

"Don't be so stubborn," Wayne said. "This is a deal I'm offering you; a full-grown elephant for just one hundred dollars."

Frank protested, "But I don't want a full-grown elephant for no hundred dollars. For one thing, where would I keep it? And the mess they make. No, sir. Count me out. An elephant I do not need."

Wayne eyed his friend closely. "Tell you what I'll do. For a hundred and fifty dollars, I'll get you two elephants!"

Frank said, "Now you're talking!"

When cows laugh, does milk come out of their noses?

—Jeff Marder

An efficiency expert was driving through the country side when he noticed an old farmer in an apple orchard feeding his pig. What he saw drove him absolutely crazy, for the farmer was holding the pig over his head and moving him from apple to apple in the trees while the pig ate happily.

The efficiency expert turned around, parked, and walked up to the farmer, saying, "Hey, there, old timer, have I got a good idea for you."

The farmer asked him what it was and the Expert continued, "Just put the pig on the ground, get a stick, knock the apples to the ground and let the pig eat them there. It sure will save a lot of time."

The old farmer thought about this while he moved his pig to another apple and finally said "Aw shucks, mister, what's time to a pig?"

I took my daughter's Montessori school class to a farm near Princeton, New Jersey. Five-year-old Claudia, who was visiting a farm for the first time, stared at a fat sow lying in a pen. Said the farmer, "She's mighty big, isn't she?"

"She sure is," said Claudia. "I just saw six little piggies blowing her up a few minutes ago."

Two young Oklahoma women met a frog on the street. "Kiss me," the frog said, "and I'll turn into an independent oil man."

One of the women picked him up and put him in her purse.

"Aren't you going to kiss him?" the other asked.

"No. A talking frog is really worth something."

—Editorial in *New York Times*

In the words of Kermit the Frog: "Time's fun when you're having flies."

I was in my office at the church one day when the phone rang. "Is the Reverend there?" a man asked.

I explained that I was a minister.

The man wanted to know which Scripture verses applied to funeral services.

I gave him several references, and he jotted them down.

"What about the `ashes to ashes, dust to dust' part?" he asked.

I read it to him slowly. Then, intending to offer him some sympathy, I inquired, "And who is the deceased?"

"My daughter's pet turtle," he replied.

After the flood subsided, Noah opened the doors of the Ark and released the animals. All living things rushed to freedom, except for two snakes who lingered in a corner. "Why don't you go forth and multiply?" asked Noah in a stern voice.

"We can't," moaned one. "We're adders!"

I think animal testing is a terrible idea; they get all nervous and give the wrong answers.

I am not a vegetarian because I love animals; I am a vegetarian because I hate plants. —A. Whitney Brown

Off-beat comedian Steven Wright offers his typically skewed perspective on a few of our animal friends:
- I spilled Spot remover on my dog. . . . Now he's gone.
- There's a fine line between fishing and standing on the shore looking like an idiot.
- I went fishing with a dotted line. . . . I caught every other fish.
- The other day when I was walking through the woods, I saw a rabbit standing in front of a candle making shadows of people on a tree.
- Yesterday I saw a chicken crossing the road. I asked it why. It told me it was none of my business.

16.
THE REST
OF THE WORLD

MUSIC

The local symphony orchestra in a small Midwestern town was rehearsing for a concert. After the last strains of Handel's *Largo* floated out, the mother of one of the violinists went up to the conductor and said, "Won't you please play Handel's *Largo?*"

"But we've just finished playing it," the conductor replied.

The woman sank back in her chair. "Oh, I wish I'd known it," she sighed. "It's my favorite piece."

Have you noticed how a concert audience will applaud a familiar encore after a few bars are played? They are applauding neither the performer nor the music. They are applauding themselves because they recognize it.   —Sigmund Spaeth

The Secret Service men were worried about security at a Washington performance of La Boheme that President Eisenhower was to attend. They inquired of Sir Rudolf Bing: "We hear the girl dies. How is she killed?"

He replied, "She dies of consumption. It isn't contagious at a distance."

During World War II, Harpo Marx, of the infamous Marx Brothers, joined an all-star company doing one-night stands for the war-bond drive. Wrote Harpo:

At Soldier Field in Chicago, we played to 110,000 people. While I was waiting to do my second bit on the show, one of the stadium hot-dog vendors came backstage to shake hands with me. "For my dough," he said, "You're the best one on the program." I felt complimented, since the other performers were Mickey Rooney, Judy Garland, Fred Astaire, Lucille Ball, Betty Hutton, Kay Kyser and his band, and José Iturbi.

"Yes sir, Mr. Marx," he added. "When you played on your harp, I sold four times as many hot dogs as when anybody else was on stage."

When the kindergarten teacher returned to her class after being absent, she asked the children how they had liked their substitute. "She was all right," said one little boy, "but she wasn't as smart as you. She had to use two hands to play the piano."

—*Sunshine Magazine*

A woman carrying a violin says to husband bearing a tuba, as they ring the neighbors' doorbell: "Now remember—if they threaten to show slides, we offer to play the background music."

A good musical comedy consists largely of disorderly conduct occasionally interrupted by talk. —George Ade

Opera is when a guy gets stabbed in the back, and instead of bleeding he sings. —Ed Gardner

ART AND LITERATURE

My friend, Murray Silverman, the owner of a priceless antiques collection, allowed a museum to exhibit his treasures. The movers packed the vases, while Murray anxiously hovered over them.

"Do be careful," he cautioned one brawny mover. "That vase is nearly two thousand years old."

"Don't worry, pal," the mover replied. "I'll treat it like it was brand new."

My cousin Tim loves art museums. Wherever he travels, he squeezes in a visit to the local art collections. Unfortunately, Aunt Kay is easily bored and tired by them.

When Tim and Kay were in Chicago, Tim dragged Kay to the Art Institute to see the famous Impressionist paintings. After only a few galleries he spotted "Sunday on the Grande Jatte" at the end of the hall. Nearly transported with ecstasy, he danced down the corridor calling: "Kay! Seurat! Seurat!"

My aunt shot back, "Whatever will be, will be."

I went to the museum where they had all the heads and arms from the statues that are in all the other museums.

—Steven Wright

Cabot Lowell Martingale, a Boston Brahmin of unquestionable social propriety and impeccable taste, had never seen, heard, or read any play by Shakespeare. When his friends learned this, they were appalled. Immediately one of them brought him an elegantly bound set of Shakespeare's complete works.

Weeks later, the two met again, and the friend said, "Well, Martingale, have you read any of Shakespeare?"

"Every word," said Martingale.

"And what did you think of him?"

"Why, I thought the man simply extraordinary. His ability with the language was almost beyond belief. I don't think there are a dozen men in Boston who could equal him."

It all depends on your point of view. Here is a tongue-in-cheek review of *Lady Chatterley's Lover* as it appeared in *Field and Stream,* November 1959:

"Although written many years ago, *Lady Chatterley's Lover* has just been reissued by Grove Press, and this fictional account of the day-by-day life of an English gamekeeper is still of considerable interest to outdoor-minded readers, as it contains many passages on pheasant raising, the apprehending of poachers, ways to control vermin, and other chores and duties of the professional gamekeeper. Unfortunately one is obliged to wade through many pages of extraneous materials in order to discover and savor these sidelights on the management of a Midlands shooting estate. In this reviewer's opinion this book cannot take the place of *J. R. Miller's Practical Gamekeeping.*"

G. K. Chesterton and several other literary figures were asked one evening what book they would prefer to have with them if stranded on a desert isle. One writer said without hesitation: "The complete works of Shakespeare." Another said, "I'd choose the Bible." They turned to Chesterton. "How about you?" And Chesterton replied, "I would choose *Thomas's Guide to Practical Ship Building.*"

To the Editor:

> I'm writing this letter,
> Quite frankly, to say
> I abhorred the column
> You wrote yesterday!
> It was weak and insipid
> And words synonymous—
> In short, it lacked courage!
>
> Yours truly,
> Anonymous.

Struggling with the English language, the foreigner was frustrated by the reasoning behind the pronunciation of words like tough, bough, though. He gave up when he read this newspaper headline: "BAZAAR PRONOUNCED SUCCESS."

—*Modern Maturity*

Did you hear about the failed attempt to start a magazine dedicated to the work of poet e. e. cummings? The project was undercapitalized.

Julie Wallace went to the post office to mail a Bible to her son at college. "Ma'am," asked the post office clerk, "does this package contain anything breakable?"

"Only the Ten Commandments," she replied.

ETC.
Here's a three-letter word
Used by more than a few
To make people think
They know more than they do.

—Richard Armour

A rejection slip sent to a writer by a Chinese economics journal was delicately phrased as follows:

"We have read your manuscript with boundless delight. If we were to publish your paper, it would be impossible for us to publish any work of a lower standard. And as it is unthinkable that, in the next thousand years, we shall see its equal, we are, to our regret, compelled to return your divine composition and beg you a thousand times to overlook our short sight and timidity."

English translation: "Don't ever send us this kind of rubbish again."

Have you seen all these modern editions of the Bible? Well, publishers still have some standards. Here are the top nine Bible publisher rejects—editions of the Bible that will not be published.

9. *The "And Then There's Some Bad News" Bible*
8. *The Reader's Digest Condensed New Testament (with Psalm and Proverb)*
7. *Scripture Lite* (every appearance of "thou shalt not" has been changed to "well, it's your decision.")
6. *The Holy Writ Pop-Up Book*
5. *The Rapper's Bible* ("In the Beginning: Word!")
4. *The First-Year Greek Student Translation*
3. *The California Valley Girl Version* ("In, like, the beginning, you know . . .")
2. *The Ig-pay Atin-lay Ulgate-vay*
1. *The Invisible Ink Bible with Secret Decoder Ring*

Cecil B. DeMille was once asked why he made so many Biblical motion pictures. He answered, "Why let two thousand years of publicity go to waste?"

I went to a bookstore and I asked the woman behind the counter where the self-help section was. She said, "If I told you, that would defeat the whole purpose."

—Brian Kiley

One time my uncle Herman from Vermont mailed an order to his butcher in Boston. First he began the note, "Kindly send two gooses." That didn't seem right, so he started over again with "Kindly send two geeses." Still he wasn't satisfied. He settled his dilemma by writing finally, "Kindly send me a goose." Then he signed his name and added a P.S.: "Send another one with it."

Man invented language to satisfy his deep need to complain.

—Lily Tomlin

It is prudent to thank an author for his book before reading it, so as to avoid the necessity of lying about it afterwards.

—George Santayana

There are seventy million books in American libraries, but the one you want to read is always out. —Tom Masson

Steven Wright's observations on art, writing, and music:
- What's another word for "thesaurus"?
- My grandfather invented Cliff's Notes. It all started back in 1912. . . . Well, to make a long story short . . .
- I play the harmonica. The only way I can play is if I get my car going really fast, and stick it out the window.
- I wrote a song, but I can't read music. Every time I hear a new song on the radio I think "Hey, maybe I wrote that."
- I'm writing an unauthorized autobiography.
- I'm writing a book. I've got the page numbers done.

COMPUTERS

NEW COMPUTER VIRUSES
- *Government Economist Virus.* Nothing works, but all your diagnostic software says everything is fine.
- *Federal Bureaucrat Virus.* Divides your hard drive into hundreds of little units, each of which do practically nothing, but all of which claim to be the most important part of the computer.
- *Paul Revere Virus.* This revolutionary virus does not horse around. It warns you of impending hard disk attack—once if by LAN; twice if by C:\>.
- *Politically Correct Virus.* Never calls itself a "virus," but instead refers to itself as an "electronic microorganism."
- *Oprah Winfrey Virus.* Your two hundred megabyte hard drive suddenly shrinks to eighty megabytes, then slowly expands back to two hundred megabytes, and then hires a personal trainer and a chef and shrinks to seventy megabytes.

- *AT&T Virus*. Every three minutes it tells you what great service you are getting.
- *MCI Virus*. Every three minutes it reminds you that you are paying too much for the AT&T virus.
- *Gallup Virus*. Sixty percent of the PCs infected will lose thirty-eight percent of their data fourteen percent of the time (plus or minus a 3.5 percent margin of error).
- *Arnold Schwarzenegger Virus*. Terminates and stays resident. It'll be back to erase your data and say, "Hasta la vista, baby!"

Applying computer technology is simply finding the right wrench to pound in the correct screw.

Three IBM staffers were on a long car trip when they got a flat tire. After they stopped and studied the situation, the sales rep said, "That does it. We need a new car."

The service rep said, "Wait! Let's switch some parts around until it works again."

The software rep said, "No. Just turn the car on and off to see if that fixes the problem." —*The Jokesmith*

DISKETTE USAGE AND CARE
- Never leave diskettes in the drive, as the data can leak out of the disk and corrode the inner mechanics of the drive. Diskettes should be rolled up and stored in pencil holders.
- Do not fold diskettes unless they do not fit into the drive. "Big" diskettes may be folded and used in "little" drives.
- Never insert a diskette into the drive upside down. The data can fall off the surface of the disk and jam the intricate mechanics of the drive.
- Diskettes cannot be backed up by running them through a photocopy machine. If your data is going to need to be backed up, simply insert two diskettes into your drive. Whenever you update a document, the data will be written onto both disks.

Diskettes should be cleaned and waxed once a week. Microscopic metal particles may be removed by waving a powerful magnet over the surface of the disk. Any stubborn metal shavings can be removed with scouring powder and steel wool. When waxing a diskette, make sure the surface is even. This allows the diskette to spin faster, resulting in better access time.

- A handy tip for more legible backup copies: keep a container of iron filings at your desk. When you need to make two copies, sprinkle iron filings liberally between the diskettes before inserting them into the drive.
- Diskettes should not be removed or inserted into the drive while the red light is on or flashing. Doing so could result in smeared or possibly unreadable text.
- If your diskette is full and needs more storage space, remove the disk from the drive and shake vigorously for two minutes. This will pack the data enough (data compression) to allow for more storage. Be sure to cover all openings with Scotch tape to prevent loss of data.
- Data access time may be greatly improved by cutting more holes in the diskette jacket. This will provide more simultaneous access points to the disk. Periodically spray diskettes with insecticide to prevent system bugs from spreading. . . .
- You can keep your data fresh by storing disks in the vegetable compartment of your refrigerator. Disks may be frozen, but remember to thaw by microwaving or briefly immersing in boiling water.
- "Little" diskettes must be removed from their box prior to use. These containers are childproof to prevent tampering by unknowledgeable youngsters.
- You can recover data from a damaged disk by using the DOS command FORMAT/U or alternately by scratching new sector marks on the disk with a nail file.
- Diskettes become "hard" with age. It's important to back up your "hard" disks before they become too brittle to use.
- Make sure you label your data. Staples are good way to permanently affix labels to your disks.

Latest computer novels:
1) *A Tale of Two CDs*
2) *Gates of Wrath*
3) *Gone with the Windows*
4) *War and PC*
5) *Moby Disk*

 Jay Leno on Campbell's nineteen new kinds of soup: "They're trying to attract a hipper, high-tech customer. The alphabet soup now has spell-check."

Unlike print, electronic text defies proverbial wisdom. You can have your cake, give it away, then eat it, and still have it.

—Richard A. Lanham

There is reason to hope that machines will use us kindly, for their existence will be in a great measure dependent on ours; they will rule us with a rod of iron, but they will not eat us.

—Samuel Butler, 1872

Technology is dominated by two types of people: those who understand what they do not manage and those who manage what they do not understand.   —Archibald Putt, 1981

Did we invent the computer because we needed very fast calculators, or did the calculators suggest to us the importance of solving problems that require such speed?   —J. David Bolter, 1984

Undeniably, some kids click with computers. The emphasis, however belongs on some—as in the phrase, some kids click with violins, or some kids click with paintbrushes. But there are no millions being spent to bring violins or paintbrushes into the schools.   —Theodore Roszak, 1986

Computerization has not made the federal government more efficient; rather, it has merely magnified the impact of its snafus. —August Bequai, 1987

Computers are a lot like the Old Testament view of God—lots of rules and not very forgiving. —Joseph Campbell, 1987

In offices across the land, all those wonderful little personal computers are being hooked together into local networks. This is sort of like having a window in your bathroom. The light is nice and the scenery can be entertaining, but you'll probably spend most of your time making sure the curtains are fully closed. The miracle of instant communication does have its down side. In the past, the company jerk with the bad sense of humor and the compulsion to comment on everything was easily avoidable. Now, electronic mail is making him an author you can't refuse.

—*"It's Not a Bug, It's a Feature!" Computer Wit and Wisdom,* compiled by David Lubar

PCs are the world's greatest medium for futzing around. They're computational catnip for obsessives, keyboard crack for neurotics and seductive time sinks for ordinary folk who just want to make sure that they've reasonably examined all their options. Why do you think we call them "users"?

—Michael Schrage

It doesn't matter how acquainted you are with a particular brand of computer. When you need to borrow someone else's, it feels like you're using their toothbrush. —Kevin Kelly

Why does it take a computer magazine six to eight weeks to change your address when you move? Don't they use computers?

—John McCormick

 **C**omputers have proved adept at handling abstract challenges like flying spaceships, playing chess, and solving quadratic equations, but housework is too hard.

—Timothy Ferris

From time to time, contractors are accosted by what seems to be religious zealots. They are really just Apple Macintosh users.

—Bill Smith

The Information Superhighway is a misnomer. First, there's no highway—there are no roadmaps, guides, rules. And second, it ain't super.

—David Martin

I heard a telling comment recently: If you torture numbers long enough, you can make them say anything.

—Cheryl Currid

I haven't had enough E-mail recently and actually had to get some real work done.

—Stewart Alsop, after a system problem prevented his mail from reaching him

The big thing today is computer dating. If you don't know how to run a computer, it really dates you.

> **I** have a spelling checker
> It came with my PC
> It plainly marks four my revue
> mistakes I cannot sea
> I've run this poem threw it
> I'm sure your please to no
> It's letter perfect in its weigh
> My checker tolled me sew

Seen on NBC: A report on "voice recognition," the ability of a computer program to recognize speech and turn it into text. An expert was being interviewed in a voice-over as the picture showed him writing a letter about this exciting new technology in the background. The expert said, "Soon voice recognition will assist in everything from electronic mail to faxes and voice mail." The computer can be seen churning away in the corner, faithfully typing out "soon voice recognition will assist in everything from electronic mail to faxes envoy smell."

HIGH (AND LOW) TECHNOLOGY

My dad just invented a new microwave television set. He can watch *60 Minutes* in twelve seconds.

Steven Wright's grasp of technology may differ from yours:
- Last night I fell asleep in a satellite dish. My dreams were broadcast all over the world.
- I just bought a microwave fireplace. . . . You can spend an evening in front of it in only eight minutes.
- I put instant coffee in a microwave and almost went back in time.

Everything is going to be automated in the future. Even Emergency 911: "Thank you for calling Emergency 911. If you're being murdered, press 1. If you're suffering from a split personality press 2, 3, and 4. If you're battling Satan, press 666. If you are being assaulted, press pound, pound, pound. If you are already dead, stay on the line, and an operator will be with you shortly."   —Adam Christing

Cordless phones are great. If you can find them.

—Glenn Foster

Banks charge a "service fee" to use an ATM. Coke machines will soon expect a tip!

—Bill Jones

From Lloyd Smith, MD, during his address at the graduation ceremony for the University of Texas Medical School at Galveston:

Then there was the man who was so imbued with the scientific method that he sent two of his children to Sunday school and kept the other two at home as controls.

The scientific theory I like best is that the rings of Saturn are composed entirely of lost airline luggage.

—Mark Russell

With every passing hour our solar system comes forty-three thousand miles closer to Globular Cluster M13 in the constellation Hercules, and still there are some misfits who continue to insist that there is no such thing as progress.

—Ransom K. Ferm

The best way to make a fire with two sticks is to make sure one of them is a match.

—Will Rogers

Comedian Yakov Smirnoff writes, "Coming from the Soviet Union, I was not prepared for the incredible variety of products available in American grocery stores. While on my first shopping trip, I saw powdered milk—you just add water, and you get milk. Then I saw powered orange juice—you just add water, and you get orange juice. And then I saw baby powder—I thought to myself, what a country!

—*America on Six Rubles a Day* (Vintage)

STUDENT STUNTS

Mother's little darling returns from his first day of school.
"Oh, I hope you didn't cry," his mother says reassuringly.
"I didn't," the little one says, "but boy, the teacher sure did."

—King Duncan

Educational television should be absolutely forbidden. It can only lead to unreasonable expectations and eventual disappointment when your child discovers that the letters of the alphabet do not leap up out of books and dance around the room with royal-blue chickens.

—Fran Lebowitz

The little darling was describing the first day of school. "We had a new teacher, and she wanted to know if I had any brothers and sisters. I told her I was an only child."
"What did she say?" the mother asked.
"She said, 'Thank goodness!'"

—King Duncan

My seven year old came home from school and asked me for a dollar. His explanation: "Our principal's leaving, so we're all chipping in to give her a little momentum."

The chemistry professor wrote the formula HNO_3 on the blackboard. Then he whirled about and pointed at a sleepy student in the back row. "Identify that formula," he insisted.
"Um, uh," stalled the unhappy student, "I've got it right on the tip of my tongue, sir."
"In that case," said the professor softly, "you'd better spit it out. It's nitric acid."

What this country really needs is some colleges that teach everything the students think they already know. —Jack Knowles

The frantic football coach begged the math professor who had flunked his quarterback on the eve of the homecoming game to give the young man another chance. Moved by the coach's sincerity, the professor agreed to give the athlete a special makeup exam.

The next day the coach and the quarterback arrived at the professor's office. Said the professor to the athlete, "I'm going to ask you just one question. How much is seven times seven?"

The young man thought for a minute and tentatively said, "Thirty-five?"

"I'm sorry," said the professor. "This is hopeless. I'll have to flunk you."

"Come on, Professor, give him a break," said the coach. "He only missed by one."

Milo Stenson, the Dean of Students at Indiana State University, informed Willis Manfred, the football coach, that his star player Malcolm Peeples was being thrown out of college. Coach dashed over to Stenson's office and said, "Dean, I'd like to know why you're expelling Malcolm."

The dean answered, "Well, we caught him cheating on a math test."

The coach asked, "How do you know he was cheating?"

"Coach," said the dean, "he was sitting next to a straight-A student, and the history professor gave a pop quiz of ten questions. The first nine answers on the two papers were identical."

And the coach said, "Well, you know, that could happen."

Dean Stenson said, "Yes, that's true. But it was the tenth answer that really sealed his fate. You see, the straight-A student answered that tenth question, 'I don't know.' And your prize player Malcolm wrote, 'I don't know, either.'"

On one occasion a student burst into his office. "Professor Stigler, I don't believe I deserve this F you've given me."

To which Stigler replied, "I agree, but unfortunately it is the lowest grade the university will allow me to award."

When he was in junior high school, my son Stephen was asked by his English teacher to give her a sentence with an object.

"You are very pretty," he answered.

"What's the object?" the teacher asked.

Stephen replied, "To get an A in English."

A college student wrote to her parents as follows:

Dear Mom and Dad,

I'm sorry to be so long in writing, but all my writing paper was lost the night the dormitory burned down. I'm out of the hospital now, and the doctor says my eyesight should be back to normal sooner or later. The wonderful boy, Bill, who rescued me from the fire, kindly offered to share his little apartment with me until the dorm is rebuilt. He comes from a good family, so you won't be surprised when I tell you we are going to be married. In fact, you always wanted a grandchild, so you will be glad to know you will be grandparents early next year.

Then she added this postscript:

Please disregard the above practice in English composition. There was no fire. I haven't been in the hospital. I'm not pregnant. And I don't have a steady boyfriend. But I did get a D in French and an F in chemistry, and I wanted you to receive the news in proper perspective.

Love,

Mary

"Papa," said the doting mother, "Junior's teacher says we should buy him an encyclopedia."

"Encyclopedia, my eye," muttered the father. "Let him walk to school like I did."

Miriam was away from home for the first time, attending a small college in Missouri. The Jewish New Year, Rosh Hashanah, was only a few days away and Miriam wanted to send her grandmother an appropriate card. She searched high and low with no luck. Finally she went to the biggest card store in town and asked, "Do you have any Rosh Hashanah cards?"

The clerk gave her an icy stare and replied snootily, "I'm sorry, we only carry Hallmark."

Then there's the father who laments the fact that three of his children are in graduate school. He's getting poorer by degrees.

Bjarne Bjorkland was examining his son's report card. "One thing can be clearly seen," he announced. "With this report card, you couldn't possibly be cheating."

CARS AND TRAFFIC

"**H**ear you've been having car trouble," said one neighbor to another.

"Yes," replied the car owner. "I bought a new carburetor that saved thirty percent on gas, a new transmission that saved fifty percent on gas, and a new set of spark plugs that saved forty percent on gas."

"So what happened?" asked the neighbor.

"After I drove about forty miles, the gas tank overflowed."

You know you're going to have a bad day when as you drive off in the morning you see surveyors from the state highway department waving at you from your new patio.

Have you noticed? Anyone going slower than you is an idiot, and anyone going faster than you is a moron.   —George Carlin

Traffic signals in New York are just rough guidelines.

—David Letterman

 A young attorney sat waiting for a red light to change. A boy rode alongside him on a moped. The boy motioned the lawyer to lower his window. As he lowered the passenger-side window, the boy leaned up and said, "Mister, that's a fine car. What kind is it?"

"A Porsche," the annoyed attorney relied.

"Does it cost a lot?" the boy asked.

"Plenty," the attorney stated.

"Is it fast?" asked the boy.

Without reply the lawyer quickly accelerated at the change of the light, leaving the youngster behind. As he increased speed, he observed the boy on the moped approaching him! And then the boy passed the Porsche, on the passenger side of the road, no less. "What has that kid got in that thing?" the lawyer wondered.

The attorney accelerated, and so did the boy. The boy passed him going very nearly twice as fast. "What is he trying to prove?" the attorney asked aloud. "Well, he won't pass me again."

He put the accelerator to the floor. In the rear view mirror he could see the boy accelerating even faster. Just as the moped was about to pass him, the frustrated attorney drove him off the road. The moped hit a large rock. The Porsche screeched to a stop, and the youngster landed close to the automobile. The embarrassed lawyer apologized, "I didn't mean to hurt you, son. I just wanted to know how you did that. Is there anything I can do for you?"

"Sure, Mister. Could you unhook my suspenders from your rear view mirror?"

Never lend your car to anyone to whom you have given birth.

—Erma Bombeck

At a personal injury suit in Texas, a man from New York was on the witness stand. While driving from Austin to San Antonio, the New Yorker's car had been struck by a beat-up old pickup truck driven by a local rancher. The New Yorker was attempting to collect damages for his injuries.

"How can you now claim to have all these injuries?" asked the insurance company's lawyer. "I notice in the report of the Texas Ranger who investigated the accident that the very first words you said to him were that you'd never felt better in your life. And yet here we are in court, you've sued my client." He said, "Can you explain that statement?"

The New Yorker replied, "Yes, sir, I think I can. After the rancher's truck hit my car, it ran into a ditch and turned over. Now, there was a mule and a dog in that truck, and they were injured worse than the rancher or me. The Texas Ranger heard the mule braying in pain and saw that it had a broken leg. So the Ranger whipped out his pistol and shot the mule right between the eyes. Then he saw that the dog was in terrible pain, so the Ranger shot him too.

"Then he came over to me and asked me, 'Sir, how are you?' And that's when I said I never felt better in my life!"

Comedian Steven Wright's unique perspective on cars and traffic:
- Yesterday I parked my car in a tow-away zone. . . . When I came back the entire area was missing.
- For a while I didn't have a car. I had a helicopter. There was no place to park it, so I just tied it to a lamp post and left it running . . .
- I had to stop driving my car for a while. The tires got dizzy.
- I replaced the headlights on my car with strobe lights. Now it looks like I'm the only one moving.
- I watched the Indy 500, and I was thinking that if they left earlier they wouldn't have to go so fast.
- I used to work in a fire hydrant factory. . . . You couldn't park anywhere near the place.
- One day, when I came home from work, I accidentally put my car key in the door of my apartment building. . . . I

turned it and the whole building started up. . . . So I drove it around. . . . A policeman stopped me for going too fast. . . . He said, "Where do you live?" I said, "Right here" . . . Then I drove my building onto the middle of a highway, and I ran outside, and told all of the cars to get out of my driveway.

- My neighbor has a circular driveway. . . . He can't get out.

I had a brand-new Mercury. I loaned it to my brother last week. I said, "Treat it as if it was your own." He sold it.

—Jimmy Edmonson, a.k.a. Professor Backwards

Two cars collided on a winding, backwoods road. The drivers got out and traded insurance information in a gentlemanly fashion. Then one driver took out a bottle and said, "Look, fellow, you seem a bit shaken up. How about a drink to steady your nerves?" The other took the proffered flask and gulped some down. Gratefully he handed it back.

When the first man simply put it away, the second asked, "Aren't you going to have any?"

The first man replied, "Not till after the police get here."

After my car skidded on wet pavement and struck a light pole, I was bruised and disheveled. When I got out of the car, I slipped and fell in some mud. The police officer who had come to the scene, pointed to an exclusive restaurant across the road and suggested that I could clean up there.

As I entered, the *maitre d'* recoiled in disgust. "Excuse me," I said, "where's the bathroom?"

"Go down the hall and turn left," replied the *maitre d'*. "When you see the sign marked 'Gentlemen,' pay no attention to it and go right inside."

The first one to see the light turn green is the driver of the second car back.

—Terry Marchal

My Uncle Irv visited New York City and was appalled by the traffic. So he came up with an ingenious plan to relieve the terrible conditions. He proposed making every cross-town street in Manhattan one way in the same direction—going west.

"What good would that accomplish?" I asked him.

He replied, "If they put my plan into effect on Monday at 9:00 A.M., by Wednesday at noon the entire problem will be New Jersey's."

A favorite Reagan yarn: A Texan was visiting a farmer in Maine. The Texan asked, "How big is your farm?" The farmer replied, "It goes from the road to that clump of trees and across to the creek. Tell me, how big is your farm?"

"Well said the Texas, "I can get in my car and drive for an hour before I can even get to the edge of my farm."

"Oh," said the Maine farmer. "I used to have a car like that myself."

Anybody in the audience with a New York license plate BL75836745895947362847456783926210284, will you kindly move it? Your license plate is blocking traffic.   —Bill Dana

Kevin was a young fellow who was quite inventive, always trying out new things. One day he thought he would see just how fast a bicycle could go before it went out of control. He pedaled as fast as he could and got the bicycle to go over thirty miles per hour. He was sure it could go at least twice as fast. So he asked his friend, Eric, who owned an old Mustang, if he could tie his bike to the bumper of his car to test his theory. His friend said, "Sure."

Kevin tied his bike to the back of the car and said to Eric, "I'll ring my bike bell once if I want you to go faster, twice if I want you maintain speed, and repeatedly if I want you to slow down."

With that, off they went. Things were going pretty well, with Eric slowly increasing his speed until he was going well over sixty miles per hour. On his bike Kevin was handling the speed just fine. Suddenly, a black Corvette came up beside them. The fellow driving the Mustang forgot all about the fellow on the bike and started drag racing the Corvette.

A little farther down the road sat Deputy Todd in his police cruiser, radar gun at the ready. He heard the two cars before his radar flashed 105 miles per hour.

He called headquarters on his radio and said, "Hey, you guys aren't going to believe this, but there's a Corvette and a Mustang racing out here on Highway 3, and there's a guy on a bike ringing his bell and waving his arms trying to pass them!"

Too bad the only people who know how to run this country are busy driving cabs and cutting hair.   —George Burns

Veterinarian Sarah Booker put a dog on the examining table to treat it for a skin irritation. The dog squirmed out of her grip, leaped off the table, sailed through the open window, and landed in the parking lot. Sarah gave chase, and was down on her hands and knees looking under the cars when the parking-lot attendant walked over.

"Oh, please help me," said the vet. "I'm looking for an itchy poochie."

"Sorry," the attendant replied. "I can't tell one Japanese car from another."   —Lowell Yoder in *The Rotarian*

HIGH (AND LOW) FINANCE

Thanks to inflation you can live in a more expensive neighborhood without going to the trouble of moving.

Who says you can't beat the odds? My lawyer friend, Bill Oakes, drove his $30,000 Cadillac to Las Vegas and returned on a $250,000 Greyhound bus!

While money isn't everything, it does keep you in touch with your children.

My tightwad Uncle Irv joined an organization that fights inflation, but he was very disappointed. An hour after he joined, they raised the dues.

My cousin Ed is so rich he has eight deadly sins. He had one custom made.

Few of us can stand prosperity. Another man's, I mean.

—Mark Twain

Uncle Irv, who was not noted for his religious devotion, needed three million dollars to clinch an important real estate deal. So he went to a local synagogue to pray for the money. By chance he knelt next to a man who was praying for one hundred dollars to pay his rent. Irv reached into his pocket for his money clip and took out a hundred dollar bill, which he pressed into the other man's hand. Overcome with gratitude, the man got up and left the sanctuary. Uncle Irv then looked heavenward and prayed, "Lord, now that I have your undivided attention . . ."

Christmas is the season when people run out of money before they run out of friends.

—Larry Wilde

Just recently my Visa card was stolen. . . . Right now it's everywhere I want to be.

—Scott Wood

Times have sure changed. Yesterday a bum asked me if I could spare $2.75 for a double cappuccino with no foam. —Bill Jones

I saw a bank that said "Twenty-Four Hour Banking," but I don't have that much time. —Steven Wright

TRAVEL

Jerome Frank, Professor of Psychiatry at Johns Hopkins University, relates, "Whenever I'm flying and I engage people in conversation, a confession is almost always forthcoming when they find out I am a psychiatrist. A few years ago, before modern security measures were installed at the nation's airports, a man I sat next to on a coast-to-coast flight told me, "I used to be deathly afraid of flying. It started after that man brought a bomb on board a flight to Denver to kill his mother-in-law. I could never stop thinking that someone on one of my flights might also be carrying a bomb."

I asked, "What did you do about it?"

He replied, "Well, I went to one of those special schools for people who are afraid of flying, and they told me there was only one chance in ten thousand that someone would be on board my flight with a bomb. That didn't make me feel much better. The odds were still too close. But then I reasoned that if there was only one chance in ten thousand that one bomb would be on the plane, there was only one chance in a hundred million that two bombs would be on board. And I could live with those odds."

So I asked, "But what good would that do you?"

"Ever since then," he quickly replied, "I carry one bomb on board myself—just to improve the odds."

The city family was looking forward to renting a summer home in the mountains and was corresponding with a property owner who had a house for rent.

"Before we agree," the woman wrote, "you must assure us that the house has a good view."

The reply came back, "From the porch you can see Johnson's service station and Peter's farm, but other than that, there's not much to look at except the mountains and lakes."

A man got on the train in Chicago and looked up the head porter. He handed him a fifty-dollar bill and said, "Now, I'm going into my berth to get some sleep, but I want you to make sure to get me up so that I can get off the train in Cincinnati." He went on to say, "I'm a very sound sleeper, and I'm hard to get up in the morning, but I'm giving you this money to make sure you get me up. Tomorrow, I'm marrying the boss's daughter in Cincinnati. It's the most important day of my life, and I have to be there."

So he went to bed, and when he woke up, the train had gone all the way to Louisville. He went looking for the porter, cussed him out, and said, "This is the maddest I've ever been. I'm so furious I could kill you!"

The porter said, "You think you're mad? You should have seen the fellow I put off in Cincinnati!"

A traveler was found by a US Customs official to be carrying a half-gallon bottle from Mexico. The official asked the man what it contained. The traveler replied, "It's just holy water. I took it from the shrine I visited. They say it causes miracles."

The inspector was suspicious and opened the bottle and took a sniff. He shouted, "This isn't holy water, it's tequila!"

The traveler lifted his eyes to the sky and cried out, "Good heavens! Another miracle!"

I have just returned from Boston. It is the only thing to do if you find yourself there.

—Fred Allen

Mr. and Mrs. Shaw were on safari in Africa, walking through the jungle. Suddenly a huge lion sprang out of the bushes and seized Mrs. Shaw, dragging her off. "Shoot!" she screamed to her husband. "Shoot!"

"I can't!" he shouted back. "I've run out of film!"

In some parts of Mexico hot springs and cold springs are found side by side—and because of the convenience of this natural phenomenon the women often bring their laundry and boil their clothes in the hot springs and then rinse them in the cold ones. A tourist, who was watching this procedure commented to his Mexican friend and guide: "I imagine that they think old Mother Nature is pretty generous to supply such ample, clean hot and cold water here side by side for their free use?"

The guide replied, "No señor, there is much grumbling because she supplies no soap."

In 1962, when John Glenn became the first American to go into orbit, his countrymen went wild with delight.

The next day, Sarah, bursting with pride and excitement, said to her friend, Rose, "And what do you think of John Glenn?"

Sarah looked bewildered and asked, "Who?"

Rose, astonished at the Sarah's ignorance of an event that was heralded on the front pages of every newspaper, said, "John Glenn! John Glenn! He just went around the world three times."

Sarah merely shrugged. "Well, if you have the money, you can afford to travel."

A man from Iowa was taking a bus tour of Nashville, Tennessee. The bus driver was pointing out the sights of the Civil War Battle of Nashville. The driver said, "Right over here a small group of Confederate soldiers held off a whole Yankee brigade." A little further along he said, "Over there a young Confederate boy, all by himself, fought off a Yankee platoon."

This went on and on until finally, the man taking the tour said, "Didn't the Yankees win anything in the battle of Nashville?"

The bus driver replied, "Not while I'm the driver of this bus, they didn't."

Fifty years ago, my Uncle Tim, then a photographer for *National Geographic,* gained considerable notoriety when he made a two-week trek, completely alone, through some of the most forbidding and unmapped wilds of the Gobi Desert, and did it without a compass!

"Nothing to it!" he airily told reporters. "You've just got to mark every jog in the route, so you can go back the way you came. Every time I changed direction, I just built a little cairn of rocks, so I'd know one way from another. It's a snap if you just leave no turn unstoned."

My wife and I went on a three-day cruise. Actually, it was more like a three-day meal. They tell you to bring just one outfit, but in three different sizes: large, extra large, and blimp.

—Robert G. Lee

Two retired church elders on a cruise sat beside each other one lunchtime. One asked, "Where did you go last year?"

The other answered, "We took a cruise around the world. Next year we'll try someplace else."

The shipwrecked mariner had spent several years on a deserted island. Then one morning he was thrilled to see a ship offshore and a smaller vessel pulling out toward him.

When the boat grounded on the beach, the officer in charge handed the marooned sailor a bundle of newspapers and told him, "With the captain's compliments. He said to read through these and let us know if you still want to be rescued."

—Bill Leverette, *On Edgar Bergen's Lap* (Peachtree Publishers)

While on his first ocean cruise, Russell Pruitt fell overboard. He was floundering in the water, shouting and waving and trying to get the attention of those on board. Finally a lawyer, a politician, and an evangelist noticed his plight.

The lawyer shouted, "Shall I prepare a suit against the cruise line on your behalf?"

The politician promised that he would press a bill in Congress next term to make sailing safer.

The evangelist said with a smile, "Yes, brother! I see your hand! Now, do I see another?"

Three people were viewing the Grand Canyon—an artist, a pastor and a cowboy. As they stood on the edge of that massive abyss, each one responded with a cry of exclamation.

"Ah," the artist said, "what a beautiful scene to paint!"

"Glory!" the minister cried. "What a wonderful example of the handiwork of God!"

"Shoot," the cowboy mused, "what a terrible place to lose a cow!"

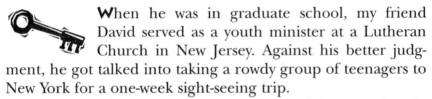

When he was in graduate school, my friend David served as a youth minister at a Lutheran Church in New Jersey. Against his better judgment, he got talked into taking a rowdy group of teenagers to New York for a one-week sight-seeing trip.

The group had reserved rooms in one of the finest hotels. When they arrived in the city they went to the hotel and registered. A bellhop led them to their rooms, which were on the 30th floor. After getting settled in their rooms they went out to see the sights. They went to Rockefeller Center, the United Nations Plaza, the Guggenheim Museum, the Empire State Building, the Statue of Liberty, etc. Finally they came back to their hotel, utterly exhausted. They went to the desk and asked for the keys to their rooms.

The clerk said, "I'm sorry, but the elevators are not running. You'll have to walk up or wait until the elevators are repaired."

They were so weary that all they could think of were the comfortable beds in their rooms. Tired as they were, they decided they would climb the thirty flights of stairs. One of them had an idea. He said, "On the way up, each of us will tell the funniest story we know." The others agreed and they started the climb. When they reached the tenth floor they were still going strong.

When they reached the twentieth floor their legs were like lead and they were panting for breath. The steps got longer and longer but they trudged on. The one whose turn it was to tell the next funny story said, "I'm sorry, I'm just too exhausted to laugh."

They trudged on in silence. When they reached the 29th floor, one of them began to laugh. He sat down on the steps and almost had hysterics. Finally, he said, "I have just thought of the funniest thing I have ever heard of in my life."

The others said, "What is it? Tell us!"

He said, "Our room keys . . . we left them in the lobby!"

The first time I flew was on a propeller plane from Chicago to Detroit. When I told the stewardess it was my first flight, she offered me a stick of gum. "For your ears," she explained over the din of the props.

When we landed, I pointed to my ears and reported, "They seem OK but couldn't you find something a little less sticky?"

"Why is there mistletoe hanging over the baggage counter?" asked the airline passenger, amid the holiday rush.

The clerk replied, "So you can kiss your luggage goodbye."

GRAB BAG

Talking to the suntanned New Mexican about the weather in Albuquerque, the tourist asked, "Doesn't it ever rain here?"

The native replied, "Mister, do you remember the story of Noah and the Ark, and how it rained forty days and forty nights?"

"Of course I do," the man answered.

"Well," drawled the Southwesterner, "we got half an inch that time."

 Says actor Tom Selleck, "Whenever I get full of myself, I remember that nice couple who approached me with a camera on a street in Honolulu one day. When I struck a pose for them, the man said, 'No, no, we want you to take a picture of us.'"

During an auction, proceedings were halted and the auctioneer announced, "A fellow in the room has just lost his wallet containing one thousand dollars. He offers two hundred bucks for its return."

Came a voice from the rear: "Two hundred and ten!"

You know you're going to have a bad day when:
- your teenager asks to wear your clothes to school on Nerd Day.
- the bird singing outside your window is a buzzard.
- you sink your teeth into a beautiful steak, and they stay there.

An inebriated man was on his hands and knees underneath a street lamp, searching the sidewalk. A friend came by and said, "Harry, what in the world are you doing out here on your hands and knees?"

"I'm hunting for my house key," Harry replied. "I lost it."

The friend got down on his hands and knees, too. "Show me where you lost it and I'll help you," he said.

"Oh, I lost it way over there in the grass," Harry said.

"Then why in the world are you looking for it out here on the sidewalk?" the friend asked.

Harry replied, "Hey, the light is better here."

Sir C. Aubrey Smith, grand old gentlemen of stage and screen, liked to dine quietly. Consequently he was rather put out when, in a Hollywood restaurant, he happened to be seated near a noisy diner who kept yelling for the waiter. "What do you have to do," demanded the pest finally, "to get a glass of water in this dump?"

The sedate, polished Sir Aubrey turned to the noisy one and quietly asked, "Why don't you try setting yourself on fire?"

A Wisconsin woman has an effective way of dealing with those unsolicited sales pitches one often gets on the telephone. Just as the salesperson gets to the spiel, the woman responds, "Oh, thank heavens!" (Big sigh of relief.) "You want to sell me something. I thought you were another collection agency."

Deborah Lester, a neighbor of mine frequently visited by Jehovah's Witnesses, asked me what she could do to escape this annoyance.

I suggested she buy an American flag, place it inside her front door, and ask such callers to pledge allegiance before their spiel. "They will refuse to honor the flag," I predicted, "and your problem will be solved."

So Deborah purchased an American flag and positioned it inside her front door. Two days later she spotted a visitor coming up the walk with paraphernalia under her arm. Soon the bell rang.

When the visitor asked for a few minutes of her time, Deborah said, "You may, but first you must pledge allegiance to the flag."

The visitor pledged allegiance to the flag inside the door, then shook her head, saying, "This is the first time I've ever been asked to pledge allegiance to the flag in all my eighteen years as an Avon lady!"

I was once invited to speak at a local Rotary club. I felt flattered by the invitation, until the master of ceremonies rose to introduce me. "Unfortunately," he said, "our original choice to be today's speaker was unable to attend." Then, in a clumsy attempt at humor, he pointed to a broken window pane which had been covered over with a piece of cardboard. "Our speaker," he said, "is like that piece of cardboard in the window. He's a substitute."

Being somewhat taken aback by the ungraceful introduction, I decided to show them: substitute or not, I would knock their socks off. And I did! When I finished the speech, I received a standing ovation.

But when the emcee returned to the lectern, his attempt to thank me was even more awkward than his introduction. "Reverend," he said, "we want you to know that you were not at all like a cardboard substitute. You were a real pane!"

That humiliation was nothing compared to what happened later. After the meeting, the club president gave me a check for one hundred dollars. I gave it back and told him to use it for his club's favorite charity. He said, "Oh, good, we can put it in our 'special' fund, the one we use to pay for really good speakers!"

God is a humorist. If you have any doubts about it, look in the mirror.
—Ken Olson

Until I was twelve, my family and I lived in a Chicago neighborhood near Garfield Park. My best friend and constant playmate was a boy my own age named Harry Joseph. When we moved, we lost contact.

Harry and I were both stamp collectors and were always engaged in swaps, each of us believing that he had gotten the better of the other. Many years later, I remember telling my wife that I often felt guilty about some of our deals. Perhaps I had taken advantage of Harry.

When I was in my early fifties, I was attending a conference in Indianapolis and called home to hear from my wife that someone named Harry Joseph was trying to contact me. "After forty years," I asked myself, "could he still be angry about the stamps?"

I phoned him at his Manhattan number and we had a marvelous conversation. He had seen me on television and tracked me down. He told me that his parents had died and that while cleaning out their basement, he had found some stamps I had sold him. These reminded him of our childhood friendship and had prompted his call. All the while I expected him to ask for a refund. Instead he asked my mailing address.

In a few days, the stamps arrived at my home as a gift from Harry.

I was so ugly when I was a kid, my imaginary playmate was ashamed to hang around with me.

You don't think times have changed? Now the Swiss Army knife has an ear-piercing tool on it.　　　　　—George Carlin

How we do admire the wisdom of those who come to us for advice.　　　　　—Ramsey Clark

Few people blame themselves until they have exhausted all other possibilities.　　　　　—Paul Porter

Remember this before you burden other people with your troubles. Half of them aren't the least bit interested, and the rest are delighted that you're getting what they think is coming to you.　　　　　—Vance Packard

Comedy is tragedy plus time.

—Carol Burnett

The only reason that some people have a secret sorrow is that the rest of us won't listen to them.

—James Forrestal

The trouble with being punctual is that nobody's there to appreciate it.

—Harold Rome

 A man who insists on having his initials embroidered on his pajamas must be uncertain of himself. Surely you ought to know who you are by bedtime.

—Christopher Morley

The cat is a saint when there are no mice about.

—Japanese proverb

Life is a tragedy to those who feel and a comedy to those who think.

"On cable TV, they have a weather channel—twenty-four hours of weather," says comedian Dan Spencer. "We had something like that where I grew up. We called it a window."

Rev. Dirk Jesse from Sidney, Ohio, passes along the following directions for how to handle stress:

- Use your MasterCard to pay your VISA bill.
- Pop some popcorn without the lid on.
- Put your toddler's clothes on him backwards and send him off to preschool as if nothing were wrong.
- Read the dictionary backwards, and look for subliminal messages.
- Bill your doctor for the time you spent in the waiting room.

Random observations from quirky comedian Steven Wright:

- I was trying to daydream, but my mind kept wandering.
- There was a power outage at a department store yesterday. . . . Twenty people were trapped on the escalators.
- I like to skate on the other side of the ice. . . . I like to reminisce with people I don't know. . . . I like to fill my tub up with water, then turn the shower on and act like I'm in a submarine that's been hit. . . . And when I get real bored, I like to drive downtown and get a great parking spot, then sit in my car and count how many people ask me if I'm leaving.
- I lost a buttonhole today.
- I met her at Macy's. She was shopping; I was putting Slinkys on the escalator.
- All of the people in my building are insane. . . . The guy above me designs synthetic hairballs for ceramic cats.
- I bought some batteries . . . but they weren't included, so I had to buy them again.
- I have a full-size map of the world. At the bottom it says "1 inch = 1 inch." I hardly ever unroll it.
- A friend of mine sent me a postcard with a satellite photo of the entire planet on it, and on the back he wrote, "Wish you were here."
- After they make Styrofoam, what do they ship it in?
- It's a small world, but I wouldn't want to paint it.
- I bought my brother some gift-wrap for Christmas. I took it to the Gift Wrap department and told them to wrap it, but in a different print so he would know when to stop unwrapping.
- I filled out an application that said "In Case Of Emergency Notify." I wrote "Doctor." . . . What's my mother going to do?
- The other day I heard that sponges grow in the ocean. Can you imagine how deep the water'd be if they didn't?
- I got a new shadow. I had to get rid of the other one. . . . it wasn't doing what I was doing.
- I forgot and left the lighthouse on all night. Next day the sun wouldn't rise.
- I went to a 7-Eleven and asked for a 2 x 4 and a box of 3 x 5s. The clerk said, "10-4!"

We should have a way of telling people that they have bad breath without hurting their feelings. "Well, I'm bored. . . . Let's go brush our teeth." Or, "I've got to make a phone call; hold this gum in your mouth."
—Brad Stine

He was so narrow-minded he could see through a keyhole with two eyes.
—Esther Forbes

Futon is a Japanese word that means "sore back." —Nick Arnette

Canadians have a tough time playing Wheel of Fortune. They keep saying "A" after every letter they ask for. —Nick Arnette

My grandson Justin pulled this one on me:
Question: What kind of shampoo do Siamese twins use?
Answer: Extra body!

He's the kind of friend who will always be there when he needs you.
—Adam Christing

Sometimes I lie awake at night, and I ask, "Where have I gone wrong?" Then a voice says to me, "This is going to take more than one night."
—Charlie Brown (*Peanuts*)

A Freudian slip is when you say one thing but mean your mother.

A great many people think they are thinking when they are merely rearranging their prejudices.
—William James

How do seedless grapes reproduce? —Mark Matlock

Lazlo's Chinese Relativity Axiom: No matter how great your triumphs or how tragic your defeats, approximately one billion Chinese couldn't care less.

 There are two kinds of people in the world: those of us who split the world into two kinds of people, and those who don't. Since I'm one of the former, here are more examples:

- People who eat pizza with a fork, and the rest of us who shovel it into our mouths with hands, elbows, and table legs.
- People who read *USA Today,* and people who read it but refuse to admit it.
- The vast group of ordinary Americans who actually work for a living, and their elected representatives.
- Those of us whose entry into the technological age has moved smoothly, and those who use America On Line.
- People who enjoy sports contests, and Raiders fans.
- Folks with a modicum of simple human civil courtesy, and the French.
- Those who listen to Michael Bolton records, and those having functioning, intact ear drums.
- Readers who regularly devour every page of each month's issue of *Vanity Fair,* and those of us with a life.
- Normal human beings with an aversion to telling outright lies while staring directly into people's faces, and tobacco lobbyists.
- Married men who learn to choke back some of their ego and tough it through the hard times in a relationship, and Larry King.
- Fine decent caring people, and Will Durst. —Will Durst

THE WORLD ACCORDING TO STUDENT BLOOPERS

Excerpted and adapted from Richard Lederer's *Anguished English*, this condensation is composed entirely of genuine, certified, authentic student fluffs, flubs, goofs, and gaffes:

- Ancient Egypt was inhabited by mummies, and they all wrote in hydraulics. They lived in the Sarah Dessert, which they cultivated by irritation. Ancient Egyptian women wore a loose-fitting garment which began just below the breasts which hung to the floor.
- The Bible is full of many interesting caricatures. Moses went up on Mt. Cyanide to get the Ten Commandments, but he died before he ever reached Canada. Jesus was born because Mary had an immaculate contraption. An epistle is the wife of an apostle.
- The Greeks were a highly sculptured people, and without them we wouldn't have history. The Greeks invented three kinds of columns: corinthian, ironic, and dorc. They also invented myths. A myth is a female moth. One myth tells us that the mother of Achilles dipped him in the river Stinks until he became intolerable.
- The Romans conquered the Geeks. Their leader, Julius Caesar, extinguished himself on the battlefields of Gaul and when the Ides of March murdered him, he expired with these immortal words upon his dying lips: "Tee hee, Brutus!"
- Then came the Middle Ages, when everyone was middle aged. King Arthur lived in the Age of Shivery, with brave knights on prancing horses and beautiful women. Magna Carta ensured that no free man should be hanged twice for the same offense. Joan of Arc was burnt to a steak. People contracted the blue-bonnet plague, which caused them to grow boobs on their necks. They also put on morality plays about ghosts, goblins, virgins, and other mythical creatures.
- Then came the Renaissance, a time of a great many discoveries and inventions. Gutenberg invented the Bible and removable type. Sir Walter Raleigh discovered cigarettes and started smoking. And Sir Francis Drake circumcised the world with a hundred-foot clipper.